The Economics of Population: Classic Writings

Julian L. Simon

editor

Transaction Publishers
New Brunswick (U.S.A.) and London (U.K.)

Library of Congress Catalog Number: 97–31565
ISBN: 1–56000–307–3
Printed in the United States of America

Library of Congress Cataloging-in-Publication Data

The economics of population : classic writings / Julian L. Simon, editor.
    p. cm.
  Includes bibliographical references
  ISBN 1–56000–307–3 (alk. paper)
  1. Population—Economic aspects. I. Simon, Julian Lincoln, 1932–
HB849.41.E264   1997
304.6—dc21   97–31565
                                                 CIP

Contents

Part 2: The Second Wave

Part 3: Twentieth-Century Classicals on Consequences

Part 4: Natural Resources

Part 5: The Determinants of Population Growth and Density

Introduction

Julian L. Simon

The aim of this introduction[1] is twofold: first, to preview some of the writings in the volume, and show how they fit with each other, second, to survey the history of premodern economic thought about population which the classical writings republished here represent. This book complements a collection of the most important modern writings on population economics, *The Economics of Population: Key Modern Writings*, that I edited, published by Edward Elgar in 1996.

The economics of population has at least as long and controversial a history as any topic in economics (as well as an exciting present). The Classical period began with the London mortality data and its analysis by John Graunt (selection 2), and the theory of William Petty (selection 3). The subject took a radical turn with the first edition of Thomas Malthus (selection 5), and then still another radical reversal with Malthus's second edition, and then with Friedrich Engels and Karl Marx (selection 14). Not much of note happened between then and the 1960s, with the interesting exception of a brief double flip-flop by John Maynard Keynes in the 1920s and 1930s (selection 17).

Population economics has often intertwined with vociferous popular debate and public policy. Both have influenced each other; public interest in the issue has induced economists to work on the subject, and has affected the direction of the their conclusions (Schumpeter, 1954; Spengler, 1978). In turn, the results of the studies of economists have influenced public debate and popular thought. Most of the professional and public interest has focused on births rather than deaths, because few people have ever questioned whether reducing the death rate is a good thing. (Amazingly, a few physicians have done so; see quotations in my 1981/1996 book.) From time to time there has also been interest in international immigration, but that topic (and internal migration) will not be covered in this book.

Perhaps more than in most branches of economics, the history of population economics includes many writings (especially in the nineteenth century) that made great advances and that may be seen as correct in light of more recent developments, but nevertheless had little or no influence upon subsequent thought. This volume includes several such works; it is not restricted to writings that have been important in the historical chain of intellectual influence. Also, in order to understand the intellectual history of population economics, I have included a few pieces of work that have been very influential but that, in light of later work, can be seen to be fundamentally wrong.

Beginning of the Premodern Period

It has always been natural and commonsensical for people (especially intellectuals) to speculate about the effects of additional people on the supply of land, food, other extractive resources, and the environment. Scraps of writing on the subject exhibiting concern about such topics as deforestation, reaching conclusions familiar to readers of the modern popular press, may be found in the classics since the ancient Greeks:

> Ever since primitive tribes had solved population problems by abortion and infanticide, people in general and social philosophers in particular never ceased to worry about them . . . the trouble arose from a relation between birth rates and death rates that was incompatible with stationary or quasi-stationary economic environments: the problem of population was one of actual or threatening overpopulation. It was from this angle that it presented itself to Plato and Aristotle. (Schumpeter, 1954, p. 250)

Spengler (1978, pp. 200–1) cites ancient Greek and Roman writers—Polybius, Plato, St. Augustine, Lucretius, and others—worrying about growth-induced depletion of soil and minerals, and deforestation, in terms that sound quite contemporary.

Real scholarship on the subject, however, began with the beginnings of classical economic theory in the seventeenth century. William Petty was the founding father of population economics. Seldom can intellectual paternity be so well established. And though his inquiries began with population economics, his influence extends far beyond this field. Observers as varied as Friedrich Hayek (in conversation) and Karl Marx (advertisement for T. Hutchinson, *Before Adam Smith*), judge Petty to be the founder of modern economics taken as a whole; if Marx and Hayek agree on a proposition, there must be something in it.[2]

Not only did Petty come first, but he did a better job of presenting some ideas than did even the other masters who came after him. An example is the idea of division of labor that Smith made so famous, and which is so grounded in population size. Smith wrote:

> To take an example, therefore, from a very trifling manufacture; but one in which the division of labour has been very often taken notice of, the trade of the pin-maker. . . . One man draws out the wire, another straights it, a third cuts it, a fourth points it, a fifth grinds it at the top for receiving the head; to make the head requires three distinct operations; to put it on is a peculiar business, to whiten the pins is another; it is even a trade by itself to put them into the paper; and the important business of making a pin is, in this manner, divided into about eighteen distinct operations, which, in some manufactories, are all performed by distinct hands, though in others the same man will sometimes perform two or three of them. (1776/1970, pp. 109–10)

Earlier Petty had written:

> . . . the Gain which is made by Manufactures, will be greater, as the Manufacture itself is greater and better . . . each Manufacture will be divided into as many parts as possible, whereby the Work of each Artisan will be simple and easier; As for Example. In the making of a Watch, If one Man shall make the Wheels, another the Spring, another shall Engrave the Dial-plate, and another shall make the Cases, then the Watch will be better and cheaper, than if the whole Work be put upon any one Man. And we also see that in Towns, and in the Streets of a great Town, where all the Inhabitants are almost of one Trade, the Commodity peculiar to those places is made better and cheaper than elsewhere . . . (1682/1899, p. 473)

Petty probably should get part of the credit for the founding of statistical demography, too, which is at the base of all empirical population economics. Many writers have speculated that Petty actually was responsible for Graunt's work. Though I doubt that, it does seem plausible that Petty was full of his original interest—London's growth—and discussed the matter with his friend Graunt. It is reasonable that Graunt would then have picked up the question, and—perhaps in consultation with Petty, or perhaps not—designed and executed the extraordinary actual inquiry which is the first systematic study of mortality and life expectancy (see selection 2).

Schumpeter (1954) provided his usual fascinating history of economic thought with respect to population; his grasp of the underlying issues also seems sound to me. These are some brief excerpts.

"Roughly speaking until the end of the sixteenth century," Schumpeter says, population growth was mainly a problem.

> In the Middle Ages the dwelling places of the lower stratum of the warrior class, the simple knights, suffered from overcrowding whenever there were no crusades, wars of the Roses, epidemics, and so on to reduce numbers; and the artisans' guilds offered livelihood for restricted numbers only and experienced perennial difficulties with ever-lengthening 'waiting lists.' (pp. 250–51)

Then there came a shift in conditions during the seventeenth and eighteenth centuries, which Schumpeter describes as follows:

> [T]he population problem became one of under-population. . . Accordingly, governments began to favor increase in population by all means at their command . . . Economists fell in with the humors of their age. With rare exceptions they were enthusiastic about 'populousness' and rapid increase in numbers.

In England, Godwin (selection 7, 1793/1820) wrote that humankind's fate is fixed by social institutions and not by immutable laws of nature. He believed that if society would reorganize itself properly, there would be no natural constraints upon population growth for a long time. This much was sound doctrine that we are relearning now from current events and data. But it was communalism rather than private property that Godwin believed to be the appropriate social organization. And it was reaction to this aspect of Godwin's thought that triggered Malthus's *Essay*.

The Classical Period

The wave of antipopulation writing that bore Malthus began in the middle of the eighteenth century, Schumpeter tells us, and its emergence is a puzzle.

> [C]onditions did not substantially change in the eighteenth century or even in the first decades of the nineteenth. Therefore, it is quite a problem to explain why the opposite attitude—which might be called anti-populationist or, to associate it with the name of the man who made it a popular success in the nineteenth century, Malthusian—should have asserted itself among economists from the middle of the eighteenth century on. Why was it that economists took fright at a scarecrow! (1954, pp. 251–52)

Schumpeter then offers an explanation of the change in mood, an explanation which is necessarily quite speculative:

> [T]he cradle of the genuinely anti-populationist doctrine was France. . . . During practically the whole of the eighteenth century France was fighting a losing battle with England. Many of her leading spirits began to accept this defeat by 1760 and to discount the opportunities for national expansion. Moreover, the outworn institutional pattern of the last half century of the monarchy was not favorable to vigorous economic development at home . . . The . . . final step . . . is to explain why anti-populationist sentiment gained a hold on the English mind in spite of the fact that exactly the opposite state of things prevailed in England . . . in the Industrial Revolution of the last decades of the eighteenth century, these short-run vicissitudes grew more serious than they had been before, precisely because the pace of economic development quickened. And some economists . . . were so impressed by them as to lose sight of the trend. (pp. 252-53)

Malthus analyzed both the causes and the consequences of population growth, welding them into a synthesis that Baumol has called "the magnificent dynamics." Malthus theorized in his first edition that an increase in income—in the form of a rise in food supply above subsistence for the mass of the population—leads to an increase in marriage and hence in births, as well as a decline in deaths.

Malthus's work provoked reply and controversy throughout the nineteenth century. One line of criticism began with the observation that during the eighteenth and nineteenth centuries in England, its overseas extensions, and some parts of Europe, population rose rapidly but the standard of living *also* rose. One explanation offered was that a greater division of labor was possible with a larger population. Another suggestion was that the independent pace of technological progress in advanced countries had been and would be greater than the pace of population growth. Malthus's first edition, and all of Ricardo's editions, however, asserted that technological progress would *not* be rapid enough to permit population growth unconstrained by death: The "law of . . . nature . . . implies a strong and constantly operating check on population from the difficulty of subsistence. This difficulty . . . must necessarily be severely felt by a large portion of mankind . . . . And the race of man cannot, *by any efforts of reason*, escape from it . . . misery is an absolutely necessary consequence of it" (Malthus, 1978/1959, p. 5, italics added). Those who believed that technological progress could and would win a "race" with population growth were naturally more sanguine about the future than was the Malthus of the first edition.

Some critics of Malthus found hope in the belief that people would increasingly limit births voluntarily—as Malthus, in the first edition, only *hoped* they might. But by the time of the second and subsequent editions of his essay Malthus came to agree that people really *might* limit families voluntarily—which, it should be noted, is equivalent to the assumption that technological progress could win a "race" with population growth. "Throughout the whole of the present work I have so far differed in principle from the former, as to suppose the action of another check to population which does not come under the head either of vice or misery; and, in the latter part I have endeavored to soften some of the harshest conclusions of the first Essay" (Malthus, 1803, p. xii of Irwin edition). Malthus even offered historical examples of voluntary fertility control, for example, the delay of marriage in Scandinavia in response to population pressures (1803, p. 81).

The shift in Malthus's theoretical position after his first *Essay* did not mean that his predictions had completely reversed: "I believe that few of my readers can be less sanguine than I am in their expectations of any sudden and great change in the general conduct of men on this subject" (5th ed., 1817/1963, p. 271). This sort of statement provided the ground—intentionally or unintentionally—for many popular and professional writers until this day to rely on the first edition's conclusions as being the essential Malthus. But there is much less of this pessimism in the fifth edition than the first, and Malthus allowed himself to end the fifth edition with the following:

> From a review of the state of society in former periods, compared with the present, I should certainly say that the evils resulting from the principle of population have rather diminished than increased . . . it does not seem unreasonable to expect that they will be still further diminished . . .
>
> On the whole, therefore, though our future prospects respecting the mitigation of the evils arising from the principle of population may not be so bright as we could wish, yet they are far from being entirely disheartening, and by no means preclude that gradual and progressive improvement in human society, which, before the late wild speculations on this subject, was the object of rational expectation. To the laws of property and marriage, and to the apparently narrow principle of self-interest which prompts each individual to exert himself in bettering his condition, we are indebted for all the noblest exertions of human genius . . . (5th ed., 1817/1963, p. 289)

This view allows for the contributions of both the check of "moral restraint" and the technological progress due to "the noblest exertions of human genius." And it projects an improving trend into the future. So Malthus himself was a powerful critic of "Malthusianism."

To corroborate my reading of Malthus, here is the conclusion of an assessment by Malthus's major modern biographer, who is a great admirer of Malthus:

> From the first to the seventh edition of *An Essay on the Principle of Population*, its author moved from an ecological to a sociological perspective . . . and—most remarkably—from an unrelenting pessimism to a cautious optimism." (Petersen, 1976, p. 373)

Malthus's importance in catalyzing the field could not be more obvious. But Schumpeter rates Malthus's intellectual contribution very low. (I would guess that his poor grading of Malthus is due in considerable part to Schumpeter's very great emphasis on intellectual priority, especially priority as established by Schumpeter's own researches, whether or not the later developer of the idea arrived at the idea independently.)

> [T]he 'Malthusian' Principle of Population sprang fully developed from the brain of Botero in 1589 . . . This path-breaking performance—the only performance in the whole history of the theory of population to deserve any credit at all—came much before the time in which its message could have spread: it was practically lost in the populationist wave of the seventeenth century. . . . the 'law of geometric progression,' . . . was suggested by Petty (1686), by Sussmilch (1740), by R. Wallace (1753), and by Ortes (1774), so that, within this range of ideas, there was nothing left for Malthus to say that had not been said before. [Non-mathematical statements came from] Franklin (1751) [and] Mirabeau (1756)—who expressed himself in his picturesque manner: men will multiply to the limits of subsistence like 'rats in a barn' (pp. 254–255)
>
> Steuart . . . presented . . . the case of the Extensive Margin: as population increases, poorer and poorer soils have to be taken into cultivation and, applied to these progressively poorer soils, equal amounts of productive effort produce progressively smaller harvests. Turgot discovered the other case of decreasing physical returns . . . the Intensive Margin: as equal quantities of [an input] are successively applied to a given piece of land, the quantities of product that result from each application will first successively increase up to a certain point at which the ratio between increment of product and increment of capital will reach a maximum. Beyond this point, however, further application of equal quantities of capital will be attended by progressively smaller increase in product, and the sequence of these decreasing increases will in the end converge toward zero. This statement of what eventually came to be recognized as the genuine law of decreasing returns cannot be commended too highly. It embodies an achievement that is nothing short of brilliant and suffices in itself to place Turgot as a theorist high above A. Smith. (pp. 259–260)

I cannot judge the extent to which Malthus's ideas were truly new or instead were derivative from prior work. But it seems clear that

Malthus did more than simply popularize well-known ideas. For example, Schumpeter gives Turgot full credit for the notion of diminishing returns. But Malthus certainly framed the issue in a very new way.

Furthermore, Malthus broke new ground with his empirical survey in his second and subsequent editions, which then influenced his theoretical analysis and his view of the future in a direction counter to his original "Malthusian" viewpoint. (See Petersen, 1979, for a judicious analysis of the course of Malthus's thinking.)

Ricardo, and later Mill, did little more than put a gloss upon first-edition Malthus, though Mill did note that "There is room in the world, no doubt, and even in old countries, for a great increase of population" (1848, Book IV, Chapter vi, #2, p. 756). But Mill adduced esthetic arguments in favor of a stationary population, saying

> [E]ven if [population growth] is innocuous, I see very little reason for desiring it . . . A population may be too crowded, though all be amply supplied with food and raiment. It is not good for man to be kept perforce at all times in the presence of his species. (1848, p. 756)

Reaction to Malthus

There were those like Godwin (1820) who believed that humankind's fate is fixed by his social institutions and not by the immutable laws of Malthus's theory. Godwin believed that if mankind would reorganize itself properly (and quite differently from the then-prevailing state of society in England and Europe) there would be no natural constraints upon population growth for a long time. (It was reaction to this aspect of Godwin's thought that triggered Malthus's *Essay*.) In the same line of thought were (and are) the Marxists. They believe that population could be too great only under capitalism, and they argue that a socialist economy could make productive use of as many people as would be born.

Alexander H. Everett[3] (selection 12 [1826]), early on pointed out the main weaknesses of Malthus's theory in the context of the U.S. experience. And he was especially clear and emphatic about the induction of technical progress by population growth.

> [A]n increase of population on a given territory is followed immediately by a division of labor; which produces in its turn the invention of new machines, an improvement of methods in all the departments of industry, and a rapid progress in the various branches of art and science. The increase effected by these improve-

ments in the productiveness of labor is obviously much greater in proportion than the increase of population, to which it is owing. (p. 26)

The literature on the economics of population passed around this observation as a stream passes around a rock in the stream bed. This was to happen again and again, as will occasionally be noted below.

Henry C. Carey (selection 12 [1840]), perhaps the first great economist in the United States, wrote at length about the positive (in both senses of the word) relationship of political organization to population density—perhaps a natural observation in a pioneer country such as the U.S. was then. He discussed the reduced cost of physical security against violence as people live closer together rather than widely scattered. And then he traced the consequent cumulative spiral:

> Population and capital continue to grow, producing a daily increasing tendency to union of action, rendering security more complete. The increasing facility of obtaining the means of support, is attended by an improvement of moral condition, and men are more disposed to respect the rights of their neighbours . . .
>
> At a later period in the progress of society, as population becomes more dense, we find the disposition to union of action constantly increasing. Men are now associated in larger communities, or nations . . . (1840, p. 98)

Carey also mentioned the increase in infrastructure such as roads or canals which accompanies increased population density (p. 102).

Engels (selection 14) recognized the importance of chemistry for agriculture—he cited Humphry Davy and Justus Liebig (Meek, p. 50)—and he was excited by the prospects of the increased capacity of given land area to support human life. It is hard to separate him from Marx, but it seems to me that Engels is the fount of this stream of thought.

> The area of land is limited—that is perfectly true. But the labour power to be employed on this area increases together with the population; and even if we assume that the increase of output associated with this increase of labour is not always proportionate to the latter, there still remains a third element—which the economists, however, never consider as important—namely, science, the progress of which is just as limitless and at least as rapid as that of population. (in Meek, p. 18)

Engels also offered a theory of the rate of growth of technology: "[S]cience advances in proportion to the body of knowledge passed down to it by the previous generation, that is, in the most normal conditions it also grows in geometrical progression" (in Meek, p. 51).

This may be an inadequate specification of the knowledge-production function, but it is a great advance over the view of a "race" between population and technology with the latter seen as simply arriving fortuitously, as Malthus saw it. So here we have another key strand in understanding the effects of population growth in the long run, the process by which resources become more abundant rather than more scarce as population and income grow.

Seeds of Modern Thought

Von Thünen (selection 25, 1826–1863/1966) described with extraordinary statistical precision the Belgian and Mecklenburg systems of cultivation, and he showed clearly how the difference in techniques used was related to population density. And his theoretical analysis explained well why different techniques are used at different distances from centers of population.

Chayanov worked out the formal utility theory, and adduced impressive data from turn-of-the-century Russian village surveys, to show that larger families caused there to be more labor expended "either by an intensification of work methods or by using more labor-intensive crops and jobs" or both (1925/1966, p. 113). But the interests of von Thünen and Chayanov were not population economics per se, and therefore perhaps it was unavoidable that their ideas were not taken into the body of population economics, but had to be rediscovered by Slicher van Bath and Boserup.

Henry George,[4] in the context of his proposal for a "single tax" on land, opposed Malthus vigorously (selection 15), though his ideas are not spelled out neatly: "[E]verywhere the vice and misery attributed to overpopulation can be traced to the warfare, tyranny, and oppression *which prevent knowledge from being utilized* and deny the security essential to production" (1879/1979, p. 123, italics added).

George noticed that there is a positive correlation between nations' population density and their level of development. And he implied that increased social capital, better social organization, increases in technology, and higher levels of human capital flow from greater density, as they also lead to further increases in population. He remarked upon a phenomenon that made a considerable impression upon economists after World War II, situations "where war or other calamity has swept away wealth, leaving population unimpaired. There is not less wealth in London today because of the great fire of 1666; nor yet is there less wealth in Chicago because of the great fire in 1870" (p. 148).

Two pithy sayings embody much of George's thinking on the subject: "No one who has seen Melbourne or San Francisco can doubt that if the population of England were transported to New Zealand, leaving all accumulated wealth behind, New Zealand would soon be as rich as England is now" (pp. 148–49). And "Both the jayhawk and the man eat chickens, but the more jayhawks the fewer chickens, while the more men the more chickens" (p. 131).

It is a tragedy—not so much for the state of knowledge as for the lives of millions of human beings affected by population policies— that the intellectual discoveries of Everett, Engels, von Thünen, Carey, Chayanov, and George (and undoubtedly other writers who also understood the core issues) have had no noticeable imprint on later writers about the subject. As is too often the case, later writers selected some existing theoretical elements for further development, and left out other elements entirely, to be lost until independently rediscovered. And the selection—in this case, as in so many others—seems to be on the basis of what is amenable to mathematical manipulation and/ or what popular opinion and sources of funding believe is true even before the work is done.

The Prevailing Orthodoxy

Despite the excellent non-Malthusian scientific works, the prevailing economic thought can fairly be considered early Malthusian throughout most of the nineteenth century, as one may see in the work of Jevons (selection 23); John Stuart Mill was the dominant figure in this tradition, extolling the stationary state (selection 13). And though when Robert Giffen gave a lecture in celebration of the fiftieth anniversary of the Royal Statistical Society's founding, he observed the great growth in population and in wealth and explained them by peace and order, growth in knowledge and agricultural productivity, and new lands, he ended as follows: "It is impossible not to revert . . . to the Malthusian theory" when the "new lands" have been "filled up" (1885/1979). And Knut Wicksell warned that "it is merely a question of time, probably only a few decades, until these countries, especially the United States, will themselves consume their entire present food surplus . . . A relatively stationary population, perhaps even a reduction in population, will, therefore, be the fate of western Europe" (1910/1976, pp. 319, 320).

In the later part of the nineteenth century, however, it becomes more difficult to characterize with any surety the dominant view of economists. In 1931 Cannan noted that "I think that the biggest change made in economic theory during the last hundred years is to be found in the treatment of Population. In 1831, Malthus was still alive and quite unrepentant" [not correct; see above] (p. 519) . . . The economic history of the hundred years has tended to bring about a very complete reversal of economists' view of this matter (p. 520) . . . All this emphasis on food is now out of date" (p. 525), though we should note that Cannan ended with "After all, the increase [in population] must stop some time," though he does not say why (p. 532). But in the 1920s, Cannan's renowned colleague John Maynard Keynes was still a very fiery Malthusian preacher about the "devil" of population growth (selection 17). And then Keynes himself reversed his views twice; we'll come back to him in a moment.

There was a resurgence of interest in population economics in the 1920s in Great Britain marked by contributions from Cannan (1928), Dalton (1928), Robbins (1927), and others. As is to be expected, given the long-run decline in the British and French birthrates, the issue was stationary and declining population rather than population growth. Some of the work displayed a very wide general grasp of the subject (e.g., Dalton, 1928, and especially Reddaway, 1937, which—aside from the empirical improvements since then—still is as good a work on aging and declining populations as has been written). But the technical approach was that of comparative statics and the concept of the "optimum population," which was something of a step backwards. Mydral called the concept of the population optimum "one of the most sterile ideas that ever grew out of our science" (1940, p. 26). But though the concept has ceased to be used much in economics, where it was developed, ecologists continue to discuss it. (see also Wicksell, 1910/ 1976). Whereas Malthus's theory was a two-variable dynamic model of the interrelated effects of income and population growth, the optimum-population notion is a static examination of the trade-off between the gains from division of labor and economies of scale, on the one hand, and the loss from diminishing returns to additional labor with a given stock of capital, on the other hand. This notion was in accord with the economics of its time, and the optimum-population theorizing was very neat even if not useful.

Keynes's writings in the pre-World War II period[5] deserve a special mention. Keynes always was intensely interested in population growth. At first he was a fiery Malthusian. In his 1920 *Economic Consequences of the Peace*, for example, he wrote:

> Before the eighteenth century mankind entertained no false hopes. To lay the illusions which grew popular at that age's latter end, Malthus disclosed a Devil. For half a century all serious economical writings held that Devil in clear prospect. For the next half century he was chained up and out of sight. Now perhaps we have loosed him again. (1920, p. 10)

Keynes was deeply concerned about what he called "the disruptive powers of excessive national fecundity" (p. 15). And he worried about supplies of raw materials, especially coal and iron (chapter IV, part II). He charged that in Russia "the disruptive powers of excessive national fecundity may have played a greater part in bursting the bonds of convention than either the power of ideas or the errors of autocracy" (p. 15). This was in accord with his general view that "The great events of history are often due to secular changes in the growth of population and other fundamental economic causes" (pp. 14, 15).

Keynes did understand that under benign social and economic circumstances, the increase in productivity could offset the increase in fertility. "One geometrical ratio might cancel another, [as] the nineteenth century was able to forget the fertility of the species in a contemplation of the dizzy virtues of compound interest" (p. 21). But this could only happen if saving cut deeply into consumption, he believed. He worried about the "pitfall" of "population still outstripping accumulation, our self-denials promot[ing] not happiness but numbers" (p. 21). Selections 17 and 20 contain Keynes's warnings of the Malthusian Devil.

Later, after he developed his "Keynesian" demand analysis, he turned around and became an enthusiast for population growth as a means of increasing effective demand, and his American colleague Hanson expanded that argument (Selection 21). Still later, Keynes arrived at being ambivalent about population growth. Though his writings on the subject were very influential, none contains material of lasting intellectual value.

Notes

1. Parts of this introduction are drawn from my various earlier works.
2. Letwin (1963) argues that the birth of a field of science should be dated when there first comes into being an *integrated* body of theory. Economics lacked such an integrated framework until Adam Smith came along to weld together the various fragmentary observations that already existed; Letwin persuasively argues that this was Smith's greatest achievement. On such a view, Smith and not Petty is the founder.
3. Salim Rashid brought Everett's work to my attention, for which I thank him.
4. Lowell Harris kindly brought George's work to my attention.
5. Petersen (1955) traces Keynes's intellectual history with respect to population.

References

Bastiat, Frederic, *Selected Essays on Political Economy* (Irvington-on-Hudson: FEE, 1964).

Cannan, Edwin, *Wealth* (London: P. S. King, 1928).

Cannan, Edwin, "The Changed Outlook in Regard to Population", *The Economic Journal*, vol. XLI, December, 1931, 520–32.

Carey, Henry C. *Principles of Political Economy* (Philadelphia: Lea and Blanchard, 1840).

Dalton, Hugh, "The Theory of Population", *Economica*, 8, 1928, 28–50.

Everett, Alexander H., *New Ideas on Population, With Remarks on the Theories of Malthus and Godwin* (New York: Augustus M. Kelley, 1970).

George, Henry, *Progress and Poverty* (New York: Robert Schalkenbach Foundation, 1879/1979), pp. 123–50.

Giffen, Robert, "Some General Uses of Statistical Knowledge," 1885, reprinted in *Population and Development Review*, 1979, pp. 319–46.

Godwin, William, *Of Population* (London: J. McGowan, 1793/1820).

Graunt, John, *Natural and Political Observations Made Upon the Bills of Mortality*, edited with an introduction by Walter F. Willcox (Baltimore: Johns Hopkins Press, 1939).

Keynes, John Maynard, *The Economic Consequences of the Peace* (New York: Harcourt, Brace, 1920).

Keynes, John Maynard, "Some Economic Consequences of a Declining Population." *Eugenics Review* 29: 1937, 13–17.

Letwin, William, *The Origins of Scientific Economics* (London: Methuen, 1963; New York: Anchor, 1965).

Malthus, Thomas R. *An Essay on the principle of population, as it affects the future improvements of society.* (London: J. Johnson, 1798).

Malthus, Thomas R., *Population: The First Essay* (Ann Arbor: University of Michigan Press, 1798/1959).

Malthus, Thomas R., *An Essay on the Principle of Population, or A View of Its Past and Present Effects on Human Happiness* (London: J. Johnson, 1803 [A new edition, very thick, enlarged]).

Malthus, Thomas R., *Principles of Population*, fifth edition (Homewood: Irwin, 1817/1963).

Meek, Ronald L., *Marx and Engels on Malthus* (Delhi: People's Publishing House, 1956).

Mill, John Stuart, *Principles of Political Economy* (London: n.p., 1848).

Myrdal, Gunnar. 1940. *Population: a problem for democracy*. Cambridge: Harvard University Press.

Petersen, William, *Malthus* (Cambridge: Harvard University Press, 1979).

Petersen, William, "John Maynard Keynes' Theories of Population and the Concept of 'Optimum,' " *Population Studies*, 8, 1955, 228–46.

Petty, William, "Another Essay in Political Arithmetic," in Charles H. Hull (ed.) *The Economic Writings of Sir William Petty* (Cambridge: Cambridge University Press, 1682/1899).

Rashid, Salim, "Malthus's *Essay on Population*: The Facts of `Super-Growth' and the Rhetoric of Scientific Persuasion," *Journal of the History of the Behavioral Sciences*, 23, January, 1987, pp. 22-36.

Robbins, Lionel, "The Optimum Theory of Population," in T. Gregory and H. Dalton (eds.), *London Essays in Economics: In Honor of Edwin Cannan* (London: Routledge, 1927).

Schumpeter, Joseph A., *History of Economic Analysis* (Oxford: Oxford University Press, 1954).

Simon, Julian L., "Economic Thought About Population Consequences: Some Reflections," *Journal of Population Economics*, 1993, 6, pp. 137–52.

Smith, Adam, *An Inquiry into the nature and causes of the wealth of nations*, edited by Edwin Cannan (New York: Modern Library, 1937).

Spengler, Joseph J., "Population Phenomena and Population Theory," in Julian L. Simon (ed)., *Research in Population Economics*, volume 1 (Greenwich: JAI Press, 1978), 197– 216.

von Thünen, Johann, *The Isolated State* (New York: Kelley, 1826–1863/1966).

Wicksell, Knut, "The Theory of Population," section translated by Monica Fong, *History of Political Economy*, vol. 8, no. 3, 1976, 311–23 (original published in 1910).

Part 1

The Classical Setting

1

History of Population Theories

Joseph J. Spengler

Ancient and Medieval Writings on Population

Germs of certain ideas which have figured prominently in recent theoretical works on population can be found in very ancient writings. The thesis that excessive growth of population may reduce output per worker, depress the level of living of the masses, and engender strife is of great antiquity. It appears in the works of Confucius and his school, as well as in the works of other schools of ancient Chinese philosophers. In fact, these writers had the concept of optimum numbers, so far as the population engaged in agriculture is concerned. They postulated an ideal proportion between land and population, any major deviation from which would create poverty. They held the government primarily responsible for maintaining such a proportion by moving people from over-populated to underpopulated areas, though they noted that governmental action was reinforced at times by spontaneous migration.

These ancient Chinese writers also paid some attention to another topic which has occupied much space in subsequent literature on population theory—namely, the checks to population growth. They observed that mortality increases when the food supply is insufficient; that premature marriage makes for high infant mortality rates; that war checks population growth; and that costly marriage ceremonies reduce the marriage rate. They did not attempt to show how the variations of mortality, fertility, and nuptiality, as well as migration, might affect the balance between population and resources.[1]

Plato and Aristotle[2] considered the question of optimum size of population in their discussions of the ideal conditions of a city-state in which man's potentialities could be fully developed and his "highest good" realized. Their treatment of this question was by no means limited to its economic aspects. The "good life" could be attained, they believed, only if the population was large enough to be economically self-sufficient and capable of defending itself, but not too large for constitutional government. Self-sufficiency required the possession of enough territory to supply the needs of the people and to make possible a moderate level of living.[3] However, neither Plato nor Aristotle inquired explicitly into the relation between population density and *per capita* output or the connexion between the size of the population and the opportunities for division of labour. Plato specified 5,040 [total population about 60,000: Ed.] as the number of citizens "most likely to be useful to all cities", because it has "fifty-nine divisors" and "will furnish numbers for war and peace, and for all contracts and dealings, including taxes and divisions of the land."[4] Aristotle was less specific with regard to the optimum number, but he held that unless the size of the population was appropriately limited, poverty would be the result, for land and property could not be increased as rapidly as population would grow; civil discord would ensue, and it would be impossible for the government to function effectively.[5]

The views of Plato and Aristotle regarding the means of controlling the size of population are noteworthy. Plato proposed to restrict births, if necessary by restraining the reproduction of those "in whom generation is affluent"; if a higher birth rate were required, he would achieve it by means of rewards, stigmas, advice and rebuke to the young men from their elders. Should the population grow too large in spite of these precautions, it could be reduced by colonization, and immigration could be used if absolutely necessary to replenish a population greatly diminished by wars or epidemics.[6] Aristotle mentioned child-exposure and abortion as suitable means of preventing an excessive number of children, and in this connection paid some attention to eugenics.[7]

The Romans, like the Chinese, viewed population questions in the perspective of a great empire rather than a small city-state. They were less conscious than the Greeks of possible limits to population growth and more alert to its advantages for military and related purposes. Perhaps partly because of this difference in outlook, Roman writers paid less attention than the Greeks to population theory, but were much concerned with the practical problem of stimulating population increase. Their attitude was indicated by their disapproval of celibacy, their writings in defence of marriage and procreation, and by their legislation aimed at raising the marriage and birth rates.[8] Cicero, touching upon this subject, rejected Plato's communism in wives and children and held that the State's population must be kept up by monogamous marriage"[9]. He listed various checks to population growth—floods, epidemics, famines, wild animals, war, revolution-—but did not attempt to state a general theory of the determinants of population increase or decrease.[10]

Medieval Christian writers considered questions of population almost entirely from a moral and ethical standpoint. Since they were concerned more with the next world than with the present, they did not stress material values. Their doctrines were mainly populationist, but they placed less emphasis than earlier Hebrew and other religious writers on maxims adjuring men to multiply and people the earth.[11] On the one hand, they condemned abortion, infanticide, child-exposure, divorce, and polygamy; on the other hand, they glorified virginity and continence, considered celibacy superior to marriage though suited only to certain persons, and frowned on second marriage.[12] Unlike the Greeks and Romans, early medieval authors did not attach great importance to population growth as a source of strength for the State, but in time, with the reappearance of Aristotle's influence, this point was again emphasized.[13] Some medieval defenders of ecclesiastical celibacy resorted to economic arguments of a vaguely proto-Malthusian character, noting the extent to which the population of the world had grown, attributing observed poverty and want to this cause, and citing pestilence, famine, war, etc., as nature's means of pruning excess population.[14] The prevailing tendency, however, was to favour population increase, as it had been in earlier times. The high rates of mortality which were found throughout the world, and the constant threat of sudden depopulation through famines, epidemics and wars predisposed ancient and medieval writers alike to favour maintenance of a high birth rate.[15]

Arguments in favour of population increase predominated in the writings of European authors on population during the early modern, as well as the medieval, period. The discovery of the New World, the increase of commerce between Europe and Asia, the rise of national states, and the Protestant Reformation[16] brought some revision of the terms of discussion of population questions, but until the latter part of the eighteenth century there was no widespread change of attitude with regard to the desirability of a large and increasing population.[17]

Two writers of the period now under consideration require special mention. One is Ibn Khaldun, a fourteenth-century Muslim author, who expounded in detail a theory of cyclical variations of population and their relation to economic, political, and social-psychological conditions.[18] Khaldun's writings, though perceptive, apparently had little influence in the East and remained unknown in the West until the nineteenth century. The other writer worthy of special note is Botero, an Italian of the sixteenth century, who set forth ably some of the arguments later developed by Malthus. Botero held that man's generative powers operate with undiminished vigour irrespective of his numbers, whereas man's capacity to produce subsistence is subject to limits. The limitation of subsistence limits population through war, strife and various secondary checks to which the struggle for a limited subsistence gives rise. Presumably, Botero believed that the limits of subsistence had been reached, and that a further increase in population could not in general augment the flow of the means of support, since he declared that the population and the supply of food had remained constant for three thousand years or longer.[19]

Mercantilist and Related Theories

The mercantilist and cameralist schools of political economy, which flourished in Europe during much of the seventeenth and eighteenth centuries, emphasized the economic, political and military advantages of a large and growing population,[20] and favoured various measures to stimulate population growth.[21] Writers in these traditions were concerned primarily with the ways and means of increasing the wealth and power of the state, and in particular its supplies of precious metals. Their aim was not to raise *per capita* income but to increase either the aggregate national income or the excess of national income over the wage-cost of production, which excess was viewed as a source of tax revenues for the state. Population growth would augment national income and at the same time depress the hourly wage rate, giving the workers an incentive to work longer hours and widening the margin between national income and wage costs. The benefit to the state would be especially great if the additional labour supply were used to develop manufactures, for manufactured goods could be exchanged abroad for gold and silver. Many writers thought that manufacturing yielded increasing returns, presumably because of the greater possibilities of division of labour in a larger population; some held that agriculture was subject to diminishing returns and that there were limits to its expansion.[22] It was generally recognized that a large labour supply was useful only if it could be employed, and certain writers stated the thesis that population was determined by the amount of employment that could be made available.

The mercantilists paid special attention to the relation between population and foreign trade. Cantillon suggested that, if the agriculture of a country could not be expanded in proportion to the population, or if such an expansion would involve diminishing returns, additional agricultural products could be obtained abroad in exchange for manufactured goods.[23] Steuart put it that "work" should be exported and "matter" imported so long as satisfactory terms of trade could be obtained; otherwise, population would have to be contained within the limits of home-produced subsistence.[24] Several writers remarked that the size of a country's population was determined by the amount of subsistence that could be produced at home or obtained abroad. Few mercantilist or cameralist writers attempted a systematic explanation of population changes, but they did discuss a variety of checks to population growth: plagues, wars, accidents, uncongenial climate, infecundity due to urbanization and other causes, vice, abortion, deferment of marriage, celibacy, monopoly, luxurious living, emigration, etc.[25]

The period in which mercantilism flourished saw the beginning of scientific analysis and measurement of population trends.[26] The first of the writers to discern an underlying order in vital statistics was Graunt, who observed "the numerical regularity of deaths and births, of the ratio of the sexes at death and birth, and of the proportions of deaths from certain causes to all deaths in successive years and in different areas; in general terms of the uniformity and predictability of many important biological phenomena in the mass".[27] Petty, more speculative than Graunt, stressed the advantages of a large population on fiscal, administrative, and economic grounds. He noted that, should the population double every 360 years, there would in 2,000 years be one person for every two acres of habitable land, and, in consequence, wars and great slaughter."[28]

Süssmilch, author of the first complete treatise on population, was influenced by the work of both Graunt and Petty.[29] Birth and death rates were regular, he observed, and numbers normally increased, although urban mortality sometimes exceeded urban natality. Süssmilch thought that population normally tended to double every century, but that the period required for doubling would lengthen as population grew. Fixing the population capacity of the world at 4,000 to 5,000 million and the present world population around 1,000 million, he inferred that population could grow without causing difficulties for at least two centuries and probably much longer if the rate of increase fell and agriculture were greatly improved. Population growth, he said, was restrained by celibacy and deferred marriage and, above all, by pestilence, war, earthquakes, floods and starvation. Because he expected only advantages from population growth, and, because he set no store by a rising standard of living, Süssmilch favoured measures which would accelerate growth.[30]

The Theories of Malthus and His Immediate Predecessors

During the last half of the eighteenth century, more and more writers on economic and social questions rejected mercantilist doctrine and, with it, the long-established idea that population growth was advantageous and should be actively encouraged by the State.[31] Particularly in England, France, and Italy, there was increasing emphasis on the dependence of population upon subsistence and increasing appreciation of the complex manner in which checks on population growth operated. Certain writers, including Cantillon and his followers, developed the thesis that population growth was dependent upon the scale of living and upon how much of the subsistence produced was available for the support of the people.[32] Few writers asserted that population was *determined* by the means of subsistence; most tended to say that, since the standard of living varied, numbers were merely *affected* by the means of subsistence. Among the checks to further growth of population mentioned were dangerous occupations, poor sanitary conditions, contraceptive practices, divorce, urbanization and hindrances to production. It was noted that with the advance of civilization, physical checks gave way somewhat to psychological checks and that the operation of checks became more complex.

The opponents of mercantilist doctrine tended, as a rule, to minimize the possible achievements of the state in augmenting subsistence and improving the lot of the people, and to favour a policy of *laissez-faire*. In this connexion, it was pointed out that, if population adjusted itself to the food supply or to the demand for labour, legislation designed to influence natural increase or migration could have little effect. Some authors, especially in England and France, opposed arrangements for poor relief on the ground that they might undermine frugality, make for labour immobility and misuse of resources, and thus increase the pressure of numbers on subsistence. These arguments were turned against such advocates of social reform as Godwin and Condorcet, in an effort to show that any benefits from reform would be cancelled by a consequent increase of population.[33]

It was in this period of reaction against mercantilist doctrine that Malthus wrote the first edition of his essay on the "principle of population"[34]. The first edition was essentially a polemic directed primarily against Condorcet's conjectures regarding the perfectibility of man, against Godwin's system of equality and his allegation that the vices of mankind originated in human institutions, and against Wallace's contention that overpopulation would develop only in the distant future. Malthus asserted "the absolute impossibility from the fixed laws of our nature, that the pressure of want can ever be completely removed from the lower classes of society"; and that schemes for social reform such as Condorcet and Godwin had proposed would only increase the number of the poor by removing existing barriers to marrige and multiplication.

Notes

1. Huan-Chang, *The economic principles of Confucius and his school* (1911), Vol. I, pp. 180, 186–187, 249–250, 297–309, 322–323, 328–330, 338–339, 345–346, 355–356, 361–362; Chi Chao, *History of Chinese political thought during the early Tain period* (1930), pp. 65-66, 128–129, 187–188; Lee, *The economic history of China with special reference to agriculture* (1921), pp. 144–146, 155–156, 159, 201, 229, 292, 416–417, 419, 436–437; Weber, *Gesammelte Aufsätze zur Religionssoziologie* (1920), pp. 276–536. That little attention was paid to the manner in which numbers are adjusted to resources is implied, for example, by the treatment of population and migration in Swann, *Food and money in ancient China* (1950), pp. 61, 126–127, 302, and Wittfogal and Chia-Sheng, *History of Chinese society: Liao, 907–1125* (1949), pp. 41–112.
2. The theories of Plato and Aristotle were treated by Moreau in "Les théories démographiques dans l'antiquité grecque" (1949). Other ancient Greek writers

had little to say about questions of population. Xenophon described certain population policies of the Lacedaemonians and Persians in his *Constitution of the Lacedaemonians* (ca. 370 B.C.), and in his *The Oeconomicus* (ca. 370 B.C.). For a brief account see Trever, *A history of Greek economic thought* (1916), Chapter 4; also Michell, *The economics of ancient Greece* (1940), paras. 40, 224, 352. Herodotus in his *History* (ca. 440 B.C.; 1921 edit.), Bk. I. paras. 58, 66, 136; Bk. II, paras. 44, 60, 87, 103–104; Bk. III, paras. 65, 108–109, 159; Bk. IV, paras. 13, 147, 150, B.C.; occasionally referred to population growth and migration, but did not discuss the causes and consequences of these phenomena. Thucydides in *History* (ca. 145 B.C.; 1919 edit.), Bk. I, paras. 1–3, made passing references to migrations caused by population pressure. See also Bilabel, *Die ionische Kolonisation* (1920), pp. 2–5.

3. Plato, *Laws* (ca. 340 B.C.; 1926 edit.), Bk. V, para. 737; Aristotle, *Politica* (ca. 354 B.C.; 1932 edit.), Bk. I, para 1; Bk. VII, para. 4. These two authors did not share the opposition of the Greek primitivists to the concentration of population in cities. Lovejoy and others (eds.), *A documentary history of primitivism and related ideas* (1935).

4. Plato, *Laws* (ca. 340 B.C.; 1926 edit), Bk. V, paras. 737–738. See also Plato, *Republic* (ca. 370–380 B.C.; 1930 edit.), Bk. II para. 372; Bk. IV, para. 423; Bk. V, paras. 459–461. A state with 5,040 citizens would have a total population of about 60,000 and, given the various amounts of territory assigned to ideal city-states a population density of 75 to 300 per square mile. Welles, "The economic background of Plato's communism" (1948). In Plato's time the density of population in Attica was about 200 per square mile, and did not permit a comfortable level of living. Glotz, "La cité grecque" (1928), pp. 29–31.

5. Aristotle, *Politica* (ca. 354 B.C.; 1932 edit.), Bk. VII, paras. 4–5; Bk. II, paras. 6–9. In the latter place Aristotle declared that failure to limit population was "a never-failing cause of poverty," and that poverty was "the parent of revolution and crime." However, in his criticism of Plato's proposed community of women and property, he did not include the later Malthusian argument that such arrangements would stimulate excessive population growth. *Ibid.*, Bk. II, paras. 1–5; von Bortkiewicz did not consider Aristotle a fore-runner of Malthus; see von Bortkiewicz, "War Aristoteles Malthusianer?" (1906). But see Moissides, "Le Malthusianisme dans l'antiquité grecque" (1932), and Himes, *Medical history of contraception* (1936), Chapter 4.

6. Plato, *Laws* (ca. 340 B.C.; 1926 edit.), Bk. V, paras. 739–741 and on colonization Bk. IV, paras. 707–709; Bk. V, para. 736; Bk. VI, para. 754. Colonization was a traditional Greek remedy for over-population. See Michell, *The economics of . . .* (1940), pp. 217–224; Isocrates, *Panegyricus* (ca. 80 B.C.; 1928 edit.), paras. 34–36.

7. See Aristotle, *Politica* (ca. 354 B.C.; 1932 edit.), Bk. VII, para. 16, where exposure of deformed children is advocated. Aristotle mentioned homosexuality as a means of population control used by the Cretans; *ibid.*, Bk. II, para. 10. For his views on colonization, see *ibid*, Bk. II, para. 11; Bk. VI, para. 5.

8. Stangeland, *Pre-Malthusian doctrines of population* (1904), Chapter I; Gonnard, *Histoire des doctrines de la population* (1923), Chapters 2-3; Ferlet, *L'abaissement de la natalité à Rome et la dépopulation des campagnes, les réformes d'Auguste* (1902), Chapters 1-4; Frank, *An economic survey of Ancient Rome* (1933), Vol I pp. 40–42; Vol. III, pp. 313–322, Vol. V, p. 130; Simkovitch, *Towards the understanding of Jesus* (1937), pp. 128 ff; Ciccotti, "Considerazioni sulle leggi

matrimoniali di Augusto" (1938); Cochrane, *Christianity and classical culture* (1944), pp. 198–201, 219–220. For examples of references to Roman population laws in the works of contemporary writers, see Suetonius, *Octavius Augustus* (ca. A.D. 123; 1914 edit.), pp. 123–287; Tacitus, *Annals* (ca. A.D. 104–109; 1931 edit.), Bk. III, paras. 25-28; and ibid. (ca. A.D. 104–109; 1937 edit.), Bk. XV, para. 19; Plutarch, *De amore prolis* (ca. A.D. 100; 1939 edit.), pp. 331–497. See also citations in Lovejoy and others (eds.), *A documentary history . . .* (1935), pp. 408–411.

9. Cicero, *De re publica* (ca. 44 B.C.; 1928 edit.) Bk. IV, para. 5.
10. Cicero, *De officis* (ca. 44 B.C.; 1913 edit.), Bk. II, para 5. The list of checks is from a non-extant work. "The destruction of human life" by Dicaerchus, a pupil of Aristotle and a primitivist. Diodorus Siculus in his *Library of history* (ca. 60 B.C., 1933 edit.), Bk. I, para. 80, attributed the large population of Egypt to the ease and cheapness of rearing children there. Pliny's works contain almost nothing about population, although they did imply that immigration might check population and that cities grew through immigration. Pliny, *Historia naturalis* (ca. A.D. 75; 1942 edit.), Bk. IV, paras. 21 and 24.
11. With the exception of certain Brahmins and Buddhists the spokesmen for the Oriental religions appear to have favoured fertility and multiplication. See Stangeland, *Pre-Malthusian doctrines . . .* (1904), Chapter 2. For the earlier Hebrew view see *Genesis*, Chapter i, verse 28; Chapter ix, verse 1; Chapter xiii, verse 6; *Leviticus,* Chapter xxvi, verse 9; *Deuteronomy,* Chapter xiv, verse 28; Chapter xvii, verse 6. Apparently, upon Palestine's becoming fully peopled, it was the preservation of the race rather than its increase that was emphasized. See Himes, *Medical history . . .* (1936), pp. 69 ff.
12. See, among the ante-Nicene writers: St. Paul, *I Corinthians* (ca. A.D. 60) Chapter vii, verses 1–40; St. Paul, *I Timothy* (ca. A.D. 66), Chapter v, verses 3, 11-14; Ignatius, "Epistle to the Philadelphians" (ca. A.D. 80; 1947 edit.), Origen, "Commentaries on Matthew" (ca. A.D. 246–248; 1903 edit.); Cyprian, "Of the discipline and advantages of chastity" (ca. A.D. 240; 1880 edit.) and Cyprian, "On works and alms" (ca. A.D. 240; 1880 edit.), Clement of Alexandria, "The miscellanies: on marriage" (ca. A.D. 170; 1869 edit.). See among the post-Nicene writers: Athemasius, "Letter 48" (ca. A.D. 354, 1892 edit.); Chrysostom, "Homilies on the gospel of St. John" (ca. A.D. 390; 1890 edit.); Cyril, "Lecture 12" (ca. A.D. 340, 1894 edit.); Basil, "Letter to a fallen virgin" (ca. A.D. 350; 1895 edit.); Ambrose, "Concerning virgins" (ca. AD. 377; 1896 edit.); Nazianzen, "On the death of his father" (ca. A.D. 374; 1894 edit.); St. Augustine, "City of God" (ca. A.D. 413–426, 1887 edit.); and St. Augustine, "Good of marriage" (ca. A.D. 400; 1887 edit.); Gregory the Great, "Book of pastoral rule: on the life of the pastor" (ca. A.D. 580; 1895 edit.); Tertullian, "Against Marcion" (ca. A.D. 200; 1868 edit.); Tertullian, "To his wife" (ca. A.D. 200; 1869 edit.); Tertullian, "On monogamy" (ca. A.D. 200, 1870 edit); Irenaeus, *Against heresies* (ca. A.D. 182–188; 1868 edit.). These writings may be found in Schopp, *The Fathers of the Church* (1946), Roberts and Donaldson (eds.), *Ante-Nicene Christian Library* (1867–1880); Schaff, *A select library of the Nicene and post-Nicene Fathers of the Christian Church* (First series, 1886; second series, 1890). See also Stangeland, *Pre-Malthusian doctrines . . .* (1904), pp. 55–82; Riquet, "Christianisme et population" (1949). Some of these views are reflected in the instructions for the clergy incorporated in the medieval handbooks of penance. McNeil and Gamer, *Medieval handbooks of penance* (1938), see for example p. 294; also Russell, *British medieval population*

(1948), pp. 159–164. The social arrangements in effect often made for the postponement of marriage, the ideal in medieval England being, according to Russell, " that a living must precede marriage." *Ibid.*, p. 164.

13. Gonnard, *Histoire des doctrines économiques* (1930), p. 41; Mombert, *Geschichte der Nationalökonomie* (1927), p. 81; Thomas Aquinas, "De regemine principum" (ca. A.D. 1260; 1939 edit.); Thomas Aquinas, "Summa theologica" (ca. A.D. 1265–1272, 1935 edit.), Question 186, Art. 4, Sec. 3.

14. Theophilus, "Theophilus to Antolychus" (ca. A.D. 170; 1867 edit.), Bk. II, para. 32; Bk. III, para. 6; Methodius, "The banquet of the ten virgins; or concerning chastity," (ca. A.D. 270; 1869 edit.); Jerome, "Letter 22" (ca. A.D. 384; 1893 edit.); Dionysius Exiguus, "Libri de creatione hominis"; (ca. A.D. 520; 1848 edit.); Tertullian, "De anima" (ca. A.D. 200; 1870 edit.); Eusebius, "Oration in praise of Constantine" (ca. A.D. 300, 1890 edit.). Raoul des Presles argued in a like manner in the fourteenth century; see Brants, *L'économie politique au moyen-age* (1895), pp. 238–240.

15. With regard to the bearing of mortality experience on both custom and collective policy concerning marriage and child-bearing, see Korherr, "Die Bevölkerungspolitik der alten Kulturvölker" (1938).

16. Luther and other leaders of the Reformation condemned celibacy, but otherwise their teachings on matters relevant to population did not greatly differ from the medieval Christian doctrines.

17. An exception should be noted in the case of England, where most writers until near the middle of the seventeenth century believed the country to be over-populated and in need of colonies to draw off the excess. For summaries of the many works relevant to population during the fifteenth and sixteenth centuries, too numerous to list here, see Knorr, *British colonial theories* (1944), pp. 41–47, 68–81; Stangeland, *Pre-Malthusian doctrines . . .* (1904), Chapter 3; also Gonnard, *Histoire des doctrines . . .* (1923), pp. 89–129; Spengler, *French predecessors of Malthus* (1942), Chapter l; Beer, *The origins of the British colonial system* (1908), Chapters 1–2.

18. Khaldun held that a densely settled population was conducive to high *per capita* income, since it permitted a greater division of labour, a greater variety of occupations, more military and political security, and more effective use of resources than could be achieved by a sparse population. Population growth was affected by what men believed the future held in store; favourable expectations made for fertility and growth while unfavourable expectations made for decline. Good economic conditions and political order stimulated population growth by increasing natality and checking mortality. The populations of states tended to undergo cyclical change. With the establishment of domination, came political order, population growth, division of labour, and rising income; in their wake came luxury, rising taxes and other changes which in several generations produced political decay, economic decline, and depopulation. Representative selections from Khaldun's "Prolegomena" are available in Issawi, *An Arab philosophy of history* (1950), Chapter 5, which is based on the Quatremère and Beirut-Cairo editions. A French translation by de Slane, *Notices et extraits de la bibliothèque imperiale et autres bibliothèques*, Vols. 19–21, appeared in 1862–68. See also Qadir, "The economic ideas of Ibn Khaldun" (1942).

19. Botero, *Delle cause della grandezza della città* (1558), pp. 220–224, 376–381.

20. The views of individual writers in these schools are summarized in dictionaries and encyclopedias of political economy. Mercantilist and cameralist views on

population are summarized in Stangeland, *Pre-Malthusian doctrines* . . . (1904), Chapters 4–6, and parts of 7–9; Gonnard, *Histoire des doctrines* . . . (1923), Part 2; Reynaud, *La théorie de la population en Italie du xvie au xviiie siècle* (1904), Part I; Furniss, *The position of the laborer in a system of nationalism* (1920), pp. 5, 31, 59, 62; Small, *The Cameralists; the pioneers of German social policy* (1909); Viner, *Studies in the theory of international trade* (1937), Chapters 1–2; Johnson, *Predecessors of Adam Smith the growth of British economic thought* (1937), especially Part 2; Heckscher, *Merkantilismen* (1931), Vol. 2, pp. 139–145; Spengler, *French predecessors* . . . (1942), Chapters 2–3, 9; Cole, *French mercantilism doctrines before Colbert* (1931), especially Chapters 1 and 4; Cole, *Colbert and a century of French mercantilism* (1939), Vol. I, pp. 19–26, 45; Cole, *French mercantilism (1683–1700)* (1943), pp. 3–6, 229–272, 284–286; Beer, *Early British economics* (1938), pp. 41, 62, 78, 183–184; Silberner, "La guerre dans la pensée économique du xvie au xviiie siècle" (1939); Wermel, *The evolution of the classical wage theory* (1939).

21. These measures included the imposition of disabilities on celibates; the employment of penalties, favours, and monetary rewards to encourage marriage and production of large families; the removal of disabilities on illegitimate children; checks to emigration and stimuli to immigration, and improvements in medicine and public health.

22. Such was the view of Serra, as stated in his "Breve trattato delle cause che possono far abbondare li regni d'oro e d'argento dove non sono miniere con applicazione al Regno di Napoli" (1613; 1913 edit.).

23. Cantillon, *Essai sur la nature du commerce en général* (1755; 1952 edit.), Chapters 15–16.

24. Steuart, *An enquiry into the priniciples of political economy* (1767), Bk. 2, Chapters 24–25. See also Johnson, *Predecessors of* . . . (1937), Chapters 11–12, 15.

25. In England, before the mid-seventeenth century, emigration to colonies was approved on the ground that it relieved population pressure at home; during the century that followed it was sometimes condemned on the ground that it reduced the size of the domestic population. This latter view was usually rejected, however, on the ground that colonies were complementary to the mother country and that emigrants to colonies brought into being supplies and markets which operated in time to increase the population capacity of the mother country. See Knorr, *British colonial* . . . (1944), pp. 41–48, 68–81. Franklin developed the argument that the American population was complementary to the British, and hence its expansion would augment the population of Britain. See Spengler, "Malthusianism in late eighteenth century America" (1935).

26. For a concise summary of the views of British writers on fecundity and factors affecting fertility, see Kuczynski, "British demographers' opinions on fertility, 1660 to 1760" (1938).

27. Willcox in his introduction to Graunt's *Natural and political observations made upon the Bills of Mortality* (1662, 1939 edit.), p. xii of introductory chapter.

28. Here Petty was under the influence of Hale's *Primitive origination of mankind* (1677), Section 11, Chapter 9. Hale, observing that population increased geometrically and could double in as few as 35 years, and that the available means of subsistence could not long sustain such a rate of growth, concluded that the growth of population was restrained by war, famine, floods, pestilence, and earthquakes. Petty's main writings are included in Hull, *The economic writings of Sir William Petty* (1899), especially Vol. 11 pp. 537–548. For Halley's life table,

which was much more complete than Graunt's skeleton table, see Halley's "An estimate of the degree of the mortality of mankind" (1693). On these writers and their relation to the originators of actuarial science see Bonar, *Theories of population from Raleigh to Arthur Young* (1931), Chapters 3–5, 7.

29. Süssmilch was influenced also by others who had noted that population grew in geometric progression, among them Nichols Scheucher, Wideburg, Euler, Whiston, Hume, Wallace, Gregory King, and Charles Davenant. Süssmilch knew Derham's Physicotheology (1723), p. 208, in which it was asserted that Divine Providence had established a balance. in the world of living creatures to which man's numbers were made to conform, somctimes apparently through plagues and war. See Bonar, *Theories of population . . .* (1931), Chapter 5. Süssmilch's contemporary, Gottfried Achenwall, and his predecessor, Herman Conring, have sometimes been honoured as the founders of statistics, though their works bear no resemblance to modern statistical studies. Conring, who stressed the military value of large populations, discussed the checks to population operating in Spain; he included emigration and celibacy among the checks. See Conring, "Examen rerum publicarum potionum totius orbis" (1677; 1926 edit.).

30. Süssmilch, *Die Göttliche Ordnung in den Veränderungen des menschlichen Geschlechte aus der Geburt, dem Tode und der Fortpflanzung desselben erwiesen* (1775), Vol. I, pp. 17 ff.

31. For summaries of late eighteenth century writings on population see Stangeland, *Pre-Malthusion doctrines . . .* (1904), pp. 224–356; Gonnard, *Histoire des doctrines . . .* (1923), pp. 160–258; Spengler, *French predecessors . . .* (1942), especially Chapters 4–9; Reynaud, La théorie de la population en Italie . . . (1904) Part 2; Bonar, *Theories of population . . .* (1931), Chapters 6–8; Wermel, *The evolution of . . .* (1939), Chapters 2–6; Knorr, *British colonial . . .* (1944), pp. 219–228. See also Vincent, "French demography in the eighteenth century" (1947). A number of writers touched upon factors affecting the location of cities, but these views are not considered here. For example, see Maunier, "Théories sur la fonction des villes" (1910).

32. In Cantillon's view the amount of subsistence produced would depend upon the uses to which proprietors put their land; while the number of people a given amount of subsistence could support would depend upon how poorly people were "content to live." See Cantillon, *Essai sur la nature . . .* (1755; 1952 edit.), Part I, Chapter 15. The full implication of this theory and its development have bcen trcated by Landry in "Une théorie négligée. De l'influence de la direction de la demande sur la productivité du travail, les salaires et la population" (1910). Landry examined the Physiocratic argument, usually denied by the contemporaries of Physiocrats, that, under certain conditions, an increase in food consumption per head or in grain exports could stimulate domestic prosperity and population growth. See Landry, "Les idées de Quesnay sur la population" (1909). Condillac pointed out that the population of a country would not exceed that number which it could nourish. The population would be less if *per capita* consumption increased; it would decrease further if land were used for production which did not increase consumption. Condillac, *Le commerce et le gouvernment* (1776), p. 252. Ferguson argued, "men will crowd where the situation is tempting, and in a few generations will people every country to the measure of its subsistence", but he added that other conditions being given, numbers would vary inversely with the "standard" according to which men wished to live, and that this standard tended to rise with civilization. Ferguson, *An essay on the history of civil society* (1767), pp. 216–

218; Chalmers, *An estimate of the strength of Great Britain during the ptesent and four preceding reigns* (1794), pp. 1–2. For other works during this period concerned with the balance of population and subsistence and its consequences for population growth, see Reynaud, *La théorie de la population en Italie* . . . (1904), pp. 109, 131, Spengler, *French predecessors* . . . (1942), pp. 230–241; Stangeland, *Pre-Malthusian doctrines* . . . (1904) pp. 227, 237–238, 266, 275 ff., 347; Smith, *An enquiry into the nature and causes of the wealth of nations* (1776; 1937 edit.), Book I, Chapter 8.

33. See Wallace, *Various prospects of mankind, nature, and providence* (1761), p. 114. Godwin denied that such could be the final outcome, while Condorcet considered the possibility only to indicate that man could cope with it. Godwin, *Political justice* (1793), Bk. 8, Chapter 7. On Condorcet see Spengler, *French predecessors* . . . (1942), pp. 259–263, Chapters 7–8; Stangeland, *Pre-Malthusian doctrines* . . . (1904), pp. 228, 273, 283, 344. See also Griffith, *Population problems of the age of Malthus* (1925), Chapter VI.

34. Malthus, An essay on the principle of population (1798). See also Griffith, *Population problems of* . . . (1925), Chapter IV. On the condition giving rise to Malthus' Essay see Nitti and Buer "The historical setting of the Malthusian controvcrsy" (1927).

2

Natural and Political Observations

John Graunt

TO THE

RIGHT HONOURABLE
JOHN Lord *ROBERTS*, Baron of

Truro, Lord *Privie-Seal*, and one of His Majestie's
most Honourable *Privie Council*.

My Lord,

Now having (I know not by what accident) engaged my thoughts upon the *Bills of Mortality*, and so far succeeded therein, as to have reduced several great confused *Volumes* into a few perspicuous *Tables*, and abridged I I such *Observations* as naturally flowed from them, into a few succinct *Paragraphs*, without any long Series of *multiloquious Deductions*, I have presumed to sacrifice these my small, but first publish'd, *Labours* unto your Lordship . . .

For with all humble submission to your Lordship, I conceive, That it doth not ill-become a *Peer of the Parliament*, or *Member of his Majestie's Council*, to consider how few starve of the many that beg: That the irreligious *Proposals* of some, to multiply People by *Polygamy*, is withall irrational, and fruitless: That the troublesome seclusions in the *Plague-time* is not a remedy to be purchased at vast

17

inconveniences: That the greatest *Plagues* of the City are equally, and quickly repaired from the Country: That the wasting of *Males* by Wars, and Colonies do not prejudice the due proportion between them and *Females*: That the Opinions of *Plagues* accompanying the Entrance of *Kings* is false, and seditious: That *London*, the *Metropolis of England*, is perhaps a Head too big for the Body, and possibly too strong: That this Head grows three times as fast as the Body unto which it belongs, that is, It doubles its People in a third part of the time: That our *Parishes* are now grown madly disproportionable: That our *Temples* are not sutable to our *Religion*: That the *Trade*, and very *City of London* removes *Westward*: That the walled City is but a one fifth of the whole Pyle:| | That the old Streets are unfit for the present frequencie of *Coaches*: That the passage of *Ludgate* is a throat too straight for the Body: That the fighting men about *London*, are able to make three as great Armies as can be of use in this *Island*: That the number of Heads is such, as hath certainly much deceived some of our *Senatours* in their appointments of Pole-money, &c. . . .

Your Lordship's most obedient, and
most faithfull Servant,

Birchen-Lane,
25 *January* 166 1/2

JOHN GRAUNT.

*   *   *

An Index of the *Positions*,
***Observations*, and *Questions* contained in this Discourse.**

* * *

The Conclusion.

It may be now asked, to what purpose tends all this laborious buzzling, and groping? To know,

1. The number of the People?
2. How many *Males*, and *Females?*
3. How many Married, and single?
4. How many *Teeming* Women?
5. How many of every *Septenary*, or *Decad* of years in *age?*
6. How many *Fighting* Men?
7. How much *London* is, and by what steps it hath increased?
8. In what time the housing is replenished after a *Plague?*
9. What proportion die of each general and perticular *Casualties?*
10. What years are Fruitfull, and Mortal, and in what Spaces, and Intervals, they follow each other?

11.   In what proportion Men neglect the Orders of the *Church,* and *Sects* have increased?
12.   The disproportion of Parishes?
13.   Why the Burials in *London* exceed the Christnings, when the contrary is visible in the Country?

To this I might answer in general by saying, that those, who cannot apprehend the reason of these Enquiries, are unfit to trouble themselves to ask them.[72]

2.   I might answer by asking; Why so many have spent their times, and estates about the Art of making Gold? which, if it were much known, would onely exalt Silver into the place, which Gold now possesseth; and if it were known but to some one Person, the same single *Adeptus* could not, nay, durst not enjoy it, but must be either a Prisoner to some Prince, and Slave to some Voluptuary, or else skulk obscurely up and down for his privacie, and concealment.

3.   I might Answer; That there is much pleasure in deducing so many abstruse, and unexpected inferences out of these poor despised Bills of *Mortality*; and in building upon that ground, which hath lain waste these eighty years. And there is pleasure in doing something new, though never so little, without pestering the World with voluminous Transcriptions.

4.   But, I Answer more seriously; by complaining, That whereas the Art of Governing, and the true *Politiques*, is how to preserve the Subject in *Peace*, and *Plenty*, that men study onely that part of it, which teacheth how to supplant, and over-reach one another, and how, not by fair out-running, but by tripping up each other's heels, to win the Prize.

Now; the Foundation, or Elements of this honest harmless *Policy* is to understand the Land, and the hands of the Territory to be governed, according to all their intrinsick, and accidental differences: as for example; It were good to know the *Geometrical* Content, Figure, and Scituation of all [73] the Lands of a Kingdom, especially, according to its most natural, permanent, and conspicuous Bounds. It were good to know, how much Hay an Acre of every sort of Meadow will bear? how many Cattel the same weight of each sort of Hay will feed, and fatten? what quantity of Grain, and other Commodities the same Acre will bear in one, three, or seven years *communibus Annis*? unto what use each soil is most proper? All which particulars I call the intrinsick value: for there is also another value meerly accidental, or extrinsick, consisting of the Causes, why a parcel of Land, lying near a good Market, may be worth double to another parcel, though but of the same intrinsick goodness; which answers the Queries, why Lands in the North of *England* are worth but sixteen years purchase, and those of the West above eight and twenty. It is no less necessary to know how many People there be of each Sex, State, Age, Religion, Trade, Rank, or Degree, *&c.* by the knowledg whereof Trade, and Government may be made more certain, and Regular; for, if men knew the People as aforesaid, they might know the consumption they would make, so as Trade might not be hoped for where it is impossible. As for instance, I have heard much complaint, that Trade is not set up in some of the *South-western*, and *North-western* Parts of *Ireland*, there being so many excellent Harbours for that purpose, whereas in several of those Places I have also heard, that there are few other Inhabitants, but such as live *ex sponte creatis*, and are unfit Subjects of Trade, as neither [74] employing others, nor working themselves.

Moreover, if all these things were clearly, and truly known (which I have but guessed at) it would appear, how small a part of the People work upon necessary Labours, and Callings, *viz.* how many Women, and Children do just nothing, onely learning to spend what others get ? how many are meer Voluptuaries, and as it were meer Gamesters by Trade? how many live by puzling poor people with unintelligible Notions in Divinity, and Philosophie? how many by perswading credulous, delicate, and Litigious Persons, that their Bodies, or Estates are out of Tune, and in danger? how many by fighting as Souldiers? how many by Ministeries of Vice, and Sin? how many by Trades of meer Pleasure, or Ornaments? and how many in a way of lazie attendance, *&c.* upon others? And on the other side, how few are employed in raising, and working necessary food, and covering? and of the speculative men, how few do truly studie *Nature*, and *Things*? The more ingenious not advancing much further then to write, and speak wittily about these matters.

I conclude, That a clear knowledge of all these particulars, and many more, whereat I have shot but at rovers, is necessary in order to good, certain, and easie Government, and even to balance Parties, and factions both in *Church* and *State*. But whether the knowledge thereof be necessary to many, or fit for others, then the Sovereign, and his chief ministers, I leave to consideration.

TABLE 1
The Table of Burials, and Christnings in London.

Anno Dom.	97 Parishes	16 Parishes	Out-Pa-rishes	Buried in all	Besides of the *Plague*	Christned
1604	1518	2097	708	4323	896	5458
1605	2014	2974	960	5948	444	6504
1606	1941	2920	935	5796	2124	66l4
1607	1879	2772	1019	5670	2352	6582
1608	2391	3218	1149	6758	2262	6845
1609	2494	3610	1441	7545	4240	6388
1610	2326	3791	1369	7486	1803	6785
1611	2152	3398	1166	6716	627	7014
	16715	**24780**	**8747**	**50242**	**14752**	**52190**
1612	2473	3843	1462	7778	64	6986
1613	2406	3679	1418	7503	16	6846
1614	2369	3504	1494	7367	22	7208
1615	2446	3791	1613	7850	37	7682
1616	2490	3876	1697	8063	9	7985
1617	2397	4109	1774	8280	6	7747
1618	2815	4715	2066	9596	18	7735
1619	2339	3857	1804	7999	9	8127
	19735	**31374**	**13328**	**64436**	**171**	**60316**
1620	2726	4819	2146	9691	21	7845
1621	2438	3759	1915	8112	11	8039
1622	2811	4217	2392	8943	16	7894
1623	3591	4721	2783	11095	17	7945
1624	3385	5919	2895	12199	11	8299
1625	5143	9819	3886	18848	35417	6983
1626	2150	3286	1965	7401	134	6701
1627	2325	3400	1988	7711	4	8408
	24569	**39940**	**19970**	**84000**	**35631**	**62114**
1628	2412	3311	2017	7740	3	8564
1629	2536	3992	2243	8771	0	9901
1630	2506	4201	2521	9237	1317	9315
1631	2459	3697	2132	8288	274	8524
1632	2704	4412	2411	9527	8	9584
1633	2378	3936	2078	8392	0	9997
1634	2937	4980	2982	10899	1	9855
1635	2742	4966	2943	10651	0	10034
	20694	**33495**	**19327**	**73505**	**1603**	**75774**

(cont.)

TABLE 1 (continued)
The Table of Burials, and Christnings in *London*.

Anno Dom.	97 Parishes	16 Parishes	Out-Pa- rishes	Buried in all	Besides of the *Plague*	Christned
1636	2825	6924	3210	12959	10400	9522
1637	2288	4265	2128	8681	3082	9160
1638	3584	5926	3751	13261	363	10311
1639	2592	4344	2612	9548	314	10150
1640	2919	5156	3246	11321	1450	10850
1641	3248	5092	3427	11767	1375	10670
1642	3176	5245	3578	11999	1274	10370
1643	3395	5552	3269	12216	996	9410
	23987	**42544**	**25221**	**91752**	**19244**	**80443**
1644	2593	4274	2574	9441	1492	8104
1645	2524	4639	2445	9608	1871	7966
1646	2746	4872	2797	10415	2365	7163
1647	2672	4749	3041	10462	3597	7332
1648	2480	4288	2515	9283	611	6544
1649	2865	4714	2920	10499	67	5825
1650	2301	4138	2310	8749	15	5612
1651	2845	5002	2597	10804	23	6071
	21026	**36676**	**21199**	**78896**	**10041**	**54617**
1652	3293	5719	3546	12553	16	6128
1653	2527	4635	2919	10081	6	6155
1654	3323	6063	3845	13231	16	6620
1655	2761	5148	3439	11348	9	7004
1656	3327	6573	4015	13915	6	7050
1657	3014	5646	3770	12430	4	6685
1658	3613	6923	4443	14979	14	6170
1659	3431	6988	4301	14720	36	5690
	25288	**47695**	**30278**	**103261**	**107**	**51502**
1660	3098	5644	3926	12668	13	6971
1661	3804	7309	5532	16645	20	8855

TABLE 2
The Table of Casualties,

The Years of our Lord	1647	1648	1649	1650	1651	1652	1653	1654	1655	1656	1657	1658
Abortive, and stillborn	335	329	327	351	389	381	384	433	483	419	463	467
Aged	916	835	889	696	780	834	864	974	743	892	869	1176
Ague, and Fever	1260	884	751	970	1038	1212	1282	1371	689	875	999	1800
Apoplex, and sodainly	68	74	64	74	106	111	118	86	92	102	113	138
Bleach		1	3	7	2					1		
Blasted	4	1			6	6			4		5	5
Bleeding	3	2	5	1	3	4	3	2	7	3	5	4
Bloudy Flux, Scouring, and Flux	155	176	802	289	833	762	200	386	168	368	362	233
Burnt, and Scalded	3	6	10	5	11	8	5	7	10	5	7	4
Calenture	1			1		2	1	1			3	
Cancer, Gangrene, and Fistula	26	29	31	19	31	53	36	37	73	31	24	35
Wolf				8								
Canker, Sore-mouth, and Thrush	66	28	54	42	68	51	53	72	44	81	19	27
Childbed	161	106	114	117	206	213	158	192	177	201	236	225
Chrisomes, and Infants	1369	1254	1065	990	1237	1280	1050	1343	1089	1393	1162	1144
Colick, and Wind	103	71	85	82	76	102	80	101	85	120	113	179
Cold, and Cough							41	36	21	58	30	31
Consumption, and Cough	2423	2200	2388	1988	2350	2410	2286	2868	2606	3184	2757	3610
Convulsion	684	491	530	493	569	653	606	828	702	1027	807	841
Cramp				1								
Cut of the Stone		2	1	3		1	1	2	4	1	3	5
Dropsy, and Tympany	185	434	421	508	444	556	617	704	660	706	631	931
Drowned	47	40	30	27	49	50	53	30	43	49	63	60
Excessive drinking			2									
Executed	8	17	29	43	24	12	19	21	19	22	20	18
Fainted in a Bath					1							
Falling-Sickness	3	2	2	3		3	4	1	4	3	1	
Flox, and small Pox	139	400	1190	184	525	1279	139	812	1294	823	835	409
Found dead in the Streets	6	6	9	8	7	9	14	4	3	4	9	11
French-Pox	18	29	15	18	21	20	20	20	29	23	25	53
Frighted	4	4	1		3		2		1	1		
Gout	9	5	12	9	7	7	5	6	8	7	8	13
Grief	12	13	16	7	17	14	11	17	10	13	10	12
Hanged, and made-away themselves	11	10	13	14	9	14	15	9	14	16	24	18
Head-ach		1	11	2		2	6	6	5	3	4	5
Jaundice	57	35	39	49	41	43	57	71	61	41	46	77
Jaw-faln	1	1			3			2	2		3	1
Impostume	75	61	65	59	80	105	79	90	92	122	80	134
Itch		1										
Killed by several Accidents	27	57	39	94	47	45	57	58	52	43	52	47
King's Evil	27	26	22	19	22	20	26	26	27	24	23	28
Lethargy	3	4	2	4	4	4	3	10	9	4	6	2
Leprosy			1								1	
Livergrown, Spleen, and Rickets	53	46	56	59	65	72	67	65	52	50	38	51
Lunatique	12	18	6	11	7	11	9	12	6	7	13	5
Meagrom	12	13		5	8	6	6	14	3	6	7	6
Measles	5	92	3	33	33	62	8	52	11	153	15	80
Mother	2					1	1	2	2	3		3

1659	1660	1629	1630	1631	1632	1633	1634	1635	1636	1629 1630 1631 1632	1633 1634 1635 1636	1647 1648 1649 1650	1651 1652 1653 1654	1655 1656 1657 1658	1629 1649 1659	In 20 Years
421	544	499	439	410	445	500	475	507	523	1793	2005	1342	1587	1832	1247	8559
909	1095	579	712	661	671	704	623	794	714	2475	2814	3336	3452	3680	2377	15757
2303	2148	956	1091	1115	1108	953	1279	1622	2360	4418	6235	3865	4903	4363	4010	23784
91	67	22	36		17	24	35	26		75	85	280	421	445	177	1306
											4	9	1	1	1	15
3	8	13	8	10	13	6	4		4	54	14	5	12	14	16	99
7	2	5	2	5	4	4	3			16	7	11	12	19	17	65
346	251	449	438	352	348	278	512	346	330	1587	1466	1422	2181	1161	1597	7858
6	6	3	10	7	5	1	3	12	3	25	19	24	31	26	19	125
								1	3		4	2	4	3		13
63	52	20	14	23	28	27	30	24	30	85	112	105	157	150	114	609
											8					8
73	68	6	4	4	1			5	74	15	79	190	244	161	133	689
226	194	150	157	112	171	132	143	163	230	590	668	498	769	839	490	3364
858	1123	2596	2378	2035	2268	2130	2315	2113	1895	9277	8453	4678	4910	4788	4519	32106
116	167	48	57					37	50	105	87	341	359	497	247	1389
33	24	10	58	51	55	45	54	50	57	174	207	00	77	140	43	598
2982	3414	1827	1910	1713	1797	1754	1955	2080	2477	5157	8266	8999	9914	12157	7197	44487
742	1031	52	87	18	241	221	386	418	709	498	1734	2198	2656	3377	1324	9073
			1	0	0	0	0	0	0	01	00	01	0	0	1	2
46	48				5	1	5	2	2	5	10	6	4	13	47	38
646	872	235	252	279	280	266	250	329	389	1048	1734	1538	2321	2982	1302	9623
57	48	43	33	29	34	37	32	32	45	139	147	144	182	215	130	827
													2		2	2
7	18	19	13	12	18	13	13	13	13	62	52	97	76	79	55	384
													1		1	
4	5	3	10	7	7	2	5	6	8	27	21	10	8	8	9	74
1523	354	72	40	58	531	72	1354	293	127	701	1846	1913	2755	3361	2785	10576
2	6	18	33	26	6	13	8	24	24	83	69	29	34	27	29	243
51	31	17	12	12	12	7	17	12	22	53	48	80	81	130	83	392
	9	1		1				3	2	3	9	5	2	2		21
14	2	2	5	3	4	4	5	7	8	14	24	35	25	36	28	134
13	4	18	20	22	11	14	17	5	20	71	56	48	59	45	47	279
11	36	8	8	5	15		3	8	7	37	18	48	47	72	32	222
35	26							4	2	0	6	14	14	17	46	051
102	76	47	59	35	43	35	45	54	63	184	197	180	212	225	188	998
		10	16	13	8	10	10	4	11	47	35	02	5	6	10	95
105	96	58	76	73	74	50	62	73	130	282	315	260	354	428	228	1639
										00	10	01				11
55	47	54	55	47	46	49	41	51	60	202	201	217	207	194	148	1021
28	54	16	25	18	38	35	20	26	69	97	150	94	94	102	66	537
6	4	1		2	2	3		2	2	5	7	13	21	21	9	67
2	2							2		2	2	1		1	3	06
8	15	94	112	99	87	82	77	98	99	392	356	213	269	191	158	1421
14	14	6	11	6	5	4	2	2	5	28	13	47	39	31	26	158
5	4			24					22	24	22	30	34	22	05	132
6	74	42	2	3	80	21	33	27	12	127	83	133	155	259	51	757
1	8	1							3	01	3	2	4	8	02	18

TABLE 2 (continued)
The Table of Casualties,

The Years of our Lord	1647	1648	1649	1650	1651	1652	1653	1654	1655	1656	1657	1658
Murdered	3	2	7	5	4	3	3	3	9	6	5	7
Overlayd, and starved at Nurse	25	22	36	28	28	29	30	36	58	53	44	50
Palsy	27	21	19	20	23	20	29	18	22	23	20	22
Plague	3597	611	67	15	23	16	6	16	9	6	4	14
Plague in the Guts				1		110	32		87	315	446	
Pleurisy	30	26	13	20	23	19	17	23	10	9	17	16
Poysoned		3		7								
Purples, and spotted Fever	145	47	43	65	54	60	75	89	56	52	56	126
Quinsy, and Sore-throat	14	11	12	17	24	20	18	9	15	13	7	10
Rickets	150	224	216	190	260	329	229	372	347	458	317	476
Mother, rising of the Lights	150	92	115	120	134	138	135	178	166	212	203	228
Rupture	16	7	7	6	7	16	7	15	11	20	19	18
Scal'd-head	2				1				2			
Scurvy	32	20	21	21	29	43	41	44	103	71	82	82
Smothered, and stifled				2								
Sores, Ulcers, broken and bruised	15	17	17	16	26	32	25	32	23	34	40	47
Shot (Limbs												
Spleen	12	17					13	13		6	2	5
Shingles												
Starved		4	8	7	1	2	1	1	3	1	3	6
Stitch					1							
Stone, and Strangury	45	42	29	28	50	41	44	38	49	57	72	69
Sciatica												
Stopping of the Stomach	29	29	30	33	55	67	66	107	94	145	129	277
Surfet	217	137	136	123	104	177	178	212	128	161	137	218
Swine-Pox	4	4	3				1	4	2	1	1	1
Teeth, and Worms	767	597	540	598	709	905	691	1131	803	1198	878	1036
Tissick	62	47										
Thrush											57	66
Vomiting	1	6	3	7	4	6	3	14	7	27	16	19
Worms	147	107	105	65	85	86	53					
Wen	1		1		2	2			1		1	2
Sodainly												

1659	1660	1629	1630	1631	1632	1633	1634	1635	1636	1629 1630 1631 1632	1633 1634 1635 1636	1647 1648 1649 1650	1651 1652 1653 1654	1655 1656 1657 1658	1629 1649 1659	In 20 Years.
70	20		3	7		6	5	8	10	19	17	13	27		77	86
46	43	4	10	13	7	8	14	10	14	34	46	111	123	215	86	529
17	21	17	23	17	25	14	21	25	17	82	77	87	90	87	53	423
36	14	1317	274	8		1			10400	1599	10401	4290	61	33	103	16384
253	402									00	00	61	142	844	253	991
12	10	26	24	26	36	21		45	24	112	90	89	72	52	51	415
						2		2	00	4	10	00	00	00		14
368	146	32	58	58	38	24	125	245	397	186	791	300	278	290	243	1845
21	14	01	8	6	7	24	04	5	22	22	55	54	71	45	34	217
441	521						14	49	50	00	113	780	1190	1598	657	3681
210	249	44	72	99	98	60	84	72	104	309	220	777	585	809	369	2700
12	28	2	6	4	9	4	3	10	13	21	30	36	45	68	2	201
												2	1	2		05
95	12	5	7	9		9		00	25	33	34	94	132	300	115	593
		24								24		2			2	26
61	48	23		20	48	19	19	22	29	91	89	65	115	144	141	504
7	20															27
7	7											29	26	13	07	68
1					1										1	2
7	14									14	19	5	13		29	51
												1				1
22	30		58	56	58	49	33	45	114	185	144	175	247		51	863
	2			1	3		1	6	1	4						15
186	214							6		6	121	295	247		216	669
202	192	63	157	149	86	104	114	132	371	445	721	613	671	644	401	3094
2		5	8	4	6	3		10		23	13	11	5	5	10	57
839	1008	440	506	335	470	432	454	539	1207	1751	2632	2502	3436	3915	1819	14236
		8	12	14	34	23	15	27		68	65	109			8	242
		15	23	17	40	28	31	34		95	93			123	15	211
8	10	1	4	1	1	2	5	6	3	7	16	17	27	69	12	136
		19	31	28	27	19	28	27		105	74	424	224		124	830
1	1			1		4				1	4	2	4	4	2	15
		63	59	37	62	58	62	78	34	221	233				63	454
															34190	229250

3

Another Essay in Political Arithmetick

William Petty

The Extract of a Letter *concerning the scope of an* Essay *intended to precede* Another Essay *concerning the* Growth *of the* City *of* (LONDON), *&c. An* Essay in Political Arithmetick, *concerning the Value and Encrease of* People *and* Colonies.

The scope of this *Essay,* is concerning People and Colonies, and to make way for *Another Essay* concerning the *Growth* of the *City* of *London.* I desire in this first *Essay* to give the World some light concerning the Numbers of People in *England,* with *Wales,* and in *Ireland*; as also, of the number of Houses, and Families, wherein they live, and of Acres they occupy.

2. How many live upon their *Lands,* how many upon their *Personal Estates,* and *Comerce,* and how many upon *Art,* and *Labour*; how many upon *Alms,* how many upon *Offices* and *Publick Employments,* and how many as *Cheats* and *Thieves*; how many are *Impotents, Children,* and *decrepit Old men.*

3. How many upon the *Poll-Taxes* in *England*, do pay extraordinary Rates, and how many at the Level[1].

4. How many Men and Women are *Prolifick,* and how many of each are Married or Unmarried.

5. What the Value of People[2] are in *England,* and what in *Ireland* at a *Medium,* both as Members of the *Church* or *Commonwealth,*

or as *Slaves* and Servants to one another; with a Method how to estimate the same, in any other *Country* or *Colony.*

6.   How to compute the Value of Land in *Colonies,* in comparison to *England* and *Ireland.*

7.   How 10 thousand People in a *Colony* may be, and planted to the best advantage.

8.   A Conjecture in what number of years *England* and *Ireland* may be fully peopled, as also all *America*, and lastly the whole habitable Earth.

9.   What spot of the *Earths-Globe* were fittest for a general and universal *Emporium*, whereby all the people thereof may best enjoy one anothers *Labours* and *Commodities.*

10.   Whether the speedy Peopling of the Earth would make
    1. For the good of Mankind.
    2. To fulfil the revealed *Will* of *God.*
    3. To what *Prince* or *State* the same would be most advantageous.

11.   An exhortation to all thinking Men to salve the Scriptures and other good Histories, concerning the *Number* of *People* in all *Ages* of the *World*, in the great *Cities* thereof, and elsewhere.

12.   An Appendix concerning the different Number of *Sea-fish* and *Wild-fowl*, at the end of every thousand years, since *Noah*'s Flood.

13.   An Hypothesis of the use of those spaces (of about 8,000 miles through) within the *Globe* of our *Earth*, supposing a shell of 150 miles thick.

14.   What may be the meaning of *Glorified Bodies,* in case the place of the Blessed shall be without the Convex of the Orb of the *fixed Stars*, if that the whole System of the *World* was made for the use of our *Earths-men. . . .*

We have spoken of the Growth of *London,* with the Measures and Periods thereof, we come next to the Causes and Consequences of the same.

The Causes of its *Growth* from 1642 to 1682, may be said to have been as followeth, *viz.* From 1642 to 1650, That Men came out of the *Countrey* to *London*, to shelter themselves from the Outrages of the Civil *Wars,* during that time; from 1650 to 1660, The *Royal Party* came to *London,* for their more private and inexpensive Living; from 1660 to 1670, the *Kings Friends* and *Party* came to receive his *Favours* after his *Happy Restauration*; from 1670 to 1680, The frequency of *Plots* and

Parliaments might bring extraordinary Numbers to the City; But what Reasons to assign for the like *Increase* from 1604 to 1642, I know not, unless I should pick out some *Remarkable Accident* happening in each part of the said *Period*, and make that to be the Cause of this *Increase* (as Vulgar People make the Cause of every Mans Sickness to be what he did last eat) wherefore, rather than so to say *quidlibet de quolibet*; I had rather quit even what I have above-said to be the Cause of *London's Increase* from 1642 to 1682, and put the whole upon some Natural and Spontaneous *Benefits* and Advantages that Men find by Living in great more than in small *Societies*; and shall therefore seek for the *Antecedent Causes* of this *Growth,* in the *Consequences* of the like, considered in greater *Characters* and *Proportions.*

Now, whereas in Arithmetick, out of two false *Positions* the Truth is extracted, so I hope out of two *extravagant* contrary Suppositions, to draw forth some solid and consistent *Conclusions, viz.*

The first of the said two Suppositions is, That the City of *London* is seven times bigger than now, and that the *Inhabitants* of it are four Millions 690 Thousand People, and that in all the other *Cities, Ports, Towns*, and *Villages,* there are but two Millions 710 Thousand more.

The other *Supposition* is, That the City of *London* is but a seventh part of its present bigness, and that the *Inhabitants* of it are but 96 Thousand, and that the rest of the Inhabitants (being 7 Millions 304 Thousand) do Co-habit thus, 104 Thousand of them in small *Cities* and *Towns,* and that the rest, being seven Millions 200 Thousand, do Inhabit in *Houses* not contiguous to one another, *viz.* in 1200 Thousand Houses, having about 24 Acres of Ground belonging to each of them, accounting about 28 Millions of Acres to be in the whole *Territory* of *England, Wales*, and the adjacent *Islands*; which any Man that pleases may Examine upon a good Map.

Now, the Question is, In which of these two Imaginary states, would be the most convenient, commodious and comfortable Livings?

But this general Question divides it self into the several Questions, relating to the following Particulars, *viz.*

1. For the *Defence* of the Kingdom against Foraign Powers.
2. For preventing the *Intestine Commotions* of *Parties* and *Factions.*
3. For *Peace* and *Uniformity* in *Religion.*
4. For the *Administration* of *Justice.*
5. For the proportionably *Taxing* of the People, and easie *Levying* the same.

6.   For *Gain* by Foraign Commerce.

7.   For *Husbandry, Manufacture*, and for *Arts* of Delight and Ornament.

8.   For lessening the Fatigue of *Carriages* and *Travelling*.

9.   For preventing *Beggars* and *Thieves*.

10.   For the Advancement and Propagation of *Useful Learning*.

11.   For *Increasing* the People by *Generation*.

12.   For preventing the Mischiefs of *Plagues* and *Contagions*. And withal, which of the said two states is most Practicable and Natural, for in these and the like particulars, do lye the *Tests* and *Touch-stones* of all *Proposals,* that can be made for the Publick Good.

First, as to *Practicable*, we say, That although our said Extravagant Proposals are both in Nature possible, yet it is not Obvious to every Man to conceive, how *London,* now seven times bigger than in the beginning of *Queen Elizabeths Reign*, should be seven times bigger than now it is, and 49 times bigger than *Anno* 1560. To which I say, I. That the present City of *London* stands upon less than 1500[1] Acres of Ground, wherefore a City, seven times as large may stand upon l0500 Acres, which is about equivalent to a Circle of four Miles and a half in Diameter, and less than 15 Miles in Circumference. 2. That a Circle of Ground of 35 Miles Semidiameter will bear *Corn, Garden-stuff, Fruits, Hay*, and *Timber,* for the four Millions 690 Thousand Inhabitants of the said City and Circle, so as nothing of that kind need be brought from above 35 Miles distance from the said City; for the Number of Acres within the said Circle, reckoning one[2] Acre sufficient to furnish *Bread* and *Drink-Corn* for every Head, and two Acres will furnish Hay for every Necessary Horse; And that the Trees which may grow in the Hedge-rows of the Fields within the said Circle, may furnish *Timber* for 600 Thousand Houses. 3. That all live Cattel and great Animals can bring themselves to the said City; and that Fish can be brought from the *Lands-end* and *Berwick* as easily as now. 4. Of *Coals* there is no doubt: And for Water, 20*s. per* Family (or 600 Thousand pounds *per Annum* in the whole) will serve this *City*, especially with the help of the *New River*. But if by Practicable be understood, that the present state may be suddenly changed into either of the two above-mentioned Proposals, I think it is not *Practicable*. Wherefore the true Question is, unto or towards which of the said two Extravagant states it is best to bend the present state by degrees, *viz.* Whether it be best to lessen or enlarge the present City? In Order whereunto we enquire (as to the first Question) which   state is most *Defensible* against *Forraign Powers*, saying, that if the above-mentioned Housing, and a border of Ground, of 3 quarters of a Mile broad, were encompassed with a Wall and Ditch of 20 Miles about (as strong as any in *Europe* which would cost but a Million, or about a Penny in the shilling of the House-Rent for one Year) what *Foraign Prince* could bring an Army from beyond Seas, able to beat, I. Our Sea-Forces, and next with Horse harrass'd at Sea, to resist all the fresh Horse that *England* could make, and then Conquer above a Million of Men, well United, Disciplin'd, and Guarded within such a *Wall*, distant everywhere 3 quarters of a Mile from the Housing, to elude the *Granadoes* and great Shot of the *Enemy*? 2. As to *Intestine Parties* and *Factions,* I suppose that 4 Millions 690 Thousand People United within this great City, could easily Govern half the said Number scattered without it, and that a few Men in Arms within the said City, and Wall, could also easily Govern the rest unarmed, or Armed in such manner as the *Soveraign* shall think fit. 3. As to *Uniformity* in *Religion*, I conceive, That if St. *Martins* Parish may (as it doth) consist of about 40 Thousand Souls, That this great City also may as well be made but as one Parish, with 7 times 130 Chappels, in which might not only be an Uniformity of Common Prayer, but in Preaching also; for that a thousand Copies of one Judiciously and Authentically Composed *Sermon* might be every Week read in each of the said *Chappels* without any subsequent Repetition of the same, as in the Case of Homilies. Whereas in *England* (wherein are near 10 Thousand Parishes, in each of which upon Sundays, Holy-days, and other Extraordinary Occasions, there should be about 100 Sermons *per Annum*, making about a Million of Sermons *per Annum* in the whole:) It were a Miracle, if a Million of Sermons Composed by so many Men, and of so many Minds and Methods, should produce *Uniformity* upon the discomposed understandings of about 8 Millions of Hearers.

4.   As to the *Administration* of *Justice*. If in this great City shall dwell the Owners of all the Lands, and other Valuable things in *England*; If within it shall be all the *Traders*, & all the *Courts*, *Offices*, *Records, Juries,* and *Witnesses*; Then it follows, that *Justice* may be done with speed and ease.

5.   As to the *Equality* and easie *Levying* of Taxes, It is too certain, That *London* hath at some time paid near half the Excise of *England*; and that the people pay thrice as much for the Hearths in *London* as those in the Countrey, in proportion to the People of each,

and that the Charge of Collecting these Duties, have been about a sixth part of the Duty it self. Now, in this great City the Excise alone according to the present Laws, would not only be double to the whole Kingdom, but also more equal. And the Duty of Hearths of the said City, would exceed the present proceed of the whole Kingdom. And as for the *Customs,* we mention them not at present.

6.   Whether more would be *gain'd* by *Foraign Commerce*[1].

The Gain which *England* makes by *Lead, Coals,* the Freight of Shipping, *&c.* may be the same, for ought I see, in both Cases. But the Gain which is made by *Manufactures,* will be greater, as the Manufacture it self is greater and better. For in so vast   a City *Manufactures* will beget one another, and each *Manufacture* will be divided into as many parts as possible, whereby the Work of each *Artisan* will be simple and easie; As for Example. In the making of a *Watch,* If one Man shall make the *Wheels,* another the *Spring,* another shall Engrave the *Dial-plate,* and another shall make the *Cases,* then the *Watch* will be better and cheaper, than if the whole Work be put upon any one Man. And we also see that in *Towns* and in the *Streets* of a great *Town,* where all the *Inhabitants* are almost of one Trade, the Commodity peculiar to those places is made better and cheaper than elsewhere. Moreover, when all sorts of Manufactures are made in one place, there every Ship that goeth forth, can suddenly have its Loading of so many several Particulars and Species as the Port whereunto she is bound can take off. Again, when the several *Manufactures* are made in one place, and Shipped off in another, the *Carriage, Postage,* and *Travelling-charges* will Inhance the Price of such *Manufacture,* and lessen the Gain upon *Foraign Commerce.* And lastly, when the Imported Goods are spent in the Port it self, where they are Landed, the Carriage of the same into other places, will create no surcharge upon such Commodity; all which particulars tends to the greater Gain by *Foraign Commerce.*

7.   As for *Arts* of *Delight* and *Ornament,*

They are best promoted by the greatest Number of *Emulators.* And it is more likely that one *Ingenious Curious Man* may rather be found out amongst 4 Millions than 400 Persons. But as for *Husbandry, viz. Tillage* and *Pasturage,* I see no Reason, but the second state (when each Family is charged with the Culture of about 24 Acres) will best promote the same.

8.   As for lessening the Fatigue of *Carriage* and *Travelling*;

The thing speaks it self, for if all the Men of Business, and all *Artisans* do Live within five Miles of each other; And if those who Live without the great City, do spend only such Commodities as grow where they Live, when the charge of Carriage and Travelling could be little.

9.   As to the preventing of *Beggars* and *Thieves*,

I do not find how the differences of the said two states should make much difference in this particular; for Impotents (which are but one in about 600) ought to be maintained by the rest. 2. Those who are unable to work, through the evil Education of their *Parents*, ought (for ought I know) to be maintained by their nearest Kindred, as a just Punishment upon them. 3. And those who cannot find Work (though able and willing to perform it) by reason of the unequal application of Hands to Lands, ought to be provided for by the *Magistrate* and *Land-Lord* till that can be done; for there needs be no *Beggars* in Countries, where there are many Acres of unimproved improvable Land to every Head, as there are in *England.* As for *Thieves,* they are for the most part begotten from the same Cause; For it is against Nature, that any Man should venture his Life, Limb, or Liberty, for a wretched Livelyhood, whereas moderate Labour will produce a better. But of this see Sir *Thomas Moor,* in the first part of his *Utopia*[1].

10.   As to the *Propagation* and *Improvement* of *Useful Learning*,

The same may be said concerning it as was above-said concerning *Manufactures* and the *Arts* of *Delight* and *Ornaments*; for in the great vast City, there can be no so odd a Conceit or Design, whereunto some Assistance may not be found, which in the thin, scattered way of Habitation may not be.

11.   As for the *Increase* of *People* by *Generation*,

I see no great difference from either of the two states, for the same may be hindred or promoted in either, from the same Causes.

12.   As to the *Plague*,

It is to be remembered that one time with another, a *Plague* happeneth in *London* once in 20 Years, or thereabouts; for in the last hundred Years, between the Years 1582 and 1682, there have been five great *Plagues, viz. Anno* 1592,1603,1625,1636, and 1665. And it is also to be remembered that the *Plagues* of *London* do commonly kill one fifth part of the *Inhabitants.* Now, if the whole People of *England* do double but in 360 Years, then the Annual Increase of the same is but 20000, and in 20 Years 400000. But if in the City of *London* there should be two Millions of People, (as there will be about 60 Years hence) then the *Plague* (killing one fifth of them, namely, 400000 once in 20 Years) will destroy as many in one Year, as the whole Nation can re-furnish in 20: And consequently the People of the Nation shall never Increase. But if the People of *London* shall be above 4 Millions (as in the first of our two *Extravagant* Suppositions is premised) then the People of the whole Nation shall lessen above 20000 *per Annum*. So as if People be worth 70*l. per* Head (as hath elsewhere been shown[1]) then the said greatness of the City will be a damage to it self and the whole Nation of 14 hundred Thousand pounds *per Annum*, and so *pro rata,* for a greater or lesser Number; wherefore to determine, which of the two *states* is best, (that is to say, towards which of the said two *states Authority* should bend the present *state*) a just Balance ought to be made between the disadvantages from the *Plague*, with the Advantages accruing from the other Particulars above-mentioned; unto which *Balance* a more exact Account of the People, and a better Rule for the Measure of its Growth is Necessary, than what we have here given, or are yet able to lay down.

Notes

1. See *Treatise of Taxes*, p. 62, note.
2. Petty reckons the "value of people" variously at more than £60, *Two Essays*, post, at £69, *Verbum Sap.*, p. 108, at £70, *Polit. Arith.*, p. 152, *Treatise of Ireland*, post, and this *Essay*, p. 476, and at £80, *O.*, p. 267.

4

Enquiry Concerning Political Justice

William Godwin

Objection To This System from the Principle of Population

Objection stated. — Opinions that have been entertained on this subject. — Population adapted to find its own level. — Precautions that have been exerted to check it. — Conclusion.

An author who has speculated widely upon subjects of government[1] has recommended equality (or, which was rather his idea, a community of goods to be maintained by the vigilance of the state), as a complete remedy for the usurpation and distress which are, at present, the most powerful enemies of human kind; for the vices which infect education in some instances, and the neglect it encounters in more; for all the turbulence of passion, and all the injustice of selfishness. But, after having exhibited this brilliant picture, he finds an argument that demolishes the whole, and restores him to indifference or despair, in 'the excessive population that would ensue'. . . .

* * *

The improvements to be made in cultivation, and the augmentations the earth is capable of receiving in the article of productiveness, can-

37

not, as yet be reduced to any limits of calculation. Myriads of centuries of still increasing population may pass away, and the earth be yet found sufficient for the support of its inabitants. It were idle therefore to conceive discouragement from so distant a contingency.

* * *

Appendix

OF HEALTH, AND THE PROLONGATION OF HUMAN LIFE

Omnipotence of mind. — Application of this principle to the animal frame. — Causes of decrepitude. — Theory of voluntary and involuntary action.— Present utility of these reasonings. — Recapitulation. — Application to the future state of society.

The question respecting population is, in some degree, connected with the subject of health and longevity. It may therefore be allowed us to make use of this occasion for indulging in certain speculations upon this article. What follows must be considered as eminently a deviation into the land of conjecture. If it be false, it leaves the system to which it is appended, in all sound reason, as impregnable as ever.

Let us then, in this place, return to the sublime conjecture of Franklin, a man habitually conversant with the system of the external universe, and by no means propense to extravagant speculations, that 'mind will one day become omnipotent over matter'. The sense which he annexed to this expression seems to have related to the improvements of human invention, in relation to machines and the compendium of labour. But, if the power of intellect can be established over all other matter, are we not inevitably led to ask why not over the matter of our own bodies? If over matter at however great a distance, why not over matter which, ignorant as we may be of the tie that connects it with the thinking principle, we seem always to carry about with us, and which is our medium of communication with the external universe? . . .

* * *

The sum of the arguments which have been here offered amounts to a species of presumption that the term of human life may be prolonged, and that by the immediate operation of intellect, beyond any limits which we are able to assign. It would be idle to talk of the absolute immortality of man. Eternity and immortality are phrases to which it is impossible for us to annex any distinct ideas, and the more we attempt to explain them, the more we shall find ourselves involved in contradiction.

To apply these remarks to the subject of population. One tendency of a cultivated and virtuous mind is to diminish our eagerness for the gratifications of the senses. They please at present by their novelty, that is, because we know not how to estimate them. They decay in the decline of life, indirectly because the system refuses them, but directly and principally because they no longer excite the ardour of the mind. The gratifications of sense please at present by their imposture. We soon learn to despise the mere animal function, which, apart from the delusions of intellect, would be nearly the same in all cases; and to value it only as it happens to be relieved by personal charms or mental excellence.

The men therefore whom we are supposing to exist, when the earth shall refuse itself to a more extended population, will probably cease to propagate. The whole will be a people of men, and not of children. Generation will not succeed generation, nor truth have, in a certain degree, to recommence her career every thirty years. Other improvements may be expected to keep pace with those of health and longevity. There will be no war, no crimes, no administration of justice, as it is called, and no government. Beside this, there will be neither disease, anguish, melancholy, nor resentment. Every man will seek, with ineffable ardour, the good of all. Mind will be active and eager, yet never disappointed. Men will see the progressive advancement of virtue and good, and feel that, if things occasionally happen contrary to their hopes, the miscarriage itself was a necessary part of that progress. They will know that they are members of the chain, that each has his several utility, and they will not feel indifferent to that utility. They will be eager to enquire into the good that already exists, the means by which it was produced, and the greater good that is yet in store. They will never want motives for exertion; for that benefit which a man thoroughly understands and earnestly loves he cannot refrain from endeavouring to promote.

Before we dismiss this subject it is proper once again to remind the reader that the substance of this appendix is given only as matter of probable conjecture, and that the leading argument of this division of the work is altogether independent of its truth or falsehood.

Note

1. Wallace: *Various Prospects of Mankind, Nature and Providence*, 1761.

5

An Essay on the Principle of Population as it Affects the Future Improvement of Society (First Edition)

Thomas R. Malthus

I think I may fairly make two postulata.

First, That food is necessary to the existence of man.

Secondly, That the passion between the sexes is necessary and will remain nearly in its present state.

These two laws, ever since we have had any knowledge of mankind, appear to have been fixed laws of our nature, and, as we have not hitherto seen any alteration in them, we have no right to conclude that they will ever cease to be what they now are, without an immediate act of power in that Being who first arranged the system of the universe, and for the advantage of his creatures, still executes, according to fixed laws, all its various operations.

I do not know that any writer has supposed that on this earth man will ultimately be able to live without food. But Mr. Godwin has conjectured that the passion between the sexes may in time be extinguished. As, however, he calls this part of his work a deviation into the land of conjecture, I will not dwell longer upon it at present than to say that the best arguments for the perfectibility of man are drawn from a contemplation of the great progress that he has already made from the savage state and the difficulty of saying where he is to stop. But towards the extinction of the passion between the sexes, no progress whatever has hitherto been made. It appears to exist in as much force at present as it did two thousand or four thousand years ago. There are individual exceptions now as there always have been. But, as these exceptions do not appear to increase in number, it would surely be a very un-philosophical mode of arguing, to infer merely from the existence of an exception, that the exception would, in time, become the rule, and the rule the exception.

Assuming then, my postulata as granted, I say, that the power of population is indefinitely greater than the power in the earth to produce subsistence for man.

Population, when unchecked, increases in a geometrical ratio. Subsistence increases only in an arithmetical ratio. A slight acquaintance with numbers will shew the immensity of the first power in comparison of the second.

By that law of our nature which makes food necessary to the life of man, the effects of these two unequal powers must be kept equal.

This implies a strong and constantly operating check on population from the difficulty of subsistence. This difficulty must fall some where and must necessarily be severely felt by a large portion of mankind.

Through the animal and vegetable kingdoms, nature has scattered the seeds of life abroad with the most profuse and liberal hand. She has been comparatively sparing in the room and the nourishment necessary to rear them. The germs of existence contained in this spot of earth, with ample food, and ample room to expand in, would fill millions of worlds in the course of a few thousand years. Necessity, that imperious all pervading law of nature, restrains them within the prescribed bounds. The race of plants, and the race of animals shrink under this great restrictive law. And the race of man cannot, by any efforts of reason, escape from it. Among plants and animals its effects are waste of seed, sickness, and premature death. Among mankind, misery and vice. The former, misery, is an absolutely necessary consequence of it. Vice is a highly probable consequence, and we therefore see it abundantly prevail, but it ought not, perhaps, to be called an absolutely necessary consequence. The ordeal of virtue is to resist all temptation to evil.

This natural inequality of the two powers of population and of production in the earth and that great law of our nature which must constantly keep their effects equal form the great difficulty that to me appears insurmountable in the way to the perfectibility of society. All other arguments are of slight and subordinate consideration in comparison of this. I see no way by which man can escape from the weight of this law which pervades all animated nature. No fancied equality, no agrarian regulations in their utmost extent, could remove the pressure of it even for a single century. And it appears, therefore, to be decisive against the possible existence of a society, all the members of which should live in ease, happiness, and comparative leisure; and feel no anxiety about providing the means of subsistence for themselves and families.

Consequently, if the premises are just, the argument is conclusive against the perfectibility of the mass of mankind.

I have thus sketched the general outline of the argument, but I will examine it more particularly, and I think it will be found that experience, the true source and foundation of all knowledge, invariably confirms its truth.

*   *   *

I said that population, when unchecked, increased in a geometrical ratio, and subsistence for man in an arithmetical ratio.

Let us examine whether this position be just.

I think it will be allowed, that no state has hitherto existed (at least that we have any account of) where the manners were so pure and simple, and the means of subsistence so abundant, that no check whatever has existed to early marriages, among the lower classes, from a fear of not providing well for their families, or among the higher classes, from a fear of lowering their condition in life. Consequently in no state that we have yet known has the power of population been left to exert itself with perfect freedom.

Whether the law of marriage be instituted or not, the dictate of nature and virtue seems to be an early attachment to one woman. Supposing a liberty of changing in the case of an unfortunate choice, this liberty would not affect population till it arose to a height greatly vicious; and we are now supposing the existence of a society where vice is scarcely known.

In a state therefore of great equality and virtue, where pure and simple manners prevailed, and where the means of subsistence were so abundant that no part of the society could have any fears about providing amply for a family, the power of population being left to exert itself unchecked, the increase of the human species would evidently be much greater than any increase that has been hitherto known.

In the United States of America, where the means of subsistence have been more ample, the manners of the people more pure, and consequently the checks to early marriages fewer than in any of the modern states of Europe, the population has been found to double itself in twenty-five years.

This ratio of increase, though short of the utmost power of population, yet as the result of actual experience, we will take as our rule, and say, that population, when unchecked, goes on doubling itself every twenty-five years or increases in a geometrical ratio.

Let us now take any spot of earth, this Island for instance, and see in what ratio the subsistence it affords can be supposed to increase. We will begin with it under its present state of cultivation.

If I allow that by the best possible policy, by breaking up more land and by great encouragements to agriculture, the produce of this Island may be doubled in the first twenty-five years, I think it will be allowing as much as any person can well demand.

In the next twenty-five years, it is impossible to suppose that the produce could be quadrupled. It would be contrary to all our knowledge of the qualities of land. The very utmost that we can conceive, is, that the increase in the second twenty-five years might equal the present produce. Let us then take this for our rule, though certainly far beyond the truth, and allow that by great exertion, the whole produce of the Island might be increased every twenty-five years, by a quantity of subsistence equal to what it at present produces. The most enthusiastic speculator cannot suppose a greater increase than this. In a few centuries it would make every acre of land in the Island like a garden.

Yet this ratio of increase is evidently arithmetical.

It may be fairly said, therefore, that the means of subsistence increase in an arithmetical ratio. Let us now bring the effects of these two ratios together.

The population of the Island is computed to be about seven millions, and we will suppose the present produce equal to the support of such a number. In the first twenty-five years the population would be fourteen millions, and the food being also doubled, the means of subsistence would be equal to this increase. In the next twenty-five years the population would be twenty-eight millions, and the means of subsistence only equal to the support of twenty-one millions. In the next period, the population would be fifty-six millions, and the means of subsistence just sufficient for half that number. And at the conclusion of the first century the population would be one hundred and twelve millions and the means of subsistence only equal to the support of thirty-five millions, which would leave a population of seventy-seven millions totally unprovided for.

A great emigration necessarily implies unhappiness of some kind or other in the country that is deserted. For few persons will leave their families, connections, friends, and native land, to seek a settlement in untried foreign climes, without some strong subsisting causes of uneasiness where they are, or the hope of some great advantages in the place to which they are going.

But to make the argument more general and less interrupted by the partial views of emigration, let us take the whole earth, instead of one spot, and suppose that the restraints to population were universally removed. If the subsistence for man that the earth affords was to be increased every twenty-five years by a quantity equal to what the whole world at present produces, this would allow the power of production in the earth to be absolutely unlimited, and its ratio of increase much greater than we can conceive that any possible exertions of mankind could make it.

Taking the population of the world at any number, a thousand millions, for instance, the human species would increase in the ratio of— 1, 2, 4, 8, 16, 32, 64, 128, 256, 512, &c. and subsistence as—1, 2, 3, 4, 5, 6, 7, 8, 9, 10, &c. In two centuries and a quarter, the population would be to the means of subsistence as 512 to 10: in three centuries as 4096 to 13, and in two thousand years the difference would be almost incalculable, though the produce in that time would have increased to an immense extent.

No limits whatever are placed to the productions of the earth; they may increase for ever and be greater than any assignable quantity; yet still the power of population being a power of a superior order, the increase of the human species can only be kept commensurate to the increase of the means of subsistence, by the constant operation of the strong law of necessity acting as a check upon the greater power.

The effects of this check remain now to be considered.

Among plants and animals the view of the subject is simple. They are all impelled by a powerful instinct to the increase of their species, and this instinct is interrupted by no reasoning or doubts about providing for their offspring. Wherever therefore there is liberty, the power of increase is exerted, and the superabundant effects are repressed afterwards by want of room and nourishment, which is common to animals and plants, and among animals, by becoming the prey of others.

The effects of this check on man are more complicated. Impelled to the increase of his species by an equally powerful instinct, reason interrupts his career and asks him whether he may not bring beings into the world, for whom he cannot provide the means of subsistence. In a state of equality, this would be the simple question. In the present state of society, other considerations occur. Will he not lower his rank in life? Will he not subject himself to greater difficulties than he at present feels? Will he not be obliged to labour harder? and if he has a large family, will his utmost exertions enable him to support them? May he not see his offspring in rags and misery, and clamouring for bread that he cannot give them? And may he not be reduced to the grating necessity of forfeiting his independence, and of being obliged to the sparing hand of charity for support?

These considerations are calculated to prevent, and certainly do prevent, a very great number in all civilized nations from pursuing the dictate of nature in an early attachment to one woman. And this restraint almost necessarily, though not absolutely so, produces vice. Yet in all societies, even those that are most vicious, the tendency to a virtuous attachment is so strong that there is a constant effort towards an increase of population. This constant effort as constantly tends to subject the lower classes of the society to distress and to prevent any great permanent amelioration of their condition.

The way in which these effects are produced seems to be this.

We will suppose the means of subsistence in any country just equal to the easy support of its inhabitants. The constant effort towards population, which is found to act even in the most vicious societies, increases the number of people before the means of subsistence are increased. The food therefore which before supported seven millions must now be divided among seven millions and a half or eight millions. The poor consequently must live much worse, and many of them be reduced to severe distress. The number of labourers also being above the proportion of the work in the market, the price of labour must tend toward a decrease, while the price of provisions would at the same time tend to rise. The labourer therefore must work harder to earn the same as he did before. During this season of distress, the discouragements to marriage, and the difficulty of rearing a family are so great that population is at a stand. In the mean time the cheapness of labour, the plenty of labourers, and the necessity of an increased industry amongst them, encourage cultivators to employ more labour upon their land, to turn up fresh soil, and to manure and improve more completely what is already in tillage, till ultimately the means of subsistence become in the same proportion to the population as at the period from which we set out. The situation of the labourer being then again tolerably comfortable, the restraints to population are in some degree loosened, and the same retrograde and progressive movements with respect to happiness are repeated.

This sort of oscillation will not be remarked by superficial observers, and it may be difficult even for the most penetrating mind to calculate its periods. Yet that in all old states some such vibration does exist, though from various transverse causes, in a much less marked, and in a much more irregular manner than I have described it, no reflecting man who considers the subject deeply can well doubt. . . .

But though the rich by unfair combinations contribute frequently to prolong a season of distress among the poor, yet no possible form of society could prevent the almost constant action of misery upon a great part of mankind, if in a state of inequality, and upon all, if all were equal.

The theory on which the truth of this position depends appears to me so extremely clear that I feel at a loss to conjecture what part of it can be denied.

That population cannot increase without the means of subsistence is a proposition so evident that it needs no illustration.

That population does invariably increase where there are the means of subsistence, the history of every people that have ever existed will abundantly prove.

And that the superior power of population cannot be checked without producing misery or vice, the ample portion of these too bitter ingredients in the cup of human life and the continuance of the physical causes that seem to have produced them bear too convincing a testimony.

But in order more fully to ascertain the validity of these three propositions, let us examine the different states in which mankind have been known to exist. Even a cursory review will, I think, be sufficient to convince us that these propositions are incontrovertible truths.

* * *

In reading Mr. Godwin's ingenious and able work on political justice, it is impossible not to be struck with the spirit and energy of his style, the force and precision of some of his reasonings, the ardent tone of his thoughts, and particularly with that impressive earnestness of manner which gives an air of truth to the whole. At the same time, it must be confessed that he has not proceeded in his enquiries with the caution that sound philosophy seems to require. His conclusions are often unwarranted by his premises. He fails sometimes in removing the objections which he himself brings forward. He relies too much on general and abstract propositions which will not admit of application. And his conjectures certainly far outstrip the modesty of nature.

The system of equality which Mr. Godwin proposes is, without doubt, by far the most beautiful and engaging of any that has yet appeared. An amelioration of society to be produced merely by reason and conviction wears much more the promise of permanence, than any change effected and maintained by force. The unlimited exercise of private judgment is a doctrine inexpressibly grand and captivating and has a vast superiority over those systems where every individual is in a manner the slave of the public. The substitution of benevolence as the master-spring and moving principle of society, instead of self-love, is a consummation devoutly to be wished. In short, it is impossible to contemplate the whole of this fair structure, without emotions of delight and admiration, accompanied with ardent longing for the period of its accomplishment. But, alas! that moment can never arrive. The whole is little better than a dream, a beautiful phantom of the imagination. These "gorgeous palaces" of happiness and immortality, these "solemn temples" of truth and virtue will dissolve, "like the baseless fabric of a vision," when we awaken to real life and contemplate the true and genuine situation of man on earth.

Mr. Godwin, at the conclusion of the third chapter of his eighth book, speaking of population, says, "There is a principle in human society, by which population is perpetually kept down to the level of the means of subsistence. Thus among the wandering tribes of America and Asia, we never find through the lapse of ages that population has so increased as to render necessary the cultivation of the earth." This principle, which Mr. Godwin thus mentions as some mysterious and occult cause and which he does not attempt to investigate, will be found to be the grinding law of necessity, misery, and the fear of misery.

The great error under which Mr. Godwin labours throughout his whole work is the attributing almost all the vices and misery that are seen in civil society to human institutions. Political regulations and the established administration of property are with him the fruitful sources of all evil, the hotbeds of all the crimes that degrade mankind. Were this really a true state of the case, it would not seem a hopeless task to remove evil completely from the world, and reason seems to be the proper and adequate instrument for effecting so great a purpose. But the truth is, that though human institutions appear to be the obvious and obtrusive causes of much mischief to mankind, yet, in reality they are light and superficial, they are mere feathers that float on the surface, in comparison with those deeper seated causes of impurity that corrupt the springs and render turbid the whole stream of human life.

Mr. Godwin, in his chapter on the benefits attendant on a system of equality, says, "The spirit of oppression, the spirit of servility, and the spirit of fraud, these are the immediate growth of the established administration of property. They are alike hostile to intellectual improvement. The other vices of envy, malice, and revenge are their inseparable companions. In a state of society where men lived in the midst of plenty and where all shared alike the bounties of nature, these sentiments would inevitably expire. The narrow principle of selfishness would vanish. No man being obliged to guard his little store or provide with anxiety and pain for his restless wants, each would lose his individual existence in the thought of the general good. No man would be an enemy to his neighbour, for they would have no subject of contention, and, of consequence, philanthropy would resume the empire which reason assigns her. Mind would be delivered from her perpetual anxiety about corporal support, and free to expatiate in the field of thought, which is congenial to her. Each would assist the enquiries of all."

This would, indeed, be a happy state. But that it is merely an imaginary picture, with scarcely a feature near the truth, the reader, I am afraid, is already too well convinced.

Man cannot live in the midst of plenty. All cannot share alike the bounties of nature. Were there no established administration of property, every man would be obliged to guard with force his little store. Selfishness would be triumphant. The subjects of contention would be perpetual. Every individual mind would be under a constant anxiety about corporal support, and not a single intellect would be left free to expatiate in the field of thought. . . .

And thus it appears, that a society constituted according to the most beautiful form that imagination can conceive, with benevolence for its moving principle, instead of self-love, and with every evil disposition in all its members corrected by reason and not force, would, from the inevitable laws of nature, and not from any original depravity of man, in a very short period, degenerate into a society, constructed upon a plan not essentially different from that which prevails in every known State at present; I mean, a society divided into a class of proprietors, and a class of labourers, and with self-love the main-spring of the great machine.

6

An Essay on the Principle of Population, or A View of Its Past and Present Effects on Human Happiness (Second and Fifth Editions)

Thomas R. Malthus

From the Introduction by Mark Blaug:

[Re] Malthus' argument in the first edition of the *Essay:* Its weakness was quickly discovered by Godwin, who pointed out that the laboring class in civilized countries seemed to be maintaining itself at a level considerably above the minimum of existence without benefit of either the positive checks or the preventive checks. Malthus, realizing that he had trapped himself by denying the possibility of any rise in the standard of living quietly gave way in the second edition of the *Essay* by recognizing the existence of a new preventive check: "moral restraint." He defined "moral restraint" as postponement of the age of marriage accompanied by strict sexual continence before marriage, and, while the other checks were frequently described as "misery and vice," the new preventive check stood alone without any moral tag attached to it. For the first time, a hopeful note crept into the argument, although Malthus always remained profoundly pessimistic about the capacity of mankind to regulate its numbers by the exercise of prudential restraint. Few readers realized that he had really abandoned his original thesis and Malthus did nothing to help them appreciate the escape clause that had now been built into the doctrine.

Any critic who produced evidence of subsistence increasing faster than population, without signs of "misery and vice," was silenced by drawing the logical implication: the working class was practicing "moral restraint." This left the critic with no reply other than to show that the average age of marriage had not increased or that the rate of illegitimate births had not fallen. Since contemporary population statistics were not adequate to verify such assertions, Malthus had furnished himself with an impregnable defense.

From the Preface to the Second Edition

Throughout the whole of the present work I have so far differed in principle from the former, as to suppose the action of another check to the population which does not come under the head either of vice or misery; and, in the latter part I have endeavoured to soften some of the harshest conclusions of the first Essay. . . .

. . . To those who still think that any check to population whatever would be worse than the evils which it would relieve, the conclusions of the former Essay will remain in full force: and if we adopt this opinion we shall be compelled to acknowledge, that the poverty and misery which prevail among the lower classes of society are absolutely irremediable.

LONDON, *June* 8, 1803

From the Preface to the Fifth Edition

This Essay was first published at a period of extensive warfare, combined, from peculiar circumstances, with a most prosperous foreign commerce.

It came before the public, therefore, at a time when there would be an extraordinary demand for men, and very little disposition to suppose the possibility of any evil arising from the redundancy of population. Its success, under these disadvantages, was greater than could have been reasonably expected; and it may be presumed that it will not lose its interest, after a period of a different description has succeeded, which has in the most marked manner illustrated its principles, and confirmed its conclusions.

From the Second Edition

It is observed by Dr. Franklin, that there is no bound to the prolific nature of plants or animals, but what is made by their crowding and interfering with each other's means of subsistence. Were the face of the earth, he says, vacant of other plants, it might be gradually sowed and overspread with one kind only, as for instance with fennel: and were it empty of other inhabitants, it might in a few ages be replenished from one nation only, as for instance with Englishmen.[1]

This is incontrovertibly true. Through the animal and vegetable kingdoms Nature has scattered the seeds of life abroad with the most profuse and liberal hand; but has been comparatively sparing in the room and the nourishment necessary to rear them. The germs of existence contained in this earth, if they could freely develop themselves, would fill millions of worlds in the course of a few thousand years. Necessity, that imperious, all-pervading law of nature, restrains them within the prescribed bounds. The race of plants and the race of animals shrink under this great restrictive law; and man cannot by any efforts of reason escape from it.

In plants and irrational animals, the view of the subject is simple. They are all impelled by a powerful instinct to the increase of their species; and this instinct is interrupted by no doubts about providing for their offspring. Wherever therefore there is liberty, the power of increase is exerted; and the superabundant effects are repressed afterwards by want of room and nourishment.

The effects of this check on man are more complicated. Impelled to the increase of his species by an equally powerful instinct, reason interrupts his career, and asks him whether he may not bring beings into the world, for whom he cannot provide the means of support.

* * *

Of the Only Effectual Mode of Improving
the Condition of the Poor

Judging merely from the light of nature, if we feel convinced of the misery arising from a redundant population on the one hand, and of the evils and unhappiness, particularly to the female sex, arising from promiscuous intercourse, on the other, I do not see how it is possible for any person who acknowledges the principle of utility, as the great criterion of moral rules, to escape the conclusion, that moral restraint, or the abstaining from marriage till we are in a condition to support a family, with a perfectly moral conduct during that period, is the strict line of duty; and when revelation is taken into the question, this duty undoubtedly receives very powerful confirmation. At the same time I believe that few of my readers can be less sanguine than I am in their expectations of any sudden and great change in the general conduct of men on this subject. . . .

However powerful may be the impulses of passion, they are generally in some degree modified by reason. And it does not seem entirely visionary to suppose that, if the true and permanent cause of poverty were clearly explained and forcibly brought home to each man's bosom, it would have some, and perhaps not an inconsiderable influence on his conduct; at least the experiment has never yet been fairly tried. Almost every thing, that has been hitherto done for the poor, has tended, as if with solicitous care, to throw a veil of obscurity over this subject, and to hide from them the true cause of their poverty. When the wages of labour are hardly sufficient to maintain two children, a man marries, and has five or six; he of course finds himself miserably distressed. He accuses the insufficiency of the price of labour to maintain a family. He accuses his parish for their tardy and sparing fulfilment of their obligation to assist him. He accuses the avarice of the rich, who suffer him to want what they can so well spare. He accuses the partial and unjust institutions of society, which have awarded him an inadequate share of the produce of the earth. He accuses perhaps the dispensations of Providence, which have assigned to him a place in society so beset with unavoidable distress and dependence. In searching for objects of accusation, he never adverts to the quarter from which his misfortunes originate. The last person that he would think of accusing is himself, on whom in fact the principal blame lies, except so far as he has been deceived by the higher classes of society. He may perhaps wish that he had not married, because he now feels the inconveniences of it; but it never enters into his head that he can have done any thing wrong. He has always been told, that to raise up subjects for his king and country is a very meritorious act. He has done this, and yet is suffering for it; and it cannot but strike him as most extremely unjust and cruel in his king and country, to allow him thus to suffer, in return for giving them what they are continually declaring that they particularly want.

Till these erroneous ideas have been corrected, and the language of nature and reason has been generally heard on the subject of population, instead of the language of error and prejudice, it cannot be said, that any fair experiment has been made with the understandings of the common people; and we cannot justly accuse them of improvidence and want of industry, till they act as they do now, after it has been brought home to their comprehensions, that they are themselves the cause of their own poverty; that the means of redress are in their own hands, and in the hands of no other persons whatever . . .

*   *   *

Of Our Rational Expectations Respecting the Future Improvement of Society

It cannot be doubted that throughout Europe in general, and most particularly in the northern states, a decided change has taken place in the operation of prudential restraint, since the prevalence of those warlike and enterprising habits which destroyed so many people. In later times the gradual diminution and almost total extinction of the plagues, which so frequently visited Europe in the seventeenth and beginning of the eighteenth centuries, produced a change of the same kind. And in this country, it is not to be doubted that the proportion of marriages has become smaller since the improvement of our towns, the less frequent returns of epidemics, and the adoption of habits of greater cleanliness. During the late scarcities it appears that the number of marriages diminished; [1800 and 1810] and the same motives which prevented many people from marrying during such a period, would operate precisely in the same way, if, in future, the additional number of children reared to manhood from the introduction of the cow-pox, were to be such as to crowd all employments, lower the price of labour, and make it more difficult to support a family. . . .

. . . [T]he prudential check to marriage has increased in Europe; and it cannot be unreasonable to conclude that it will still make further advances. If this take place without any marked and decided increase of a vicious intercourse with the sex, the happiness of society will evidently be promoted by it; and with regard to the danger of such increase, it is consolatory to remark that those countries in Europe, where marriages are the latest or least frequent, are by no means particularly distinguished by vices of this kind. It has appeared, that Norway, Switzerland, England, and Scotland, are above all the rest in the prevalence of the preventive check; and though I do not mean to insist particularly on the virtuous habits of these countries, yet I think that no person would select them as the countries most marked for profligacy of manners. Indeed, from the little that I know of the continent, I should have been inclined to select them as most distinguished for contrary habits, and as rather above than below their neighbours in the chastity of their women, and consequently in the virtuous habits of their men. . . .

From a review of the state of society in former periods, compared with the present, I should certainly say that the evils resulting from the principle of population have rather diminished than increased, even under the disadvantage of an almost total ignorance of the real cause. And if we can indulge the hope that this ignorance will be gradually dissipated, it does not seem unreasonable to expect that they will be still further diminished. The increase of absolute population, which will of course take place, will evidently tend but little to weaken this expectation, as every thing depends upon the relative proportion between population and food, and not on the absolute number of people. In the former part of this work it appeared that the countries, which possessed the fewest people, often suffered the most from the effects of the principle of population; and it can scarcely be doubted that, taking Europe throughout, fewer famines and fewer diseases arising from want have prevailed in the last century than in those which preceded it.

On the whole, therefore, though our future prospects respecting the mitigation of the evils arising from the principle of population may not be so bright as we could wish, yet they are far from being entirely disheartening, and by no means preclude that gradual and progressive improvement in human society, which, before the late wild speculations on this subject, was the object of rational expectation. To the laws of property and marriage, and to the apparently narrow principle of self-interest which prompts each individual to exert himself in bettering his condition, we are indebted for all the noblest exertions of human genius, for every thing that distinguishes the civilised from the savage state. A strict inquiry into the principle of population obliges us to conclude that we shall never be able to throw down the ladder, by which we have risen to this eminence; but it by no means proves, that we may not rise higher by the same means. The structure of society, in its great features, will probably always remain unchanged. We have every reason to believe that it will always consist of a class of proprietors and a class of labourers; but the condition of each, and the proportion which they bear to each other, may be so altered, as greatly to improve the harmony and beauty of the whole. It would indeed be a melancholy reflection that, while the views of physical science are daily enlarging, so as scarcely to be bounded by the most distant horizon, the science of moral and political philosophy should be confined within such narrow limits, or at best be so feeble in its influence, as to be unable to counteract the obstacles to human happiness arising from a single cause. But however formidable these obstacles may have appeared in some parts of this work, it is hoped that the general result of the inquiry is such, as not to make us give up the improvement of human society in despair. The partial good which seems to be attainable is worthy of all our exertions; is sufficient to direct our efforts, and animate our prospects. And although we cannot expect that the virtue and happiness of mankind will keep pace with the brilliant career of physical discovery; yet, if we are not wanting to ourselves, we may confidently indulge the hope that, to no unimportant extent, they will be influenced by its progress and will partake in its success.

Note

1. Franklin's Miscell. p. 9.

7

Of Population

William Godwin

[L]et us consider a little attentively how it is that the increase of population, by procreation only, is to produce the effect of making provisions too scanty. The first start of this increase must be by an addition to the number of infants. But infants do not in their first years consume any great quantity of animal or vegetable food. The increasing demand therefore for the means of subsistence can only come upon us gradually. And the means of subsistence, by the doctrines of the Essay on Population, are susceptible of an increase, regular, progressive and unlimited, though only in an arithmetical ratio. It is not therefore any actual increase in the number of candidates, that renders the means of subsistence in an old country too limited for the fair supply of its inhabitants. But, if it is not any thing actual, then it is something apprehended. To this conclusion we must come at last. If it is the tendency to increase in population beyond the practicable increase in the means of subsistence that keeps down the numbers of mankind, then it must be the apprehension of that increase. But how can that be, since Mr. Malthus in the year 1798 had the honour to discover the geometrical ratio, and since all the statesmen of ancient and modern times up to that memorable era, were persuaded, with Dr. Paley, that "the decay of population is the greatest evil that a state can suffer," and considered the main *desideratum* in politics as being, to

59

increase the number of their fellow-citizens? Thus it has been no reality, but the apprehension of what no man apprehended, that has carried on the most extensive system of infanticide, and strangled the progeny of the human race, to an amount which it is difficult to conceive, but which any man who will be at the trouble of applying the geometrical ratio from the first planting of this island, or peopling of the world, may easily put down, if he can procure a sheet of paper large enough to contain the figures that represent it.

To help the imagination of the reader in this point, I will present him with two authentic calculations on the subject.

The first is to be found in Morse's American Gazetteer. Under the article, "New York City," he has the following words: "Should the population of this city proceed in the same ratio through this century, as it has the last twenty years, the number of its inhabitants will be 5,257,493:" thus raising by anticipation, in the course of less than a century, a comparatively humble town, with a population, at the moment of the author's writing his book, as it appears, of 83,500 persons, to somewhat towards the double of the computed population of Pekin.

My next example shall be taken from the pen of Mr. Malthus himself, who, in a book just published, entitled, Principles of Political Economy Considered, has the following passage. "If any person will take the trouble to make the calculation, he will see that, if the necessaries of life could be obtained without limit, and the number of people could be doubled every twenty-five years, the population, which might have been produced from a single pair since the Christian era, would have been sufficient, not only to fill the earth quite full of people, so that four should stand upon every square yard, but to fill all the planets of our solar system in the same way, and not only them, but all the planets revolving round the stars which are visible to the naked eye, supposing each of them to be a sun, and to have as many planets belonging to it as our sun has[1]."

And this is the doctrine, which has seriously deluded the gravest statesmen of England and of Europe for the last twenty years, has reared its motley front in courts and parliaments, and been judged worthy to be made the foundation of legislative measures, and of codes of practical administration and jurisprudence to mankind!

The spirit of Mr. Malthus' theory bears a striking resemblance to the policy employed in training coach-horses, upon whose heads their manager is accustomed to fasten a pair of blinkers, that they may attend to nothing on either side, but see only straight before them. It is surely worth while that we should endeavour to trace the effects of the geometrical ratio, as it must have operated in ages past. We live, as I have often had occasion to repeat, in an unpeopled world. How come this, upon the principles of the Essay on Population? What was it that stopped the increase of population in ancient times before the existence of records?

I have abundantly shewn, if population is kept down by the narrow limits within which the means of subsistence are at present confined, that this restraint arises out of civil institutions, the inequality of mankind, and the accumulation of property, landed property especially, in few hands. But this system of policy had a beginning. It is the offspring of refinement. The soil of the earth was once as free, once probably a great deal freer, than it is now in the territory of the United States of North America. Every man might have land at a very cheap rate. Every man might have land perhaps for nothing. And then, by the principle I have already explained, that each man in civilized society is born with the power of producing a much greater quantity of food than is necessary for his own subsistence, I see nothing that upon the principle of the Essay on Population should have arrested the progress of population, till the earth, the known world, was "cultivated like a garden." I call on Mr. Malthus to explain this phenomenon. I call on Mr. Malthus to account for what we see, an unpeopled world.

But perhaps the disciples of the geometrical ratio will say that, in this state of things, population was not arrested, as the fundamental principle of the Essay on Population affirms that the operation of this ratio is not stopped in North America. Perhaps the whole world once "swarmed with human beings," as the eyewitnesses of the first discovery of South America affirm of that quarter of the world, "as an anthill swarms with ants." If this is true, surely the thought of it is enough to make one serious. The earth might easily, upon our present systems of husbandry and cultivation, be made to subsist thirty times the number of human creatures that now inhabit it. Therefore it did contain thirty times the number of its present inhabitants. Therefore twenty-nine thirtieths of the human race have already been struck out of the catalogue of the living. And it is in this wreck of a world, almost as desolate as if a comet from the orbit of Saturn had come too near us, that Mr. Malthus issues his solemn denunciations, warning us on no consideration to increase the numbers of mankind.

The reader is aware that he is not to take the above statements as the enunciation of my own opinions. I give them only as the fair consequences of the theory of the Essay on Population. I give them only as results which Mr. Malthus must either account for or elude. And I therefore give them as considerations to which I might have trusted singly for the overthrow of Mr. Malthus's positions, if the world had not appeared so infatuated on the subject, as to impose on me the necessity of an elaborate refutation of the most groundless paradoxes that ever were started.

*   *   *

I by no means undertake to assert, that there is absolutely no tendency in the human species to increase, though I certainly think, that the idea of guarding ourselves against the geometrical ratio, is just as sagacious and profound, as that of Don Quixote's fighting with the windmills. All I affirm is, that the evidence we yet possess is against the increase: and I think it is the business of the true statesman and practical philanthropist in the mean time to act on such evidence as we have. It will be time enough to hunt our species out of the world, and "stop the propagation of mankind," when we see such danger, as no man up to the present time can have any solid reason to apprehend.

The business therefore of the true statesman and practical philanthropist under this head is extremely simple. Let us take it for granted that England and Wales at this moment contain ten millions of inhabitants. Let us assume with Mr. Malthus, that there are not at present provisions within the country to subsist this number. Certain it is, that, practically speaking, and looking to the distribution only, all are not adequately subsisted. The proper enquiry is, how this is to be remedied: and scarcely any man, considering the state of our soil, its cultivated and uncultivated parts, will venture to deny that a remedy may be accomplished, whether it shall be by certain wise changes in the mechanism of society, or by breaking up more ground, and rendering that which is already inclosed more available to its genuine purposes.

This speculation brings us back to the feelings of unsophisticated humanity, which it is the clear tendency of Mr. Malthus's theory to expel out of the world. He says, No, we must not increase the happiness of our contemporaries, lest by so doing we should immeasurably increase the candidates for happiness and subsistence. He would starve the present generation, that he may kill the next.

In the mean while, the idle dream of his ratios being dispelled, human nature is itself again. We return to the morality of our ancestors. We return to the morality of the Christian religion, and of all the religious leaders and legislators from the beginning of the records of mankind. Wherever I meet a man, I meet a brother. I recognise in him the image of the all-perfect. I see a creature, "fearfully and wonderfully made," and admire the exquisiteness of the workmanship. I do not think of effacing God's image, or of neglecting and superciliously setting light by that on which he has affixed his seal. I do not seek to suppress the most natural impulses of a human being, and turn the world into a great monastery. No: if it is ever unwise for man to marry (and unfortunately this is too true in a variety of instances), it is not owing, as Mr. Malthus impiously would have us to believe, to any thing in the original and indestructible laws of nature, but to the partiality and oppressiveness of human institutions.

It is the duty of legislators, and was always so understood, till Mr. Malthus came with his wild theory, built upon the erroneous construction of what was seen in one corner of the earth, and in flagrant opposition to all other evidence, and upon his perversion of the idea of subsistence,—I say, it is the duty of legislators, to deal tenderly with the life of man, not brutally and rashly to extinguish that, which all their art can never revive again, to cherish it as the apple of the eye, to believe that when they cut off a man, they impair so far the nerves by which a nation is sustained, and to tremble and hesitate before they take on themselves so awful a responsibility. Mr. Malthus's theory on the contrary would persuade us to hail war, famine and pestilence, as the true friends of the general weal, to look with a certain complacent approbation upon the gallows and massacre, and almost to long for the decimation of our species, that the survivors might be more conveniently accommodated.

Note

1. *Principles of Political Economy*, p. 227.

8

The Principles of Political
Economy and Taxation

David Ricardo

[I]t appears then that wages are subject to a rise or fall from two causes:—

First, the supply and demand of labourers.

Secondly, the price of the commodities on which the wages of labour are expended.

In different stages of society, the accumulation of capital, or of the means of employing labour, is more or less rapid, and must in all cases depend on the productive powers of labour. The productive powers of labour are generally greatest when there is an abundance of fertile land: at such periods accumulation is often so rapid that labourers cannot be supplied with the same rapidity as capital.

It has been calculated that under favourable circumstances population may be doubled in twenty-five years; but under the same favourable circumstances the whole capital of a country might possibly be doubled in a shorter period. In that case, wages during the whole period would have a tendency to rise, because the demand for labour would increase still faster than the supply.

In new settlements, where the arts and knowledge of countries far advanced in refinement are introduced, it is probable that capital has a tendency to increase faster than mankind; and if the deficiency of labourers were not supplied by more populous countries, this tendency would very much raise the price of labour. In proportion as these countries become populous, and land of a worse quality is taken into cultivation, the tendency to an increase of capital diminishes; for the surplus produce remaining, after satisfying the wants of the existing population, must necessarily be in proportion to the facility of production, viz. to the smaller number of persons employed in production. Although, then, it is probable that under the most favourable circumstances, the power of production is still greater than that of population, it will not long continue so; for the land being limited in quantity, and differing in quality, with every increased portion of capital employed on it there will be a decreased rate of production, whilst the power of population continues always the same.

In those countries where there is abundance of fertile land, but where, from the ignorance, indolence, and barbarism of the inhabitants, they are exposed to all the evils of want and famine, and where it has been said that population presses against the means of subsistence, a very different remedy should be applied from that which is necessary in long settled countries where, from the diminishing rate of the supply of raw produce, all the evils of a crowded population are experienced. In the one case, the evil proceeds from bad government, from the insecurity of property, and from a want of education in all ranks of the people. To be made happier they require only to be better governed and instructed, as the augmentation of capital, beyond the augmentation of people, would be the inevitable result. No increase in the population can be too great, as the powers of production are still greater. In the other case, the population increases faster than the funds required for its support. Every exertion of industry, unless accompanied by a diminished rate of increase will add to the evil, for production cannot keep pace with it.

With a population pressing against the means of subsistence, the only remedies are either a reduction of people or a more rapid accumulation of capital. In rich countries, where all the fertile land is already cultivated, the latter remedy is neither very practicable nor very desirable, because its effort would be, if pushed very far, to render all classes equally poor. But in poor countries, where there are abundant means of production in store, from fertile land not yet brought into cultivation, it is the only safe and efficacious means of removing the evil, particularly as its effect would be to elevate all classes of the people.

The friends of humanity cannot but wish that in all countries the labouring classes should have a taste for comforts and enjoyments, and that they should be stimulated by all legal means in their exertions to procure them. There cannot be a better security against a super-abundant population. In those countries where the labouring classes have the fewest wants, and are contented with the cheapest food, the people are exposed to the greatest vicissitudes and miseries.

Part 2

The Second Wave

9

New Ideas on Population with Remarks on the Theories of Malthus and Godwin

Alexander H. Everett

It is remarkable . . . that Mr. de Sismondi, although he disputes the principles of Malthus which alone lend some appearance of probability to his practical conclusions, seems nevertheless to acquiesce in these conclusions, in themselves certainly not very attractive, nor very consonant with common opinion. He has the same panic terror of the excessive increase of population, the same jealousy of the operation of charity, public and private, and the same anxiety to discourage matrimony among the poor and middling classes . . .

> [From Sismondi] We are suffering in almost every part of Europe the calamity of an excessive population, which we have no means of supporting. For this calamity we are indebted to the imprudent zeal of our governments. With us religious instruction, legislation, the organisation of society, all combine to produce an increase of population, for the maintenance of which no means had previously been provided.

. . . It is sufficiently notorious, that an increase of population on a given territory is followed immediately by a division of labor; which produces in its turn the invention of new machines, an improvement of methods in all the departments of industry, and a rapid progress in the various branches of art and science. The increase effected by these improvements in the productiveness of labor is obviously much greater in proportion than the increase of population, to which it is owing. . . .

The ultimate effect of an increase of population in such a community, if continued for any length of time, would however probably be to effect a transition to an easier and more civilized mode of living. . . .

The increase of population on an unoccupied territory only increases the quantity of rude labor and of its products, but leaves the productiveness of labor and the comparative abundance of its products as before. On a limited territory, the same cause introduces the new element of skill, the effects of which, in augmenting the productiveness of labor, and the abundance of its products, are unbounded and incalculable.

The result, in the latter case, is naturally a great and immediate extension of manufactures and commerce. The fine productions of skilful labor, after satisfying the demand of the neighboring nations, are carried to the most distant parts of the world, and bring back the coarser natural productions to be used for consumption or wrought up into these fine fabrics. This exchange is advantageous to both parties, and especially to the civilised or populous community. The labor of a single member of such a society will perhaps purchase the product of that of a hundred barbarian hunters. A few glass beads, which may be valued at nothing, are converted, by the help of the machinery employed in navigation, into a princely fortune. To facilitate these exchanges, some of the inhabitants of the populous nations fix themselves in foreign countries. At first they generally return after realising the immediate object of their expedition. But as the settlements which they make for commercial purposes gradually become more agreeable places of residence, many persons are induced to remain, and establish themselves for life. In this way emigration and colonisation are introduced in connexion with manufactures and commerce. In the new settlements that are thus formed, labor is applied with skill, and is proportionally productive: while population, encouraged by the high state of civilisation, proceeds with rapidity. These flourishing establishments are naturally employed almost wholly in agriculture; and resort to the mother-country, in order to exchange its fruits for the fine products of taste and art. Thus the rapid growth of these young scions, instead of exhausting the parent stock, gives it new health and vigor; and a dense and increasing population on a limited territory, instead of bringing with it any danger of scarcity, is not only an immediate cause of greater abundance to the nation where it exists, but a principle of prosperity and civilisation to every part of the world. The history of most of the populous nations with which we are acquainted confirms the truth of these remarks: and they are illustrated in a particular manner by that of Great Britain and the United States of America. If well grounded, they are decisive of the whole question, in regard to the influence of the increase of population upon the supply of the means of subsistence, and prove conclusively that the theory of Mr. Malthus is not only erroneous, but directly the reverse of the truth; and that an increase of population, instead of being, as he maintains, the chief cause of all the physical and moral evil to which we are exposed, is, on the contrary, the real and only active principle of national wealth and happiness.

10

Summary of the Differences between Malthus and Gray

William Petersen

Malthus	Gray
Population has a natural tendency to overincrease—that is, to increase faster than subsistence.	Population has a tendency to increase but not to overincrease, for any increase carries in itself the power of fully supplying its various wants.
The natural growth of population is according to a geometric ratio, that of subsistence only according to an arithmetic one.	The natural growth of population depends upon the circumstances, but uniformly results in a growth of subsistence nearly the same as its own.
The amount of subsistence regulates the amount of population.	Population regulates subsistence as completely as it does clothing, housing, and other goods.

Malthus	Gray
Population increases more or less rapidly according to the abundance of subsistence.	Superabundance, or an excess of subsistence, has a defecundating and depopulating effect.
Population increase tends to overstock and thus to diminish the total employment to be divided among the available work force.	The increase of population tends uniformly to increase the demand for hands and thus employment.
The increase of population has a certain natural tendency to promote poverty.	The increase of population has therefore a uniform tendency to increase income and wealth, and over time by an increasing proportion.
The diseases and evils generated by the increase of population are chiefly those springing from a scarcity of food and from poverty.	The diseases and evils generated by an increase of population are chiefly those which spring from luxury, or an excess of subsistence.

Source: Adapted from Gray, 1818, pp. 10–12 by William Petersen, *Malthus* (Cambridge: Harvard UP, 1979), p. 79.

11

The Happiness of States, or An Inquiry Concerning Population

Simon Gray

1. *All species of circuland are productive of wealth, and enlarge the source of wealth, according to their quantum of chargeability, or their price rate: and all for precisely the same reasons.* 2. *Population regulates the amount of subsistence, as completely as that of clothing, housing, or any other branch of the supply. And* 3. *The increase of population is the original cause of all permanent increase of employment and wealth, and invariably creates a new additional average quantity of both, which,* caeteris paribus, *keeps enlarging in proportion to the new numbers.*

These great, these benevolent and cheering principles of nature, the source of such an infinite variety of happiness, though they have been for the most part either overlooked, or denied, by statisticians, have an absolutely necessary existence upon her arrangements.

* * *

The Influence of Government on the Increase of Population

There are some who seem disposed to attribute the increase of population almost entirely to the influence of a free and good government. I should reckon it much more like the actual fact to attribute a free and good government to the increase of population. This increase, by its influence in expanding the mind, and promoting science, and by its spreading wealth and its concomitant, a consciousness of independence, throughout the great mass, either makes at length the form of government free, or constrains it to act liberally.

That a good government assists in promoting the increase of population, is true; for, by maintaining internal tranquillity and rendering property secure, it promotes early marriage. Such, however, is the force of the all-meliorating influence of the increase of population, that, if government does not, by its injurious or tyrannical conduct, succeed in checking this principle, it alone will do the rest.

* * *

Principles and Results of Population

Man in the uncivilized state is rather unprolific. The artificial stimulants created by civilization, are required to render the progress of his numbers at all rapid. And to a certain rate of populousness at least, these stimulants, produced by civilization and the increase of population, quicken the rate of his increase.

In the savage or hunter's state, which is the most pure from mixture, population appears in general to be nearly stationary. In the pastoral state, which is also found sometimes very pure, the increase of population is quickened, but it is still very slow. In the third or agricultural state, which is occasionally, in a thin rate of numbers to territory, found pretty pure, it becomes very rapid. And in the fourth or commercial state, which is almost uniformly found very mixed, the increase is seldom so rapid as in the third. But in all these states, whether more pure or more mixed, the increase is found to be according to no regular ratio in regard to time, but according to the force of the stimulating, checked by the counteracting circumstances. . . .

Population regulates the supply of subsistence, clothing, houses, and all other articles which it requires, as far as this is dependent upon its will.

While it has a tendency to increase, as has been stated, *it has no tendency to over-increase*, either with respect to subsistence, employment, or wealth. It completely regulates the supply of the first; and its increase uniformly augments the average quantum of the second and third.

1. *It has no natural tendency to increase faster than subsistence*, as has been supposed by Mr. Malthus and others. This is proved incontestably by the superabundance of the materials of that supply, the fully sufficient number of suppliers, and the average price of subsistence. After the increase of numbers for at least 4000 years, perhaps barely one eighth of the materials is exhausted or fully used. Indeed, scarcely a single region of any great extent has yet attained its complement. Nor in any country that has reached the agricultural state, however populous, is there now found, or ever has been found, any average deficiency, which home or foreign cultivation could not supply. And so far is the number of suppliers from being, on the average, inadequate, that a considerable portion of those born and bred up among the class of cultivators, is constantly obliged, from a deficiency in their mode of employment, to have recourse to other modes. There is an incessant emigration of circulators from the country to towns. The price of subsistence, also, though it rises too high and falls too low occasionally, like that of other articles, is, on an universal average, at a fair rate compared with the general average prices of all kinds of circuland.

2. *The increase of population augments the average quantum of employment*. The new members not only have the same demands to employ one another as the old, but, combined with the latter, assist in multiplying the wants of all; and thus the increase of numbers is always creating new varieties of circuland. It consequently withdraws suppliers from the old modes. These still remain demanders of the old articles, while they furnish new ones which do not interfere with the former. Actual results in real life amply confirm this. With an increasing population the natural wants do not diminish, while the artificial are found to be continually augmenting. The thicker its rate and the more rapid its increase, the more constantly are all employed. There is a perpetual emigration, in search of employment, from thinner peopled districts and countries to those which are better peopled; while the more populous a state is, unless from special circumstances, the smaller is the average number of emigrants. The more crowded the population of a district or country also, the greater is the demand for machinery. In very thinly peopled districts human labour is more than sufficient to furnish the supplies for the regular demand. In thickly peopled districts it is utterly inadequate to the purpose; and the more populous they are, though in all lines the hands grow more expert and adroit, the more deficient of itself is it found.

The increase of population *is the great, indeed the sole original cause of the permanent increase of wealth.* The new comers, instead of trespassing on the funds of the old, add to their resources. The increase of numbers, by augmenting the demand faster than the supply, enables the various circulators not only to obtain more constant employment, but a better rate of price. The power of production, and consequently of reproduction, keeps constantly increasing in strength with the number of circulators.

The more crowded the mass, caeteris paribus *the more mutual stimulus is crated, and the richer is the whole.*

The result is, *that every increase in the number of circulators, on a given extent of territory, necessarily tends to increase it, and not merely according to the average quantity of the former dividend, but also according to a new average quantity, which is augmented in proportion to the new numbers, and the rate per square mile.*

The increase of population is *also the grand source of civilization.* By varying the employments of men, and affording them a more ample scene, as well as stronger inducements, to exert themselves, it gradually calls the various powers of the human mind more into action. At the same time it gives more scope and influence to the reasoning faculty. It thus tends gradually to improve both the talents and the manners of circulators. . . .

Though population has been hitherto gradually augmenting, it probably carries in its own increase the means of ultimately checking that increase. The populating causes seem evidently to gain on the antipopulating by the aid of increasing civilization, at least to a certain rate of populousness per square mile. Beyond that rate, from the increase of towns and of sedentary employments, and from the general prevalence of luxury, it is probable, the latter, both of the defecundating and positively depopulating kinds, will become powerful enough fully to counteract the former, and prevent the earth from reaching her universal complement, by rendering population throughout her various regions stationary, if not retrogressive. *At present, in districts that have approached or passed their complement, any farther increase seems not to be indigenous, but to spring from immigration.* It is not unlikely, but the equalizing of the two opposite powers may take place when the large town population, or the population of towns of 5000 souls and upwards, is equal to that of the country throughout all the districts connected nationally or commercially. . . .

A View of the Effects of the Increase of Population.

On concluding a work, one of the principal objects of which is to answer the grand question respecting population—*Does the increase of it tend to promote the attainment of the great object of a nation's pursuit, social happiness, or to counteract this?* it will be proper to exhibit a view of the effects of the increase of population in detail. This is as interesting as it is important.

The increase of population gives rise not only to the fond affections between the sexes, which produce so much happiness, but to many of the social connexions, from which so great a share of human enjoyment is derived. It tends directly to increase that purest and most virtuous class of pleasures, the domestic.

It gives existence, and, of course, a capability of happiness, to a greater number of beings. And these additional beings are by no means ungrateful in return. Their happiness serves to increase the happiness that formerly existed.

The increase of population operates towards correcting the bad effects of the progress of wealth and luxury. It cannot take place without a general practice of early marriage. And nothing tends so much to national virtue, or to general temperance, sobriety, frugality, and decency of manners, as marrying young. Late marriage leads directly to illicit amours, and all the dissoluteness of manners and extravagance, which springs from them.

The increase of population tends to regulate more completely the supply of food, and to render men less dependent on the natural fertility of the soil, and even on the climate. It augments subsistence, either in the district in which it takes place, or others that are at a distance, but have a commercial connexion with the former. It effects this by enlarging the demand as well as the means of supplying it. By the one the cultivator is stimulated to exert himself; while the additional quantity of capital and of skill, which it produces, affords him the other, and enables him to cultivate more steadily and successfully, to render every species of soil fertile, and to improve the advantages, which weather, though unfavourable to subsistence in one form, may bring to it in another. We uniformly find, that in proportion as population increases or decreases, agriculture flourishes or declines, and luxury, or the use of too large a quantity of subsistence in the various forms, prevails more or less among the members. Instead of an increase of population tending, as the subsistencians suppose, to diminish the average quantity of food consumed, and of course, procured, it uniformly tends to augment that average. . . .

The increase of population necessarily adds to the wealth of a country. From its natural effect in multiplying wants and the means of supplying them, it raises a greater portion of the whole population above poverty; and, by adding to the circuland of these individuals, necessarily augments the sum total of this, the circuland of the nation. There are other causes besides an increase of population that tend to increase the wealth of a state, such as certain natural circumstances and peculiar modes of employment arising out of these, which have a powerful effect on the circulandary movement and the quantum of circuland: these, however, must, perhaps uniformly, be combined with an increase of population to be permanently effective. But an increase of population, of itself, tends to accelerate the movement of circulation, and to augment the quantum of circuland. It consequently necessarily adds to the wealth of a larger proportional number. With respect to countries as well as districts, a greater population, *caeteris paribus*, will tend to increase the wealth of a greater proportion of the individuals. Were Switzerland, which is not what we call a manufacturing country, four times as populous as it is, even if we could suppose that it had no more modes of employing its new population than it has already, a greater proportion of its people would rise in the scale of wealth, than that which rises at present. Or if Great Britain, which is one of the highest manufacturing countries in Europe or the world, were to reach double the amount of her present population, while she kept increasing in populousness at the rate which she has done of late years, a proportion of her people much beyond the double of the present number would advance in that scale.

The increase of population is, in truth, the great predisposing cause of wealth[1]. Modes of employment are the machinery by which this cause operates. The ratio of increase of circuland will of course be in some degree regulated by these, but it always tends to create or extend those means; and perhaps no natural or political circumstances can be so unfavourable, but population, if it can be kept going on, will at length conquer them, and introduce an increase of wealth and wealthy employments into the country.

These observations are justified by the circumstances of every country on earth. *Caeteris paribus*, from the savage states, which have so small a population, up to the most populous, the average wealth of a country and of its individuals is in proportion to the quantity of population per square mile: and it is in proportion to the quantity of population, that different districts of the same country are rich and poor. Switzerland is poorer than the Low Countries and than Holland. Wales and Scotland are poorer than England. The Highlands of Scotland are poorer than the Lowlands. And both England and Scotland are richer now than they were a hundred years ago, because their population is greater and more rapidly increasing. Their population has increased during that period to double the amount, but their wealth, both capital and that portion appropriated to expenditure, has increased fully five-fold, and probably in a much greater ratio. The increase in wealth is not to be measured by the increase of the home population alone in these instances, it is true, more than in others; but the latter is the principal cause. It operates with greater or less force, according as it meets with circumstances more or less favourable, or is more or less connected with foreign population. . . .

What perhaps tends to lead so many wrong with respect to the increase of population, as if it actually tended to increase poverty, is the striking difference between the poorer and richer classes in highly peopled districts. They do not consider, that the great wealth of the rich classes springs from an increasing population as the original cause, and that the great body of the poorer classes in populous countries is not poor in reality, but only by comparison with these. It is the general poverty, it is the very equality in poverty, in thinly peopled districts, that makes us think the poorest in more tolerable circumstances. Where all are low in the scale of wealth, the very poor do not seem to be so, because they do not seem to be very different from their neighbours. They appear to be in tolerable circumstances, because few are in comfortable. If we inquire into the circumstances of the poorer ranks in Middlesex and other populous districts of Great Britain, which by contrast so offend us with the appearance of poverty, we shall find, that they have incomes on an average twice, or even thrice, the amount of those of the same classes in thinly inhabited countries, or even in the less populous districts of our own island. The average income derived from manual labour in London, at present (1818), is above a pound a week; and in many districts, where the price of articles, excepting house-rent, is not materially different, though the style of living is, half a pound is the full average among the peasants, and in some thinly peopled districts only seven or eight shillings. . . .

In sum, with respect to wealth, from the savage state, which consists of a small population spread over a vast extent of country, and where, of course, all are poor, up to the highest peopled states, the average income, with some exceptions arising out of peculiar circumstances, is proportionally greater according as the population increases on the same quantity of territory: and wealth becomes more general in the community, according as the increase of population is more rapid. It is the increase of population, that first forces savages to have recourse to artificial cultivation and introduces distinct ideas of property; and it is the increase of population that directly or indirectly creates all the wealth additional to that of the mere savage state, found in the most thinly peopled as well as the most populous country. All springs from populousness and the increase of population, and the effects which these produce in society.

The increase in population is also the grand cause of the civilization of society, as well as of all the fine arts and intellectual pursuits, which spring from this. By dividing, or elementizing, and varying employments, by accumulating capital, enlarging income, and creating demands for intellectual articles, if the expression may be used, it opens a more extensive and varied scene for the exertions of the human mind. And it is in proportion to the populousness and the rapidity of increase in the population of a state, that civilization, in its numerous pleasing forms, is found to flourish.

The increase in population is thus the source of the wealth and civilization of society, and all the advantages arising from these. And it is generally in proportion to the ratio of the increase, that subsistence, and the superfluities of subsistence or luxuries, wealth and civilization, increase also in a nation: and in proportion as population decreases, a nation becomes ill-fed, poor, and partly uncivilized again.

The increase of population produces its effects not chiefly by the harsh influence of increasing poverty and famine, as the abettors of that melancholy system, which throws a hateful gloom over the whole mass of nature's arrangements and results, the antipopulation theory, would insinuate; nor at all. Its influence is as kindly and cheering as it is powerful. It operates not by impoverishing but enriching; and not by causing scarcity but by creating abundance. It is constantly infusing new vigour among all classes of the community, by means of an increasing demand and increasing wealth, the consequence of an increase of consumers and suppliers. This increase thus tends to quicken the circulandary movement and to augment the circuland. By meliorating the present circumstances of the circulators, and holding up to their view a more extended market, it also kindles hope and brightens future prospects, and thus inspires all the industrious members of the community with additional activity in their respective employments. . . .

Populousness and the increase of population tend to enable a greater proportion of a nation to reach comforts, and to make them more cleanly, as well as industrious. This is effected by the increase of wealth, and that activity with which, as has just been observed, a rapidly increasing circulation inspires the whole national body, by employing them agreeably and brightening their prospects. The supposed state of population also brings the inhabitants more under the eye of one another, and the females become more jealous of being outdone. Increasing means and the conduct of richer neighbours give person of all ranks a taste for what is tidy and comfortable. The same causes operate in producing national activity and industry. The higher price of the new species of labour, which population in its progress is constantly introducing, urges every one to exert himself. The increase in the expenses of the style of living also stimulates even the slothful on to activity. . . .

Thinly peopled states, if slowly increasing, stationary, or decreasing, are almost without an exception dirty and idle; and populous states, if increasing, are likewise, with few exceptions, cleanly and active. Those exceptions are formed merely by unfavourable political or religious circumstances. But if population keeps increasing, it will at length vanquish even these.

Populousness and a rapidly increasing population, by the variety of mental employments, which they give rise to, prove the source of greater happiness to those minds formed by nature for such exercises, as well as exalt the national intellect. There is a great variety of genius and disposition among men; and individuals are never so happy, nor are they so likely to be successful, as when they are employed in the peculiar lines for which they are fitted by nature. The greater the population, the greater the variety of its employments, particularly of the kind which require mind. In thinly peopled states such employments are few; and in stationary or decreasing states, if populous, from the growing national languor, and the decrease of the stimulating power, the mind itself becomes despondent and weak; and though the former mental sorts of exercises may be still indulged in, it is not with the former energy and spirit.

The increase of population tends to enlarge states, at least to a certain extent. The accumulation of power derived from it, and the ambition arising from this accumulation, throw down by degrees the limits of petty states. From the earliest periods of history we find, that population in its progress has gradually destroyed the limits of small states, indeed all limits but those of an immovable, powerful, and strongly marked natural character. . . .

[T]he increase of population tends naturally to subsist, clothe, and lodge the great body more comfortably, to employ them more agreeably, to cultivate their minds, and to assist the cause of science as well as of virtue. It operates equally to increase wealth and advance civilization. . . .

The Conclusion

It has been found, that not only does the increase of population tend to the increase of wealth and other means of happiness, but that the former increase operates on the latter with an influence, the ratio of which is constantly augmenting. Instead, therefore, of withdrawing inducements to early marrying, or throwing obstacles in the way of it, as has been urged by the antipopulation theorists, and naturally, according to their principles, every proper inducement ought to be held out to it.

It has been found also, that the permanent increase of population is the directing cause of a permanent increase of food: that man, from the time he becomes a cultivator, becomes a regulator of subsistence, and a regulator possessed of sufficient power; for an increase of population carries within itself ample means of supplying itself up to the *ne plus ultra* of the increase of subsistence. This leads to the same practical conduct as the former result: for, as population thus cannot increase too fast, there is no necessity, as the subsistencians imagine, for retarding marriage.

It may be given as an axiom in statistics, that *the grand all-meliorating cause in society is the increase of population.* And the practical maxim of the sound statistician will be *to take care of population, as population will take care of subsistence, and of all other species of the supply.* Indeed, one of the leading objects of every enlightened statesman will be to increase population, and, consequently, to promote early marriage, by every means in his power. For, increased population, and wealth, with all that is politically good, will immediately or ultimately follow. But if population decrease, or even if it becomes stationary, the reverse will take place. A rapidly increasing population is an incontestable proof of a flourishing country: a stationary one, unless the country have reached at least the half of its complement, is a proof that its progress in acquiring wealth and other means of happiness, is doubtful; and a decreasing one is the most decisive of all proof, that it is going to decay and becoming more poor. . . .

The inquirer, at concluding, may be permitted to say, that the result of his inquiry respecting one great point essentially connected with his subject, has been particularly satisfactory to himself. It is pleasing to have found, that the *increase of population tends to increase wealth and other means of happiness in a new and additional proportion.* This truth dissipates at once the gloom shed over the human horizon from a theory, which, by checking marriage, would have operated, as far as acted upon, to promote vice and reduce a nation to poverty. It has also rescued man out of the hands of subsistence, as a regulator of his numbers, and restored him to his real place, as the regulator of what feeds him as much as of what clothes or lodges him. It has proved that what is most congenial to our natural feelings, in a measure that so essentially affects all mankind, is right. It has thrown a bright and steady light over human prospects; and by the encouragement which it claims for marriage has joined with every thing else to show, that what tends to promote virtue, tends also to promote the happiness of states.

Note

1. And yet there are some who found theories on the supposition, that the increase of population has rather a tendency to increase poverty. This fancy must arise from calculating, that 16 divided among 4 averages four to each; but if a fifth was added, while the 16, as these theorists calculate, become only perhaps 18, the new number would average only 3 3/5. But from the natural effects of an increase of population on the circulandary movement, the probability is, that in all countries beyond the mere savage state, there would be 21 or more to divide, so that the average share would be 4 1/5, or more, or at least, above 4.

12

Principles of Political Economy, Vol. 1

Henry C. Carey

In the early stages of society, men are widely scattered over the land, and with difficulty obtain, by the cultivation of the superior soils, scanty supplies of indifferent food. Unable to draw near together, because of the difficulty of obtaining subsistence, they are unable to unite together for protection. Land is abundant, but food and clothing are scarce. Men are carried off and enslaved, and their property is confiscated. Security of person and property is unknown. No law is known but that of force. By degrees, as capital increases, they are enabled to obtain increased supplies from a diminished surface, owing to the facility with which they cultivate the inferior soils, and are thus enabled to live in closer connexion with each other. They now associate together for mutual assistance. Laws are instituted for the purpose of determining and securing the enjoyment of the rights of person and property. Their political condition is improved, in consequence of *union of action*, the result of an increase of population and capital. They are still, however, obliged to give a considerable *proportion* of their time for the defence of the community, and to contribute much of the proceeds of their labour for the support of those who are employed in the maintenance of security.

With the further increase of population and capital, we find different small communities establishing intercourse, and gradually associating with each other for the maintenance of peace and order.

When each small community was compelled to depend upon itself, every man was obliged to hold himself in readiness to bear arms; but the association of ten or twenty such communities, while securing internal peace, gives strength sufficient to secure them in some measure against violence from abroad, and diminishes the proportion of the labour of each individual required for the public service. Increased security enables men to apply their labour more productively, and the diminution in the amount of contributions enables them to retain a larger *proportion* of the increased product. Population and capital continue to grow, producing a daily increasing tendency to union of action, rendering security more complete. The increasing facility of obtaining the means of support, is attended by an improvement of moral condition, and men are more disposed to respect the rights of their neighbours. The increased extent of the community, and the difference in the interests of the occupants of the extended territory now united in one system, render it more difficult to produce general excitement, the consequence of which is, that occurrences that would have led to war between the small communities, are peaceably arranged among larger ones. There is a constantly increasing tendency to peace abroad and at home. Instead of finding in each village a chief exercising the powers of government, and having under his control officers and soldiers, a single one performs the same service for the little state, the greater strength of which diminishes the necessity for employing men in carrying arms, and for interfering with the rights of the people, for the purpose of obtaining the means of paying them.

With improvement in the physical and moral condition of man, he becomes daily more and more aware of what those rights are, and more and more able to assert them, while those who are charged with the duties of government become daily more and more sensible of the necessity of avoiding interference with his exercise of them.

At a later period in the progress of society, as population becomes more dense, we find the disposition to union of action constantly increasing. Men are now associated in larger communities, or nations, and the numerous petty chiefs of earlier times are replaced by a single officer, termed king, emperor, or president. Peace and free intercourse now prevail throughout large masses. The consciousness of strength diminishes still further the necessity for maintaining armies, and for raising taxes for their support. Internal peace and diminished taxation enable men to increase their capital, and to apply their powers still more productively, while the diminishing wants of the government require a constantly diminishing proportion of that product, leaving a constantly increasing proportion to be divided between the capitalist and the labourer.

There is a daily diminution in the necessity for interfering with the enjoyment of perfect security of person and property, and a daily increase of the productive power, arising out of a tendency to united action, that is the natural consequence of increased wealth. Man passes gradually from a state of slavery to that of perfect freedom, exercising full and uncontrolled power over his own action and thoughts, over the employment of his time, and over the proceeds of his labour, while abstaining from interference with the exercise of similar rights by his neighbours. Free and secure himself, and obtaining by his own exertions the means of improving his own condition, he is desirous of aiding his neighbours to do the same, and ready to unite them in repelling any assaults to which they may be subjected, rather than to attempt himself to lessen their enjoyment of the rights of person and property. Thus—

Increase of wealth, by enabling men to cultivate the inferior soils, also enables them to draw nearer together, and to associate for the maintenance of peace and for securing each other in the enjoyment of the rights of person and property, thus improving their political condition. Peace and security tend to promote the growth of wealth, and the further improvement of the physical, moral, and political condition of man.

On the other hand—

Decrease of wealth, by diminishing the power of obtaining the means of subsistence, compels men to disperse themselves over the land; prevents them from associating for the maintenance of peace and security, and thus deteriorates their political condition. Insecurity and war tend to diminish the growth of wealth, and to deteriorate the physical, moral, and political condition of man.

The most perfect freedom of thought and action tends to produce the most rapid increase of the power of producing wealth, and the most rapid increase of the productive power tends to establish the most perfect freedom.

———

Casting our eyes over the earth, we observe the various communities differing widely in political condition, and those differences having apparently little connexion with the destiny of population. Thus freedom is unknown in South America, in Mexico, and in Russia, where population is widely scattered, while enjoyed in the United States, where population is but little more dense; and but little known in France, and in Germany, where it is dense, while enjoyed in England where the proportion of population to land is still greater, and it is unknown in Bengal where that proportion is greatest.

When, however, we compare these several nations with themselves, at different periods, we find uniformly that as population and capital increase, slavery and restrictions of all kinds pass gradually away, enabling the people to acquire political rights and influence. The moral and physical condition of *the few* is constantly improving; their political condition, so far as regards the exercise of power over *their own actions and their own property*, is unimpaired; but there is a daily diminution in their power to control *the actions of others*, or to direct the application of the product of their labour. The relative position of the two parties is constantly changing.

In every nation in which has existed security of person and of property, tending to enable its members to employ their labour productively, there has been a steady diminution in the proportion of those exercising power over their fellow men, and in the amount of power exercised, accompanied by a constant increase in the control exercised by the whole body of the people over their own actions, and over the movements of the government. . . .

It is sufficiently obvious that increased wealth has tended to give to *the many*, power to demand equality of political rights, but the *modus operandi* is yet to be shown. Like all other of the operations of nature, it will be found exceedingly simple, and the power with which she acts in this case, will be seen to be, as in all others, in the direct ratio of the simplicity of the means employed.

Our readers have seen that with every increase in the ratio of capital to population, there is an increase in the value of labour as compared with capital, and an increased competition on the part of the owners of the latter for the employment of labourers, the consequence of which is that with every such increase the labourer is enabled to retain *an increased proportion* of the commodities he produces, leaving to the landlord, or other capitalist, a constantly *decreasing proportion*: and, *vice versa*, that with every diminution in the ratio of capital to population, the proportion of the landlord increases, and that of the labourer falls, producing in the one case a constantly increasing tendency to equality of physical condition, and in the other to inequality. We propose now to show how the change in the mode of distribution that thus takes place, influences the political condition of both parties, enabling the labourer gradually to exercise the same control over his actions that is exercised by the capitalist over his property.

Land being the source from which all wealth must be derived, it is, at an early period of society, appropriated by those whose physical or intellectual powers enable them to obtain the mastery over portions of their fellow men, who are compelled to cultivate the portions assigned to them, receiving in return such allowance of food and clothing as may be awarded to them. The few are masters, and the many are slaves.

In this stage of society, population is widely scattered, and there is no capital in the form of roads or canals by which men are enabled to perform exchanges, or even to meet together for the promotion of any object tending to improve their condition.

* * *

The proposition with which our First Part concluded was,

"That, as capital increases, population becomes more dense, and the inferior soils are brought into action with a constantly increasing return to labour, men are enabled to benefit by the co-operation of their neighbours, and habits of kindness and good feeling take the place of the savage and predatory habits of the early period. Poverty and misery gradually disappear, and are replaced by ease and comfort. Labour becomes gradually less severe, and the quantity required to secure the means of subsistence is diminished, by which he is enabled to devote more time to the cultivation of the mind. His moral improvement keeps pace with that which takes place in his physical condition, and thus the virtues of civilization replace the vices of savage life."

We had, however, evidence that population had in many countries increased in density without either physical or moral improvement having taken place, and to ascertain the causes thereof, it became necessary to prosecute the inquiry just completed, the result of which we now offer to the reader in the following propositions.

I. That security of person, and perfect freedom of action—security of property, and perfect freedom in its employment—are essential to the productive application of labour.

II. That man associates with his fellow man with a view to obtain security.

III. That in the infancy of society, when population is thinly scattered over the land, and when the superior soils only are cultivated, a very large *proportion* of the labour of the community is employed in the endeavour to maintain security, which nevertheless exists in a very limited degree.

IV. That with the increase of capital man is enabled to draw nearer to his fellow man; population becomes more dense, and a *constantly increasing security* is obtained at the cost of a *constantly diminishing proportion* of the labour of the community.

V. That, therefore, while labour is constantly increasing in its productive power, a constantly increasing *proportion* is left to be divided between the labourer and the capitalist.

VI. That with this diminution in the proportion required for the maintenance of security, there is a constant diminution in the *necessity* for interference with the modes of employing either person or property.

VII. That the power of accumulating capital is constantly increasing, accompanied by a constant diminution in the *proportion* of the product of labour that can be claimed by the capitalist for permitting it to be used.

VIII. That, therefore, with the increase of population and of capital, there is a constant diminution in *the proportion* required by *both government and capitalist*, attended by a constant increase in the proportion, and a rapid increase in *the quantity, retained by the labourer.*

IX. That such have been the results observed in France, England, and the United States, as population has increased in density.

X. That such are likewise the results as we compare the *different portions of each country*, one with another.

XI. That such would likewise be the case as we compared the several countries, one with another, were it not that the policy of the several nations has been essentially different. . . .

XIII. That every improvement in the *quality* is attended by a diminution in the *quantity* and severity of labour.

XIV. That it is also accompanied by a diminution in the proportion of the product thereof that can be claimed by the owner of capital.

XV. That there is therefore a constant tendency to approximation in the condition of the labourer and capitalist.

XVI. That while the labourer experiences a constantly increasing facility in becoming a capitalist, the constant diminution in the severity of application and the constant increase of reward offer to the owner of capital great inducements to exertion.

XVII. That the *constant reduction in the proportion of the latter*, although attended by a constant *increase of quantity*, being also accompanied by *a constant improvement in the general standard of living*, produces a *necessity* for the exertion of his faculties.

XVIII. That thus with the increase of population and of capital there is a constant improvement in the condition of both labourer and capitalist, attended by a constantly increasing necessity for the exertion of their talents, and producing a constantly increasing facility for passing upwards from the one class to the other, as is seen in England and still more in the United States.

XIX. That where the increase of population is attended by a *diminution* in the ratio which capital bears thereto, there is a *constant deterioration* in the condition of both labourer and capitalist, accompanied by a *depression in the general standard of living*. The smaller capitalists become labourers. The reward of talent is constantly falling. The distance between the highest and lowest classes of society is constantly increasing, attended by a constantly increasing difficulty in passing upwards from the one class to the other, as is seen in India.

XX. That wars and unproductive expenditure, and restrictions upon the employment of labour and capital, tend to perpetuate and to increase inequality of condition, and to maintain a low standard of living, while peace, economy, and freedom of action tend to remove inequalities, and to exalt the general standard of living.

XXI. That with increased facility in providing for physical wants, there is a constant increase in the proportion of the product of labour that may be applied to the promotion of intellectual and moral improvement.

XXII. That accordingly with the growth of population and of wealth, there is a constant increase in the proportion which the institutions for education and for religious instruction bear to the population, and an equally constant increase in the disposition to aid in supporting them.

XXIII. That there is likewise an increase in the disposition to provide relief for the aged and infirm, and those who, by other causes, are rendered unable to provide for themselves.

XXIV. That thus with the physical improvement of man we find a constant improvement in his moral and intellectual condition, as is shown in the United States and England.

XXV. That with physical deterioration we find a constant moral and intellectual deterioration, as is shown in India.

XXVI. That wars and unproductive expenditure, and restraints upon the employment of labour and capital, tend to prevent both physical and moral improvement.

XXVII. That the maintenance of perfect security of person and of property, and of perfect freedom in the employment of both, is attended by increased productiveness of labour, rapid growth of capital, and great moral and intellectual improvement, and that both capitalist and labourer are benefited thereby, whereas every diminution of security and every interference with the mode of employment of either person or property tends to diminish production, to prevent the growth of capital, and to prevent improvement. . . .

XXXIV. That high wages and high profits of capital, and a high physical and moral condition should accompany density of population, but that wars and unproductive expenditure may prevent increase of capital and improvement of condition, as is the case in India—or retard them, as in France.

XXXV. That a constant continuance of peace and moderation of expenditure may enable even a scattered population to attain a high moral and physical condition, as is seen in the United States, and particularly in that portion styled New England.

13

Principles of Political Economy

John Stuart Mill

This impossibility of ultimately avoiding the stationary state—this irresistible necessity that the stream of human industry should finally spread itself out into an apparently stagnant sea—must have been, to the political economists of the last two generations, an unpleasing and discouraging prospect; for the tone and tendency of their speculations goes completely to identify all that is economically desirable with the progressive state, and with that alone. . . .

Even in a progressive state of capital, in old countries, a conscientious or prudential restraint on population is indispensable, to prevent the increase of numbers from outstripping the increase of capital, and the condition of the classes who are at the bottom of society from being deteriorated. Where there is not, in the people, or in some very large proportion of them, a resolute resistance to this deterioration—a determination to preserve an established standard of comfort—the condition of the poorest class sinks, even in a progressive state, to the lowest point which they will consent to endure. The same determination would be equally effectual to keep up their condition in the stationary state, and would be quite likely to exist. Indeed, even now, the countries in which the greatest prudence is manifested in the regulating of population, are often those in which capital increases least rapidly. Where there is an indefinite prospect of employment for increased numbers, there is apt to appear less necessity for prudential restraint. If it were evident that a new hand could not obtain employment but by displacing, or succeeding to, one already employed, the combined influences of prudence and public opinion might in some measure be relied on for restricting the coming generation within the numbers necessary for replacing the present.

I cannot, therefore, regard the stationary state of capital and wealth with the unaffected aversion so generally manifested towards it by political economists of the old school. I am inclined to believe that it would be, on the whole, a very considerable improvement on our present condition. I confess I am not charmed with the ideal of life held out by those who think that the normal state of human beings is that of struggling to get on; that the trampling, crushing, elbowing, and treading on each other's heels, which form the existence type of social life, are the most desirable lot of human kind, or anything but the disagreeable symptoms of one of the phases of industrial progress. It may be a necessary stage in the progress of civilization, and those European nations which have hitherto been so fortunate as to be preserved from it, may have it yet to undergo. . . .

There is room in the world, no doubt, and even in old countries, for a great increase of population, supposing the arts of life to go on improving, and the capital to increase. But even if innocuous, I confess I see very little reason for desiring it. The density of population necessary to enable mankind to obtain, in the greatest degree, all the advantages both of co-operation and of social intercourse, has, in all the most populous countries, been attained. A population may be too crowded, though all be amply supplied with food and raiment. It is not good for man to be kept perforce at all times in the presence of his species. A world from which solitude is extirpated, is a very poor ideal. Solitude, in the sense of being often alone, is essential to any depth of meditation or of character; and solitude in the presence of natural beauty and grandeur, is the cradle of thoughts and aspirations which are not only good for the individual, but which society could ill do without. Nor is there much satisfaction in contemplating the world with nothing left to the spontaneous activity of nature; with every rood of land brought into cultivation, which is capable of growing food for human beings; every flowery waste or natural pasture ploughed up, all quadrupeds or birds which are not domesticated for man's use exterminated as his rivals for food, every hedgerow or superfluous tree rooted out, and scarcely a place left where a wild shrub or flower could grow without being eradicated as a weed in the name of improved agriculture. If the earth must lose that great portion of its pleasantness which it owes to things that the unlimited increase of wealth and population would extirpate from it, for the mere purpose of enabling it to support a larger but not a better or a happier population, I sincerely hope, for the sake of posterity, that they will be content to be stationary, long before necessity compels them to it.

It is scarcely necessary to remark that a stationary condition of capital and population implies no stationary state of human improvement. There would be as much scope as ever for all kinds of mental culture, and moral and social progress; as much room for improving the Art of Living, and much more likelihood of its being improved, when minds ceased to be engrossed by the art of getting on. Even the industrial arts might be as earnestly and as successfully cultivated, with this sole difference, that instead of serving no purpose but the increase of wealth, industrial improvements would produce their legitimate effect, that of abridging labour. Hitherto it is questionable if all the mechanical inventions yet made have lightened the day's toil of any human being. They have enabled a greater population to live the same life of drudgery and imprisonment, and an increased number of manufacturers and others to make fortunes. They have increased the comforts of the middle classes. But they have not yet begun to effect those great changes in human destiny, which it is in their nature and in their futurity to accomplish. Only when, in addition to just institutions, the increase of mankind shall be under the deliberate guidance of judicious foresight, can the conquests made from the powers of nature by the intellect and energy of scientific discoverers, become the common property of the species, and the means of improving and elevating the universal lot.

*   *   *

But is it the fact, that these tendencies are not counteracted? Has the progress of wealth and industry no effect in regard to cost of production, but to diminish it? Are no causes of an opposite character brought into operation by the same progress, sufficient in some cases not only to neutralize, but to overcome the former, and convert the descending movement of cost of production into an ascending movement? We are already aware that there are such causes, and that, in the case of the most important classes of commodities, food and materials, there is a tendency diametrically opposite to that of which we have been speaking. The cost of production of these commodities tends to increase.

This is not a property inherent in the commodities themselves. If population were stationary, and the produce of the earth never needed to be augmented in quantity, there would be no cause for greater cost of production. Mankind would, on the contrary, have the full benefit of all improvements in agriculture, or in the arts subsidiary to it, and there would be no difference, in this respect, between the products of agriculture and those of manufactures. The only products of industry, which, if population did not increase, would be liable to a real increase of cost of production, are those which, depending on a material which is not renewed, are either wholly or partially exhaustible; such as coal, and most if not all metals; for even iron, the most abundant as well as most useful of metallic products, which forms an ingredient of most minerals and of almost all rocks, is susceptible of exhaustion so far as regards its richest and most tractable ores.

When, however, population increases, as it has never yet failed to do when the increase of industry and of the means of subsistence made room for it, the demand for most of the productions of the earth, and particularly for food, increases in a corresponding proportion. And then comes into effect that fundamental law of production from the soil, on which we have so frequently had occasion to expatiate; the law, that increased labour, in any given state of agricultural skill, is attended with a less than proportional increase of produce. The cost of production of the fruits of the earth increases, *caeteris paribus*, with every increase of the demand.

No tendency of a like kind exists with respect to manufactured articles. The tendency is in the contrary direction. The larger the scale on which manufacturing operations are carried on, the more cheaply they can in general be performed. Mr Senior has gone the length of enunciating as an inherent law of manufacturing industry, that in it increased production takes place at a smaller cost, while in agricultural industry increased production takes place at a greater cost. I cannot think, however, that even in manufactures, increased cheapness follows increased production by anything amounting to a law. It is a probable and usual, but not a necessary, consequence.

As manufactures, however, depend for their materials either upon agriculture, or mining, or the spontaneous produce of the earth, manufacturing industry is subject, in respect of one of its essentials, to the same law as agriculture. But the crude material generally forms so small a portion of the total cost, that any tendency which may exist to a progressive increase in that single item, is much over-balanced by the diminution continually taking place in all the other elements; to which diminution it is impossible at present to assign any limit.

The tendency, then, being to a perpetual increase of the productive power of labour in manufactures, while in agriculture and mining there is a conflict between two tendencies, the one towards an increase of productive power, the other towards a diminution of it, the cost of production being lessened by every improvement in the processes, and augmented by every addition to population; it follows that the exchange values of manufactured articles, compared with the products of agriculture and of mines, have, as population and industry advance, a certain and decided tendency to fall. Money being a product of mines, it may also be laid down as a rule, that manufactured articles tend, as society advances, to fall in money price. The industrial history of modern nations, especially during the last hundred years, fully bears out this assertion.

Whether agricultural produce increases in absolute as well as comparative cost of production, depends on the conflict of the two antagonist agencies, increase of population, and improvement in agricultural skill. In some, perhaps in most, states of society, (looking at the whole surface of the earth,) both agricultural skill and population are either stationary, or increase very slowly, and the cost of production of food, therefore, is nearly stationary. In a society which is advancing in wealth, population generally increases faster than agricultural skill, and food consequently tends to become more costly; but there are times when a strong impulse sets in toward agricultural improvement. Such an impulse has shown itself in Great Britain during the last twenty or thirty years. In England and Scotland agricultural skill has of late increased considerably faster than population, insomuch that food and other agricultural produce, notwithstanding the increase of people, can be grown at less cost than they were thirty years ago: and the abolition of the Corn Laws has given an additional stimulus to the spirit of improvement. In some other countries, and particularly in France, the improvement of agriculture gains ground still more decidedly upon population, because though agriculture, except in a few provinces, advances slowly, population advances still more slowly, and even with increasing slowness; its growth being kept down, not by poverty, which is diminishing, but by prudence.

Which of the two conflicting agencies is gaining upon the other at any particular time, might be conjectured with tolerable accuracy from the money price of agricultural produce (supposing bullion not to vary materially in value), provided a sufficient number of years could be taken, to form an average independent of the fluctuations of seasons. This, however, is hardly practicable, since Mr Tooke has shown that even so long a period as half a century may include a much greater proportion of abundant and a smaller of deficient seasons than is properly due to it. A mere average, therefore, might lead to conclusions only the more misleading, for their deceptive semblance of accuracy. . . .

* * *

Influence of the Progress of Industry and Population on Rents, Profits, and Wages

Continuing the inquiry into the nature of the economical changes taking place in a society which is in a state of industrial progress, we shall next consider what is the effect of that progress on the distribution of the produce among the various classes who share in it. . . .

Let us first suppose that population increases, capital and the arts of production remaining stationary. One of the effects of this change of circumstances is sufficiently obvious: wages will fall; the labouring class will be reduced to an inferior condition. The state of the capitalist, on the contrary, will be improved. With the same capital, he can purchase more labour, and obtain more produce. His rate of profit is increased. The dependence of the rate of profits on the cost of labour is here verified; for the labourer obtaining a diminished quantity of commodities, and no alteration being supposed in the circumstances of their production, the diminished quantity represents a diminished cost. The labourer obtains not only a smaller real reward, but the product of a smaller quantity of labour. The first circumstance is the important one to himself, the last to his employer. . . .

The new element now introduced—an increased demand for food— besides occasioning an increase of rent, still further disturbs the distribution of the produce between capitalists and labourers. The increase of population will have diminished the reward of labour: and if its cost is diminished as greatly as its real remuneration, profits will be increased by the full amount. If, however, the increase of population leads to an increased production of food, which cannot be supplied but at an enhanced cost of production, the cost of labour will not be so much diminished as the real reward of it, and profits, therefore, will not be so much raised. It is even possible that they might not be raised at all. The labourers may previously have been so well provided for, that the whole of what they now lose may be struck off from their other indulgences, and they may not, either by necessity or by choice, undergo any reduction in the quantity or quality of their food. To produce the food for the increased number may be attended with such an increase of expense, that wages, though reduced in quantity, may represent as great a cost, may be the product of as much labour, as before, and the capitalist may not be at all benefited. On this supposition the loss to the labourer is partly absorbed in the additional labour required for producing the last instalment of agricultural produce; and the remainder is gained by the landlord, the only sharer who always benefits by an increase of population. . . .

* * *

Agricultural skill and knowledge are of slow growth, and still slower diffusion. Inventions and discoveries, too, occur only occasionally, while the increase of population and capital are continuous agencies. It therefore seldom happens that improvement, even during a short time, has so much the start of population and capital as actually to lower rent, or raise the rate of profits. There are many countries in which the growth of population and capital is not rapid, but in these agricultural improvement is less active still. Population almost everywhere treads close on the heels of agricultural improvements, and effaces its effects as fast as they are produced. . . .

Agricultural improvement may thus be considered to be not so much a counterforce conflicting with increase of population, as a partial relaxation of the bonds which confine that increase.

Note

1. [In the 1848 edition the preceding passage ran as follows: The northern and middle states of America are a specimen of this stage of civilization in very favourable circumstances; having, apparently, got rid of all social injustices and inequalities that affect persons of Caucasian race and of the male sex, while the proportion of population to capital and land is such as to ensure abundance to every able-bodied member of the community who does not forfeit it by misconduct. They have the six points of Chartism, and they have no poverty: and all that these advantages seem to have done for them is that the life of the whole of one sex is devoted to dollar-hunting, and of the other to breeding dollar-hunters.]

14

On Malthus

Friedrich Engels

The Myth of Overpopulation

Malthus . . . asserts that population constantly exerts pressure on the means of subsistence; that as production is increased, population increases in the same proportion; and that the inherent tendency of population to multiply beyond the available means of subsistence is the cause of all poverty and all vice. For if there are too many people, then in one way or another they must be eliminated; they must die, either by violence or through starvation. . . .

Is it necessary for me to give any more details of this vile and infamous doctrine, this repulsive blasphemy against man and nature, or to follow up its consequences any further? Here, brought before us at last, is the immorality of the economists in its highest form. . . .

We shall destroy the contradiction simply by resolving it. With the fusion of those interests which now conflict with one another, there will disappear the antithesis between surplus population in one place and surplus wealth in another, and also the wonderful phenomenon—more wonderful than all the wonders of all the religions put together—that a nation must starve to death from sheer wealth and abundance; and there will disappear too the crazy assertion that the earth does not possess the power to feed mankind. . . .

Malthus puts forward a calculation upon which his whole system is based. Population increases in geometrical progression—1+2+4+8+ 16+32, etc. The productive power of the land increases in arithmetical progression—1+2+3+4+5+6. The difference is obvious and horrifying—but is it correct? Where has it been proved that the productivity of the land increases in arithmetical progression? The area of land is limited—that is perfectly true. But the labour power to be employed on this area increases together with the population; and even if we assume that the increase of output associated with this increase of labour is not always proportionate to the latter, there still remains a third element—which the economists, however, never consider as important—namely, science, the progress of which is just as limitless and at least as rapid as that of population. For what great advances is the agriculture of this century obliged to chemistry alone—and indeed to two men alone. Sir Humphry Davy and Justus Liebig? But science increases at least as fast as population; the latter increases in proportion to the body of knowledge passed down to it by the previous generation, that is, in the most normal conditions it also grows in geometrical progression—and what is impossible for science? But it is ridiculous to speak of overpopulation while "the valley of the Mississippi alone contains enough waste land to accommodate the whole population of Europe", while altogether only one-third of the earth can be described as cultivated, and while the productivity of this third could be increased sixfold and more merely by applying improvements which are already known.

*   *   *

A Declaration of War Upon the Proletariat

[T]he most open declaration of war of the bourgeoisie upon the proletariat is Malthus' Law of Population and the New Poor Law framed in accordance with it. We have already alluded several times to the theory of Malthus. We may sum up its final result in these few words, that the earth is perennially overpopulated, whence poverty, misery, distress, and immorality must prevail; that it is the lot, the eternal destiny of mankind, to exist in too great numbers, and therefore in diverse classes, of which some are rich, educated, and moral, and others more or less poor, distressed, ignorant, and immoral. Hence it follows in practice, and Malthus himself drew this conclusion, that charities and poor-rates are, properly speaking, nonsense, since they serve only to maintain, and stimulate the increase of, the surplus population whose competition crushes down wages for the employed; that the employment of the poor by the Poor Law Guardians is equally unreasonable, since only a fixed quantity of the products of labour can be consumed, and for every unemployed labourer thus furnished employment, another hitherto employed must be driven into enforced idleness, whence private undertakings suffer at cost of Poor Law industry; that, in other words, the whole problem is not how to support the surplus population, but how to restrain it as far as possible. Malthus declares in plain English that the right to live, a right previously asserted in favour of every man in the world, is nonsense. . . .

Population and Communism

There is, of course, the abstract possibility that the number of people will become so great that limits will have to be set to their increase. But if at some stage communist society finds itself obliged to regulate the production of human beings, just as it has already come to regulate the production of things, it will be precisely this society, and this society alone, which can carry this out without difficulty. It does not seem to me that it would be at all difficult in such a society to achieve by planning a result which has already been produced spontaneously, without planning, in France and Lower Austria. At any rate, it is for the people in the communist society themselves to decide whether, when, and how this is to be done, and what means they wish to employ for the purpose. I do not feel called upon to make proposals or give them advice about it. These people, in any case, will surely not be any less intelligent than we are.

15

Progress and Poverty

Henry George

[E]verywhere the vice and misery attributed to overpopulation can be traced to the warfare, tyranny, and oppression which prevent knowledge from being utilized and deny the security essential to production. . . .

The strength of the reproductive force in the animal and vegetable kingdoms—such facts as that a single of pair of salmon might, if preserved from their natural enemies for years, fill the ocean; that a pair of rabbits would, under the same circumstances, soon overrun a continent; that many plants scatter their seeds by the hundred fold, and some insects deposit thousands of eggs; and that everywhere through these kingdoms each species constantly tends to press, and when not limited by the number of its enemies, evidently does press, against the limits of subsistence—is constantly cited, from Malthus down to the textbooks of the present day, as showing that population likewise tends to press against subsistence, and, when unrestrained by other means, its natural increase must necessarily result in such low wages and want, or, if that will not suffice, and the increase still goes on, in such actual starvation, as will keep it within the limits of subsistence.

But is this analogy valid? . . .

Does not the fact that all of the things which furnish man's subsistence have the power to multiply many fold—some of them many thousand fold, and some of them many million or even billion fold—

while he is only doubling his numbers, show that, let human beings increase to the full extent of their reproductive power, the increase of population can never exceed subsistence? . . .

Of all living things, man is the only one who can give play to the reproductive forces, more powerful than his own, which supply him with food. Beast, insect, bird, and fish take only what they find. Their increase is at the expense of their food, and when they have reached the existing limits of food, their food must increase before they can increase. But unlike that of any other living thing, the increase of man involves the increase of his food. If bears instead of men had been shipped from Europe to the North American continent, there would now be no more bears than in the time of Columbus, and possibly fewer, for bear food would not have been increased not the conditions of bear life extended, by the bear immigration, but probably the reverse. But within the limits of the United States alone, there are now forty-five millions of men where then there were only a few hundred thousand, and yet there is now within that territory much more food per capita for the forty-five millions than there was then for the few hundred thousand. It is not the increase of food that has caused this increase of men; but the increase of men that has brought about the increase of food. There is more food, simply because there are more men.

Here is a difference between the animal and the man. Both the jayhawk and the man eat chickens, but the more jayhawks the fewer chickens, while the more men the more chickens. Both the seal and the man eat salmon, but when a seal takes a salmon there is a salmon less, and were seals to increase past a certain point salmon must diminish; while by placing the spawn of the salmon under favorable conditions man can so increase the number of salmon as more than to make up for all he may take, and thus, no matter how much men may increase, there increase need never outrun the supply of salmon.

In short, while all through the vegetable and animal kingdoms the limit of subsistence is independent of the thing subsisted, with man the limit of subsistence is within the final limits of earth, air, water, and sunshine dependent upon man himself. . . .

Granted that man is only a more highly developed animal; that the ring-tailed monkey is a distant relative who has gradually developed acrobatic tendencies, and the humpbacked while a far-off connection who in early life took to the sea—granted that back of these he is kin to the vegetable, and is still subject to the same laws as plants, fishes, birds, and beasts. Yet there is still this difference between man and all other animals—he is the only animal whose desires increase as they are fed; the only animal that is never satisfied. The wants of every other living things are uniform and fixed. The ox of to-day aspires to no more than did the ox when man first yoked him. The sea gull of the English Channel, who poises himself above the swift steamer, wants no more better food or lodging than the gulls who circled round as the keels of Caesar's galleys first grated on a British beach. Of all that nature offers them, be it ever so abundant, all living things save man can take, and care for, only enough to supply wants which are definite and fixed. The only use they can make of additional supplies or additional opportunities is to multiply.

But not so with man. No sooner are his animal wants satisfied than new wants arise. Food he wants first, as does the beast; shelter next, as does the beast; and these given, his reproductive instincts assert their sway, as do those of the beast. But here man and beast part company. The beast never goes further; the man has but set his feet on the first step of an infinite progression—a progression upon which the beast never enters; a progression away from and above the beast.

The demand for quantity once satisfied, he seeks equality. The very desires that he has in common with the beast become extended, refined, exalted. It is not merely hunger, but taste, that seeks gratification in food; in clothes, he seeks not merely comfort, but adornment; the rude shelter becomes a house; the undiscriminating sexual attraction begins to transmute itself into subtle influences, and the hard and common stock of animal life to blossom and to bloom into shapes of delicate beauty. As power to gratify his wants increases, so does aspiration grow. . . .

Passing into higher forms of desire, that which slumbered in the plant and fitfully stirred in the beast, awakes in the man. The eyes of the mind are opened, and he longs to know. He braves the scorching heat of the desert and the icy blasts of the polar sea, but not for food; he watches all night, but it is to trace the circling of the eternal stars. He adds toil to toil, to gratify a hunger no animal has felt; to assuage a thirst no beast can know. . . .

[B]esides the positive and prudential checks of Malthus, there is a third check which comes into play with the elevation of the standard of comfort and the development of the intellect, is pointed to by many well-known facts. The proportion of births is notoriously greater in new settlements, where the struggle with nature leaves little opportunity for intellectual life, and among the poverty-bound classes of older countries, who in the midst of wealth are deprived of all its advantages and reduced to all but an animal existence, than it is among the classes to whom the increase of wealth has brought independence, leisure, comfort, and a fuller and more varied life. . . .

If the real law of population is thus indicated, as I think it must be, then the tendency to increase, instead of being always uniform, is strong where a greater population would give increased comfort, and where the perpetuity of the race is threatened by the mortality induced by adverse conditions; but weakens just as the higher development of the individual become possible and the perpetuity of the race is assured. In other words, the law of population accords with and is subordinate to the law of intellectual development, and any danger that human beings may be brought into a world where they cannot be provided for arises not from the ordinances of nature, but form social maladjustments that in the midst of wealth condemn men to want. . . .

I assert that in any given state of civilization a greater number of people can collectively be better provided for than a smaller. I assert that the injustice of society, not the niggardliness of nature, is the cause of the want and misery which the current theory attributes to overpopulation. I assert that the new mouths which an increasing population calls into existence require no more food than the old ones, while the hands they being with them can in the natural order of things produce more. I assert that, other things being equal, the greater the population, the greater the comfort which an equitable distribution of wealth would give to each individual. I assert that in a state of equality the natural increase of population would constantly tend to make every individual richer instead of poorer. . . .

The power of any population to produce the necessaries of life is not be measured by the necessaries of life actually produced, but by the expenditure of power in all modes.

There is no necessity for abstract reasoning. The question is one of simple fact. Does the relative power of producing wealth decrease with the increase of population?

The facts are so patent that it is only necessary to call attention to them We have, in modern times, seen many communities advance in population. Have they not at the same time advanced even more rapidly in wealth? We see many communities still increasing in population. Are they not also increasing their wealth still faster? Is there any doubt that while England has been increasing her population at the rate of two per cent per annum, her wealth has been growing in still greater proportion? Is it not true that while the population of the United States has been doubling every twenty-nine years her wealth has been doubling at much shorter intervals? Is it not true that under similar conditions—that is to say, among communities of similar people in a similar stage of civilization—the most densely populated community is also the richest? Are not the more densely populated eastern states richer in proportion to population than the more sparsely populated western or southern states? Is not England, where population is even denser than in the eastern states of the Union, also richer in proportion? Where will you find wealth devoted with the most lavishness to nonproductive use—costly buildings, fine furniture, luxurious equipages, statues, pictures, pleasure gardens and yachts? Is it not where population is densest rather than where it is sparsest? Where will you find in largest proportion those whom the general production suffices to keep without productive labor on their part—men of income and of elegant leisure, thieves, policemen, menial servants, lawyers, men of letters, and the like? Is it not where population is dense rather than where it is sparse? Whence is it that capital overflows for remunerative investment? Is it not from densely populated countries to sparsely populated countries? These things conclusively show that wealth is greatest where population is densest; that the production of wealth to a given amount of labor increases as population increases. These things are apparent wherever we turn our eyes. On the same level of civilization, the same stage of the productive arts, government, etc., the most populous countries are always the most wealthy. . . .

The richest countries are not those where nature is most prolific; but those where labor is most efficient—not Mexico, but Massachusetts; not Brazil, but England. The countries where population is densest and presses hardest upon the capabilities of nature, are, other things begin equal, the countries where the largest proportion of the produce can be devoted to luxury and the support of the nonproducers, the countries where capital overflows, the countries that upon exigency, such as war, can stand the greatest drain. . . .

Wealth will not bear much accumulation; except in a few unimportant forms it will not keep. The matter of the universe, which, when worked up by labor into desirable forms, constitutes wealth, is constantly tending back to its original state. Some forms of wealth will last for a few hours, some for a few days, some for a few months, some for a few years; and there are very few forms of wealth that can be passed from one generation to another. Take wealth in some of its most useful and permanent forms—ships, houses, railways, machinery. Unless labor is constantly exerted in preserving and renewing them, they will almost immediately become useless. Stop labor in any community, and wealth would vanish almost as the jet of a fountain vanishes when the flow of water is shut off. Let labor again exert itself, and wealth will almost as immediately reappear. This has been long noticed where war or other calamity has swept away wealth, leaving a population unimpaired. There is not less wealth in London today because of the great fire of 1666; nor yet is there less wealth in Chicago because of the great fire in 1870. On those fire-swept acres have arisen, under the hand of labor, more magnificent buildings, filled with greater stocks of goods; and the stranger who, ignorant of the history of the city, passes along those stately avenues would not dream that a few years ago all lay so black and bare. The same principle—that wealth is constantly re-created—is obvious in every new city. Given the same population and the same efficiency of labor, and the town of yesterday will possess and enjoy as much as the town founded by the Romans. No one who has seen Melbourne or San Francisco can doubt that if the population of England were transported to New Zealand, leaving all accumulated wealth behind, New Zealand would soon be as rich as England is now; or, conversely, that if the population of England were reduced to the sparseness of the present population of New Zealand, in spite of accumulated wealth, they would soon be as poor. Accumulated wealth seems to play just about such a part in relation to the social organism as accumulated nutriment does to the physical organism. Some accumulated wealth is necessary, and to a certain extent it may be drawn upon in exigencies; but the wealth produced by past generations can on more account for the consumption of the present than the dinners he ate last year can supply a man with present strength. . . .

[W]hether we compare different communities with each other, or the same community at different times, it is obvious that the progressive state, which is marked by increase of population, is also marked by an increased consumption and an increased accumulation of wealth, not merely in the aggregate, but per capita. And hence, increase of population, so far as it has yet anywhere gone, does not mean a reduction, but an increase in the average production of wealth.

And the reason of this is obvious. For, even if the increase of population does reduce the poor of the natural factor of wealth, compelling a resort to poorer soils, etc, it yet so vastly increases the power of the human factor as more than to compensate. Twenty men working together will, where nature is niggardly, produce more than twenty times the wealth that one man can produce where nature is most bountiful. The denser the population the more minute becomes the subdivision of labor, the greater the economies of production and distribution, and, hence, the very reverse of the Malthusian doctrine is true . . .

[T]he great cause of the triumph of the [Malthusian] theory is, that, instead of menacing any vested right or antagonizing any powerful interest, it is eminently soothing and reassuring to the classes who, wielding the power of wealth, largely dominate thought. At a time when old supports were falling away, it came to the rescue of the special privileges by which a few monopolize so much of the good things of this world, proclaiming a natural cause for the want and misery which, if attributed to political institutions, must condemn every government under which they exist.

The Malthusian doctrine parries the demand for reform, and shelters selfishness from question and from conscience by the interposition of an inevitable necessity. . . .

I go to the heart of the matter in saying that there is no warrant, either in experience or analogy, for the assumption that there is any tendency in population to increase faster than subsistence. The facts cited to show this simply show that where, owing to the sparseness of population, as in new countries, or where, owing to the unequal distribution of wealth, as among the poorer classes in old countries, human life is occupied with the physical necessities of existence, the tendency to reproduce is at a rate which would, were it to go on unchecked, some time exceed subsistence. But it is not a legitimate inference from this that the tendency to reproduce would show itself in the same force where population was sufficiently dense and wealth distributed with sufficient evenness to life a whole community above the necessity of devoting their energies to a struggle for mere existence. Nor can it be assumed that the tendency to reproduce, by causing poverty, must prevent the existence of such a community; for this, manifestly, would be assuming the very point at issue, and reasoning in a circle. And even if it be admitted that the tendency to multiply must ultimately produce poverty, it cannot from this alone be predicated of existing poverty that it is due to this cause, until it be shown that there are not other causes which can account for it—a thing in the present state of government, laws, and customs, manifestly impossible.

16

Design for Utopia

Charles Fourier

Among the inconsistencies and the blunders of modern policy, there is nothing more shocking than the neglect to legislate upon the equilibrium of population, upon the proportion of the number of consumers to the productive forces. It were vain to discover the means of increasing the product four or even five-fold, if the human race were condemned to multiply as it does to-day; constantly to accumulate a mass of people, three or four times as great as that to which it ought to be limited in order to maintain the graduated comfort of the different classes.

In every age, the equilibrium of population has been the stumbling-block, or one of the stumbling-blocks, of civilised policy. Already the ancients, who had so many uncultivated regions around them which could be colonised, found no other remedy for the exuberance of population than to tolerate the exposure and destruction of infants, the killing of superfluous slaves,—which was resorted to by the virtuous Spartans,—or having them perish in naumachies for the amusement of Roman citizens, proud of the fine name of free men, but very far removed from filling the *rôle* of just men.

More recently, we have seen modern politicians confess their discomfiture regarding the problem of population. I have quoted Stewart, Wallace, and Malthus, the only writers worthy of attention upon this subject, because they acknowledge the helplessness of science. Their wise views upon the vicious circle of population are stifled by economic jugglers, who shove aside this problem as they do so many others. Stewart, more honest, has treated it very well in his hypothesis of an island, which, being well cultivated, was able to support 1,000 inhabitants of unequal fortune, in comfort; but, says he, if the population swells to 3,000 and 4,000; to 10,000 and 20,000, how is it to be supported?

The answer given is, that colonisation must be resorted to, multitudes of people sent away; this is to quibble with the question; for if the entire globe were inhabited, peopled to the full, whither could the swarms of colonists be sent?

The sophists answer, that the globe is not all peopled, and will not be so very soon; that is one of the subterfuges of the Owen sect, which, promising happiness, evades the problem of the equilibrium of population, and says that it will take at least 300 years for the earth to be peopled to its FULL CAPACITY. They are mistaken; it will take only 150 years. However that be, it is retreating before a problem to relegate its solution to the future, 300 years hence, and without guaranteeing that the solution will be found then. Besides, granting that it would be 300 years before the earth were fully peopled, such a theory would still be a very imperfect one,—the theory of a happiness or pretended happiness which should disappear at the end of 300 years through a defect in social policy, through the exuberance of population.

Now, as it is certain that this scourge will not tarry 300 years and that it will appear at the end of 150 years,—under the conditions of universal peace and general plenty which will be brought about by the associative state,—the scheme of this new order must provide very effective means to prevent excess of population, to reduce the number of inhabitants of the globe to a just proportion between means and needs—to about 5 milliards, without the danger of seeing the population increase to 6, 7, 8, 10, 12 milliards; an exuberance which would be inevitable should the entire globe introduce the civilised *régime*.

Part 3

Twentieth-Century Classicals
on Consequences

17

Population and Unemployment

John Maynard Keynes

Sir William Beveridge's interesting address, under this title, before the British Association has revived discussion on a matter which, whatever way it touches our hopes or our prejudices, must surely trouble the thoughts of anyone who concerns himself with political or social purpose. Sir William, in common with many other people, dislikes the idea of Birth Control; but, like the good economist he is, he remains on the broad issue a sound Malthusian. "Nothing that I have said," he finally concludes, "discredits the fundamental principle of Malthus, reinforced as it can be by the teachings of modern science." His main themes were, first, that we must not be too ready to argue from unemployment to over-population, instancing the excellence of employment in Germany to-day, "a nation which assuredly should be suffering from over-population if any nation is"; and, secondly, that an *obiter dictum* of mine in "The Economic Consequences of the Peace" about the state of affairs in 1900–1910 was unjustifiably pessimistic.

I will deal elsewhere with the criticism personal to myself. My main point in the brief passage taken by Sir W. Beveridge as his text was that the pre-war balance in Europe between population and the means of life was, for various reasons, already precarious; and from this I do not think that he seriously dissents. But I also threw out the suggestion that the turning-point in the strongly favourable developments of the latter half of the nineteenth century may have come about the year 1900. The suggestion is one which it is not easy either to refute or to establish, and the exact date is a matter of historical interest, and not one of decisive importance in relation to the present state of the world. But, in any case, Sir William Beveridge's statistics do not touch me, inasmuch as my suggestion related to the "equation of exchange" between the manufactured products of the Old World and the raw produce of the New, an indication to which his particular figures, since they nearly all deal with raw produce, are not relevant. I shall discuss this statistical point, giving the evidence on which my statement was based, in the December issue of the "Economic Journal," where those interested will also have the advantage of reading the full text of Sir William Beveridge's address.

Let us, however, turn to Sir William's first point, namely, the relation of unemployment to over-population. I agree with him that it would be rash to argue straight from one to the other. Unemployment is a phenomenon of maladjustment, and the maladjustment may be due to causes which have nothing to do with population;—as, for example, the maladjustment due to a transition, through deflation of purchasing power, from a higher to a lower price-level, or that due to the necessity of changing over from supplying one type of outside market to supplying another because of a sudden change in the relative wealth and requirements of the rest of the world. Each of these influences is probably responsible for an important part of the existing unemployment in Great Britain.

But, on the other hand, unemployment may be a symptom of a maladjustment very closely connected with population—namely, that which results from an attempt on the part of organized labour, or of the community as a whole, to maintain real wages at a higher level than the underlying economic conditions are able to support. The most alarming aspect of the prolongation and the intensity of the existing unemployment is the possibility that transitory influences may not wholly explain it, and that deep causes may be operating which interfere with our continuing ability to maintain in these islands an expanding population at an improving standard of life. The doubt is a dreadful one. Our social aims and objects flow from the opposite assumption, and are rendered futile by its negation. What is the use or the purpose of all our strivings if they are to be neutralized or defeated by the mere growth of numbers? Malthus's Devil is a terrible Devil because he undermines our faith in the real value of our social purposes, just as much now as when Malthus loosed him against the amiable dreams of Godwin. The *primâ facie* case for doubting our ability to provide during the present generation for growing numbers at an improving standard, and for seeing some corroboration of this doubt in the present state of our labour market and of our staple industries, is so serious that it is frivolous to think we can dismiss it by mentioning that unemployment is not *necessarily* due to over-population and by pointing to the disastrous example of Germany, where the nation's submission, under the overwhelming pressure of events, to a drastic lowering of their standard of life and the impairment of their capital resources has put away this particular symptom for the time being.

No statistics can be decisive on such a matter unless they extend over a period long enough to eliminate other influences,—which means that their final answer may be too late to determine policy. But it is useful to keep ourselves reminded from time to time of one or two simple and well-known figures. In 1851 the population of Great Britain was about 21,000,000; in 1901, 37,000,000; and in 1921, 43,000,000. Thus, the population which is growing old is the remnant of a population not much more than half the size of the population which is growing up. Several conclusions follow from this.

(1) Although the birth-rate is materially lower than it was half a century ago, nevertheless the absolute number of daily births in Great Britain to-day is nearly double the number of deaths.

(2) The fact that the average age of the population is less than it would be in a stationary population means that the proportion of old people of pensionable age, which the community will have to support as time goes on, will tend to increase to a figure not far short of double what it is at present.

(3) Most important of all, the supply of adult labourers will continue to increase sharply for a generation to come, irrespective of the contemporary birth-rate, because the number of boys now growing up to working age will greatly exceed year by year that of the old men dying or reaching pensionable age. In round numbers the male population between twenty and sixty-five years of age is now between 14,000,000 and 15,000,000. In the course of the next twenty years the boys (already born) entering these age limits will exceed by between 4,000,000 and 5,000,000 the old men passing out. That is to say, we shall have to find, within this short period, employment, equipment,

and houses for 25–30 per cent. more working-class families than at present; and the net productivity of these additional hands will have to support a larger proportion of old people, and, if the present birth-rate continues, as large a proportion of children. Now that this surplus already exists, emigration may be a palliative. As a continuing policy, however, emigration is a ruinous expedient for an old country, as is obvious when one considers that, if the males are shipped abroad, a corresponding number of females must be sent also, and that the cost per head of rearing and educating a child up to working age is a heavy charge for which the country will get no return of productivity if the youth then emigrates.

(4) Very few of our staple export industries are operating above their pre-war level of ten years ago. and some of them, notably textiles, are seriously below it. Most of these industries are well satisfied if they see a prospect ahead even of their former level of activity in normal times. Their difficulties are increased in some cases by the fact that the American demand for certain essential raw materials has risen more than the total supply, and that America is able to pay a higher price than we can. We cannot rely, unless the material conditions of the rest of the world greatly improve, on finding markets for a much larger quantity of goods at as good a net return to ourselves. With Europe's present prospects, and with the growing tendency of the New World to keep its advantages to itself, we are not entitled to rely on so great an advance in our own opportunities.

These *primâ facie* grounds, for fear and hesitation, and for straining our minds to find a way out, are not disposed of by the fact that many improvements are conceivable, other than restriction, which would postpone or alleviate the problem. Sir William Beveridge concluded his address, after admitting and emphasizing the dangers of our economic situation, by urging that the cure was to be found not in Birth Control, but in Peace and World Trade resuming their sway. He might have mentioned many other desirable things which would put off the evil day,—a greater accumulation of capital, the swifter progress of science, a raising of the acquired and inborn endowments of the average man, more commonsense, intelligence, and public spirit.

But it is not safe to leave the question of numbers unregulated, in the mere hope that we may be rescued by one of these conceivable, but as yet unrealized, improvements. And even if we do realize them, is it not discouraging that they should only operate to compensate an increase of numbers, when they might, if there had been no increase, have availed to improve the lot of the average man?

Is not a country over-populated when its standards are lower than they would be if its numbers were less? In that case the question of what numbers are desirable arises long before starvation sets in, and even before the level of life begins to fall. Perhaps we have already sacrificed too much to population. For is not the improvement in the average conditions of life during the past century very small in comparison with the extraordinary material progress of that period? Does it not seem that the greater part of man's achievements are already swallowed up in the support of mere numbers?

It is easy to understand the distaste provoked by particular methods, and the fear inspired by any proposal to modify the *laisser-faire* of Nature, and to bring the workings of a fundamental instinct under social control. But it is strange to be untroubled or to deny the existence of the problem for our generation.

18

The Changed Outlook
in Regard to Population

Edwin Cannan

Times change, and economic theories change with them. We need
no longer be ashamed of the fact, as we were inclined to be in the old
days, when our colleagues in other Sections of the Association pro-
fessed to despise us for disagreeing among ourselves and perpetually
overthrowing conclusions arrived at by our predecessors. We hear less
now of the certainty and finality of the other sciences, and can face
their exponents unabashed, confident that theories may be useful for
leading us on towards the truth without being immutable and exempt
from revision.

I think that the biggest change made in economic theory during the
last hundred years is to be found in the treatment of the subject of
Population. In 1831, Malthus was still alive, and quite unrepentant for
the shock he had given the public thirty-three years earlier by his
*Essay on the Principle of Population as it affects the future Improve-
ment of Society*. No one, it is true, any longer attached much importance to his doctrine of the inherent incompatibility of the ratios in
which it was possible for population and food to increase, but the
disfavour with which he regarded what he considered the natural tendency of population to increase was shared by most of the economists
of the orthodox school, who had adopted the theory of diminishing

returns to agriculture which was evolved in England from the local conditions of the very "short period" of the Napoleonic war.

That theory, not as now taught in a form which makes it innocuous, but as taught in the early years of the nineteenth century, purported to show that the natural limitation of fertile and well-situated land must necessarily mean that the more numerous the people, the more difficult it must be for them to feed themselves. It was admitted that there were counteracting circumstances, summed up as "the progress of civilisation," which, in fact, had throughout history prevented the growing population of the civilised world from actually finding it more difficult to feed itself, but these circumstances were regarded as making only temporary headway against the general tendency, and not, like it, as being a law of nature. J.S. Mill, in his *Principles of Political Economy with some of their Applications to Social Philosophy*, which, though not made into a book until seventeen years after, was really thought out before 1831, and represents the ideas of 1800 to 1830 better than any other work, even ventured to assert that though the people of his time were better off than the people of a thousand years before, they would have been still better off if the increase of population had been less.

The economic history of the hundred years has tended to bring about a very complete reversal of economists' view of this matter.

The hundred years began with developments which threw great discredit on the fundamental assumption of the old school that the extension of human occupation of land necessarily meant that less fertile and less well-situated land must be occupied as numbers grew. It was easy for men who saw arable cultivation creeping over barren hills in England and stony "bogs" in Ireland to believe in that theory when Chicago was a collection of Indian huts, and Broadway, New York, a rough cart-track to a farm, but the application of steam to ships and railways enabled mankind to extend easily over an immense area of land more fertile than much of what was occupied before. And as for situation, not only did the improvement in transport, coupled with the violations of natural geography involved in the cutting of the great ship canals, bring the "more distant" lands nearer the "market," it also eventually brought "the market" to the "more distant" lands.

So we no longer think of the first cradle of the human race (or the first cradles of the human races if there are more than one) as the most fertile and well-situated spot (or spots) from which men have gradually been forced outwards. You probably all know the opinion of the British Army in Mesopotamia, expressed by the sergeant who was told by an officer that he was now on the very site of the Garden of Eden: "Well, Sir, all I can say is that if this was the Garden of Eden it's no wonder the twelve apostles mutinied." Though the sergeant was evidently not a well-read man, the change of view had reached even him.

In the later part of the hundred years scientific discovery in various directions has led to a complete change of emphasis in regard to the importance of what the old economists used to call "improvements." The old economists thought of hedges and ditches, drains, and a few other trifles of that kind which would enable corn to be more easily produced from European fields, and just a little of better breeding of cattle and sheep. These were things which might, they believed, interrupt for a time, now and then, the general downward drift of the returns to agricultural industry, but could not do more than that. Modern science has changed our outlook. We set no bounds to the possibilities of improvement. We expect to make unwholesome areas healthy, and to modify vegetables as well as animal products so that they will better serve our needs. Primitive mankind presumably fought and killed some of the now extinct carnivora; advanced mankind fights and will kill the locusts and the smaller insects which have hitherto prevented much use being made of some of the most fertile areas of the world. We smile now at the suggestion made in 1898 from the Presidential chair of the Association, that it would soon become very difficult to increase much further the production of wheat.

Thus, even if we still expected population to increase very rapidly, we should not believe, as J.S. Mill did, that it "everywhere treads close on the heels of agricultural improvement, and effaces its effects as fast as they are produced" (*Principles*, Bk. IV. ch. iii § 5). But in fact, Cotter Morrison's cry, made only a generation ago, that all would be well if only we could stop for a few years "the devastating torrent of babies" would seem grotesque to-day, for we do not now expect rapid increase of population to continue much longer, even if it becomes progressively easier to obtain subsistence.

The approach of reduction in the rate of growth of population began to show itself in England in the second half of the 1871-80 decade, when the annual number of births became nearly stationary after the rapid increase recorded down to 1876. But the public takes little notice of the supply of people furnished by the births. Just in the wooden way in which illiterate farmers and unbusinesslike old ladies look at their balances at the bank, so the public looks at the censuses. The census of 1881 showed an increase of 14.36 per cent. in the decade, which was higher than that shown by any of the censuses except those of 1821 and 1831, which were probably unduly swollen by the diminishing incompleteness of the enumerations. In 1881-91, in spite of high emigration, the rate of increase of population was still regarded as the normal thing which everyone should expect. The Royal Commission on the Water Supply of the Metropolis in 1893 deliberately rejected the reasonable suggestion that the rate of increase in Greater London might continue to fall as it had already begun to do, and relying on a continuance of observed increase, estimated the probable population in the present year, 1931, at two and three-quarter millions more than the recent census has shown it to be.

But I had noticed that the old rapid increase in the annual number of births seemed to have come to an end, and working on the ages of the people as recorded in successive censuses, I put before Section F of the Association at its meeting in Ipswich in 1895, a paper (subsequently published in the *Economic Journal* for December in that year) in which I estimated the number of persons who would be living at each census up to that of 1951 on the assumptions that migration, mortality, and, not the rate, but the absolute number of births remained stationary. I found that on these hypotheses the population of England and Wales would stop increasing during the present century, and would have only a trifling increase after 1941. The paper suggested that this was, at any rate, not improbable.

Hostile critics derided what they called my "prophecy," and for some time events were unfavourable to me. Emigration fell off enormously, mortality decreased, and the births increased slightly, so that the census of 1901 showed an increase of 12.17 per cent. in the decade, the absolute increase of three and a half millions being the largest recorded. But the situation was not fundamentally altered, since the increase of births was due entirely to the drop in emigration, which had caused a larger proportion of persons of parental age to remain in the country. At the 1901 Meeting of the British Association and in the *Fortnightly Review* of March 1902, I returned to the charge with a paper on the "Recent Decline of Natality in Great Britain," in which, using a method of weighting the annual numbers of marriages by their proximity to the births recorded for each year—a method which seems to have been beneath the notice of the mathematical statisticians of that period—I was able to show, I think conclusively, that the number of children resulting from each marriage was falling steadily and rapidly, and insisted with more emphasis than before on the "considerable probability of the disappearance of the natural increase of population—the excess of births over deaths—in Great Britain within the present century."

The decade 1901-11 was indecisive; the ratio of increase was smaller than in any of its ten predecessors, but the absolute amount of increase just topped that of 1891-1901, and the number of births till 1908 or 1909 seemed to indicate some recovery of natality. But this was illusory. Even before the War the births had got down again to the level of 1876. The War sent them tumbling down to about three-quarters of that number, and now, after a wild but very short-lived recovery when the Army returned from abroad, they seem inclined to settle at the War figure—three-quarters of the number attained more that fifty years ago, when the total population was twenty-six millions instead of forty millions, as it is now. The ratio of births, legitimate and illegitimate, to my weighted figure of marriages which was just over $4^1/_2$ fifty years ago, fell gradually and steadily to $3^1/_4$ before the War caused it to collapse. (See the Appendix.)

It was commonly supposed by many of those to whom percentages serve rather to hide than to expose the facts on which they are based, that the diminution of births was being counterbalanced by the decline of infant mortality. It is true, of course, that diminution of infant mortality mitigates the effect of decline of natality, but the degree in which it can do so obviously decreases as the rate of infant mortality falls. When that rate is 500 per thousand, as it probably was here in the reign of Queen Anne, and may be still in great parts of Africa, a cutting down of births by 25 per cent. can be counteracted completely by a drop of one-third in the infantile mortality rate. But when the infant mortality rate is down to 100 per thousand, it would have to fall to nothing at all in order to counteract a decline of only 10 per cent. in the number of births. In fact, the rate has fallen in England and Wales from about 140 to about 70 in the fifty years from 1881, and this drop to one-half only balances about one-fifth of the decline in the number of births.

Though there were eminent dissentients only a few years ago, statisticians are now agreed that in the absence of some great and unexpected change, the increase of population in England and Wales will come to an end at a very early date. Even the lay public has been to some extent enlightened and rather shocked by the recent census announcements that the population of Scotland has actually decreased in the last ten years, and that of England and Wales has increased only 2,061,000, as against 3,543,000 in the ten years from 1901-11, though the emigrants have been 324,000 less.

The same change is observable in some degree in other Western European countries and our own oversea offshoots. The cause of it—birth control—will doubtless in time affect the rest of the world, so that while we may expect considerable increase—even an increase much more rapid than at present, owing to decrease of huge infant mortality—to take place among the more backward peoples for another half-century at least, there is no reason whatever for expecting the population of the world to "tread close on the heels of subsistence" in the future, even if it may be correctly regarded as having done so in the past.

This change in our expectations involves many changes of emphasis, both in the theory of production and in that of distribution.

Two of them are perfectly obvious. First, the need, which J. S. Mill and most of his contemporaries and immediate predecessors felt so strongly, for insisting on the due restriction of population, has completely disappeared in the Western countries. Economists do not now require to talk as if the first duty of men and women was to refrain from propagating their race. Secondly, the need for insisting on the desirability of saving has become less pressing. A rapidly increasing population requires a rapidly increasing number of tools, machines, ships, houses, and other articles of material equipment in order merely to maintain without improving its economic condition, while at the same time the maintenance of a larger proportion of children renders it more difficult to make the required additions. To a stationary population saving will still be desirable for the improvement of conditions, but it need no longer be insisted on as necessary for the mere maintenance of the existing standard.

But there are other changes of equal importance which are more likely to be overlooked. One is in regard to the weight which we attach to the different kinds of production. In the middle of the eighteenth century, "subsistence," and what we should consider a very coarse and inadequate subsistence probably seriously deficient in vitamins, appeared so much the most important economic good that the French *économistes* insisted on calling all labour which did not get something out of the soil *stérile* or barren; and our own Adam Smith, with all his common sense, while admitting the manufacturing class into the ranks of "productive" labourers, insisted on excluding domestic servants, physicians, guardians of law and order, and all other workers who did not make up material objects, or who were not employed for profit (he never was quite sure which criterion he meant to stand by). The great Christian philosopher, Paley, believed that nothing more than a "healthy subsistence" was required for perfect happiness. Even Malthus and his immediate disciples, when they insisted on the desirability of the working-class having a high standard of comfort, seem to have done so more because this would prevent the "misery" of semi-starvation for adults and absolute starvation for infants than because there is a direct advantage in being comfortable. Ricardo said "the friends of humanity cannot but wish that in all countries the labouring classes should have a taste for comforts and enjoyments," not apparently because comforts and enjoyments are good in themselves, but because "there cannot be a better security against a superabundant population," the population being superabundant, in his opinion, when it is subject to famine.

All this emphasis on food is now out of date. We no longer look forward to a future in which increasing population will be forced by the operation of the law of diminishing returns to devote a larger and ever larger proportion of its whole labour force to the production of food. We know that even in the past, with a rapidly increasing population, the returns to agricultural industry have increased so much that civilised mankind has been able to feed itself better and better, while giving a smaller and ever smaller proportion of its whole labour force to the production of bare subsistence; and we can reasonably expect that the increase in the productiveness of agricultural industry will be at least as great in the future, so that under the combined influence of the "narrow capacity of the individual human stomach" and the stationary number of stomachs, not only a smaller and ever smaller proportion, but a small and smaller absolute number of workers will be able to raise food for the whole.

Even the politicians, who for the most part follow the economists with a sixty or seventy years' lag, are beginning to realise the change, and are losing their enthusiasm for schemes for "settling more people on the land," either in colonies or at home, and thereby increasing the already excessive depreciation of agricultural compared with manufactured products. The numerous subsidies which they still give to agriculture are mostly of an eleemosynary character intended to relieve distress, and the encouragement which they give to agricultural production is only an incidental effect, unintended and often deplored. They are defended, not on the ground that they increase food, but because they are supposed to increase employment.

The necessary change of emphasis applies not only as between food and other things, but also as between most primary and most finishing industries. In face of rapidly growing knowledge and slowly growing or stationary population, it is inevitable that the "staple" or "heavy" industries which provide materials should decline relatively to those which provide finished goods and services. The demand for each of such things as pig-iron and yards of cloth is easily satiated; and so also, no doubt, is the demand for cricket-bats and chauffeurs. But the minor or "lighter" industries are susceptible of an indefinite multiplication which makes the demand for their products, taken as a whole, insatiable. Increase a person's power of spending, and he will not increase his purchases in weight or bulk so much as in refinement of form, so that a richer people will devote a less proportion of their labour to producing things like pig-iron and bricks. Moreover, the mere fact of the disappearance of rapid increase of population tends to increase the proportion of demand which can be satisfied from scrap without fresh primary production. So, given a stationary population with rapidly increasing knowledge applied to production, we may expect the already observable tendency towards a less proportion of the whole labour-force being employed in the "heavy industries" and a larger in the lighter industries to become more pronounced. Perhaps we see this even now in the slight drift of industrial population from the North to the South of England which appears to be taking place.

Another change of emphasis, of little importance on the Continent, where the West-Ricardian theory of rent never took real root, but of great importance in England and other English-speaking areas, is in respect of the landowners' share of the community's income. The disappearing bugbear of diminishing returns carries away with it the vampire rural landlord, who was supposed to prosper exceedingly when diminution of returns made food scarce and dear. You all know the famous passage in which J.S. Mill described the landlords as they

appeared to him and the school which he, a little belatedly, represented:—

> "The ordinary progress of a society which increases in wealth is at all times
> tending to augment the incomes of landlords; to give them both a greater amount
> and a greater proportion of the wealth of the community, independently of any
> trouble or outlay incurred by themselves. They grow richer, as it were, in their
> sleep, without working, risking, or economising." (*Principles*, Bk. V. ch. ii §5.)

Perhaps the disciple went a little beyond his master, Ricardo, in
asserting so roundly that in a prosperous society the landlords must
tend to get a larger and ever larger *proportion* of the whole income,
but there can be no doubt that this was the impression which the
Ricardian school conveyed to the public, and which formed the foundation for Henry George's scheme of land nationalisation and the
agitation for land-value taxation. If the school had only meant to teach
that the land became more valuable absolutely—in the sense of being
worth a larger absolute amount of commodities rather than a larger
proportion of all the commodities and services constituting the
community's income—they could not have supposed land so peculiar,
since it would share this characteristic with many other things—with
anything which was more limited in supply than the generality.

To grasp the completeness of the change of view which has taken
place in the last hundred years, we must notice that Mill and the whole
school which he represented were thinking not of the few lucky landlords who have inherited land which has been selected by nature or
accident as the site of a city, but of the ordinary rural agricultural
landlords. So far have we moved that the land-value taxers of to-day
quite cheerfully propose to exempt all "purely agricultural value" from
the imposition which they advocate.

Envy of the happy owners of such urban land as rises in value more
than enough to recoup what they and their predecessors in title paid in
road making, sewering and other expenses of "development" plus loss,
if any, in waiting for income, still plays a part in contemporary politics, but the economist foresees that there will be at any rate less of
such rise of value when the adult population ceases to increase and the
demand for additional houses and gardens consequently disappears.
He realises that if any such rise continues, it will be due to the people
being not only able, as they doubtless will be, to occupy a larger area
with their houses and gardens, but also desirous of doing so. He will

think this quite possible, but will not be confident about it, when he reflects that the vast spread of villadom may be only a temporary phenomenon, and that the married couples of the future, childless or with small families, may be more content with flats in towns and little bungalows with tiny curtilages right in the country.

The disappearance from economic theory of the picture of the vampire landlord taking an ever-increasing proportion of the whole produce of industry which was itself decreasing per head of workers, leaves the theoretic arena open for discussion of the sharing of the whole produce between earnings of work and income derived from possession of property of all kinds.

As to this, the economists of a hundred years ago had nothing to say. If they thought of the question at all, they mixed it up hopelessly with the rate of interest on capital, imagining property to receive a smaller proportion when the rate of interest fell, and *vice versa*. The Socialists, who in fact followed them the more closely the more they denounced them, failed completely to clear up the confusion, and it dominates the mind of the lay public even now—much, I admit, to the discredit of the economists, who should have taught that public better.

While there are no statistics on the subject worth much, and none covering any considerable area either of place or time, past history is sufficiently known to assure us that increasing civilisation has in fact, made the aggregate share of property grow faster than that of labour, the obvious cause of this being that useful things constituting property have grown faster than population, and so much faster that what decline of the rate of interest has taken place has not been sufficient to counteract the tendency. The most primitive people had scarcely any tools, and their buildings, if any, could be erected in a few hours. Ownership certainly did not then give a claim to about one-third of the whole income, as statistics suggest that it does in modern Western countries.

There is nothing to show that this tendency will be either reversed or intensified by a cessation of the growth of population. The cessation will, of course, tend to reduce the desirability of additional equipment; a large part of the additions of the past have been required simply to enable the additional people to be provided with tools, houses, and other instruments of production or enjoyment. But additions to equipment will be made with less sacrifice of immediate enjoyable income than before, so that the increase of quantity may be sufficient to counteract the decline in the value of the units. Moreover, it is quite impossible to say what the tendency of invention may be in the future—whether to enhance or to diminish the value of additional material equipment.

But the history of the last hundred years suggests that this question of the division of income between property and labour is losing whatever importance it possessed. The economists and socialists of a hundred years ago were little removed from the time when it was common to talk of the "labouring poor," as if society was pretty sharply divided into poor workers on the one side and rich owners of property on the other. There were, indeed, some members of the propertied classes who were poor, but they were offshoots of the wealthier families rather than members of the proletariat with a little property. How innocent the mass of the people were of the crime of owning anything you may realise if you recollect that none of the agencies with which we are familiar for enabling them to invest had then got beyond the embryo stage. Friendly societies, co-operative societies, building societies, savings banks, are all modern growths. Before their advent a worker could, of course, become a small master—never, I think, a small mistress—and from a small master grow to be a big master, but if for any reason this was not open to him, what could he do with savings, supposing he was able to make any? Put them in a stocking, or the thatch, or under the garden soil, and if they happily escaped accident there, and accumulated sufficiently, give them to an attorney of doubtful honesty to be lent out on mortgage. I remember only about fifty years ago being told by a booking-clerk at a moorland station, about a hundred miles from London, how two old women had recently paid for return tickets to London in threepenny-bits, and by a solicitor that an old man from the same district had just brought him for investment on mortgage a large sum in gold which he had so far been keeping in the thatch of his cottage. All this is now changed, and when property, as a whole, and not merely the large property-owners, is attacked, the great investing agencies of the "working classes" become formidable opponents and are supported by the small direct investors who have been helped by them.

And while many of the working-class have become property owners, many of the propertied class have become the paid servants of public companies and other institutions, so that the old sharp distinction between the wage-earner and the capitalist is become a thing of the past, and the division of income between property and labour is no longer a division between two classes composed of different individuals, but a division between two sources of income largely possessed by the same individuals.

Thus, in Distribution, emphasis on the old categories of land, capital and labour is rapidly becoming obsolete and is being replaced by emphasis on individual riches and poverty, however arising. No longer do we think of relieving poverty by improving the terms of the general bargain which theory conceives labour as making with capital; we are much more likely to meet with arguments that individual poverty is being caused by this general bargain being too much in favor of the wage-earners. It is no longer the lowness of standard earnings that worries the philanthropic economist, but the fact that so many people are unable to rank themselves among recipients of those wages. Emphasis is on unemployment.

Unemployment is not really a very modern phenomenon. The crowds of beggars who collected their daily dole in the Middle Ages from the monasteries and from private wayfarers and householders were, perhaps, as large a proportion of the population as the normal registered unemployed of to-day. The "distresses" of the period just preceding a hundred years ago seem to have been accompanied by enormous unemployment, but we have no reliable statistics, and the loose statements, such as that in Birmingham in 1817, one-third of the workpeople were wholly unemployed and all the rest on half-time, do not help us much. But so far as I know, it has never been contended that history shows unemployment to be greater when population (or even population of working age) is rapidly increasing.

Yet it is common to talk of "the difficulty of providing employment for a rapidly increasing population," and some eminent authorities quite recently endeavoured to console the public by alleging that the coming decline in the growth of numbers will greatly alleviate the present situation in regard to unemployment.

I believe this to be a profound error, based on an elementary misconception of the origin of demand. The old proverb, "With every mouth God sends a pair of hands" is true and valuable, but no more so than its converse, "With every pair of hands God sends a mouth." The demand for the products of industry is not something outside and independent of the amount of products. The demand for each product depends on the supply of products offered in exchange for it, and the demand for all products depends on the supply of all products. Consequently, there is not the slightest danger of the working population ever becoming too great for the demand for its products taken as a whole.

Unemployment arises not from insufficient demand for the products of industry as a whole, but from the number of persons offering to work in particular branches of industry being in excess of the number admissible, having regard to the conditions and wages which are required to satisfy both the would-be workers who are unemployed and the persons already in employment. If the unemployed will not take what employers would offer them, the case is simple, and it is only a little more complicated if they are willing to take, and the employers are willing to give, something less than what is paid to the persons already employed; but the two parties are prevented from coming to terms on that basis by the fact that those already employed would go out on strike if the additional contingent was accepted at a lower rate than that which they themselves are receiving.

Now one of the commonest causes of such a situation is a falling off of demand for the products of a particular branch of industry. The fact that the demand for any product, let us say coal, for example, falls off, is a good reason for fewer persons being employed in that branch of industry and more in other branches. If the diminution of demand is very gradual, the necessary reduction in personnel can be effected by a cessation of recruiting. Many a branch of industry has gradually wilted away in this manner without much inconvenience or hardship to anyone. But if the diminution is more sudden, unemployment results owing to the natural reluctance of persons skilled, or at any rate experienced, in the particular branch of industry to leave it and try for employment in some other. The thoughtless outsider is apt to say that both the unemployed and those who are still employed in the branch should accept lower wages, and so, by cheapening the product, extend the demand for it. As a temporary palliative this may sometimes be reasonable, but it is evidently never the best final solution of the difficulty. It is not reasonable that a trade should be continuously worse paid than others merely because the demand for its products was once bigger than it has become. What the diminution of demand calls for is a redistribution of labour force, fewer persons being allotted to the branch of industry of which the products are less in demand, and more persons to the other branches.

But when population is increasing, absolute diminutions of demand are likely to be somewhat fewer, and somewhat less acute when they do occur, than when population is stationary. If, for example, by the introduction of oil, or more economical consumption, the average person's demand for coal is reduced by one-tenth, in a stationary population the total demand for coal would be reduced by one-tenth; but if the population in the same time increased 12 per cent., the total demand would be not reduced but slightly increased, and there would be no employment difficulty.

We ought, therefore, not to imagine that a stationary or declining population will rid us of the trouble of unemployment. It will provide more rather than less reason for promoting mobility of labour in place and occupation, and we shall have to take more care, rather than less, than at present to secure that arrangements which seem superficially desirable do not hinder that mobility.

It is inevitable, I suppose, that the question will be asked whether cessation of the growth of population is to be regarded as a good or an evil turn in human history. But the limitations of economics and perhaps of human nature prevent any straight answer being given. Nationalists in each nation want their own nation to increase in comparison with others; if they think of the others' interests at all, they say and believe that it will be promoted by the predominance of their own nation. We can get no further that way, since the pretension of each is contradicted by the pretensions of the others. If we try to avoid this obstacle by saying that we will ignore national and racial differences, and assume either that somehow the generally fittest will grow at the expense of the others, or that each as well as the whole will have stationary numbers, we still have to face the fact that our conception of the distinction between economic welfare and welfare of other kinds is nebulous in the extreme, and that if it was clearer, we should not know—I think we never can know—how much of the one should be regarded as equal to a given quantity of the other.

Different persons will give different answers. Some agree with Paley that ten persons with sufficient subsistence must be in possession of more welfare than a single millionaire; others with J.S. Mill that the world turned into a "human anthill" would be an undesirable place of residence. The same person will give different answers according to his mood at the moment. Personally, I spent my early boyhood in a town which throughout my life has been the most prosperous in England, and I have long lived in another which, having added motor manufacture to education in its old age, has lately been growing nearly as fast, and sometimes when I contemplate their growth, I feel a little like G. R. Porter when he wrote the *Progress of the Nation*, during the period 1800 to 1831. At other times, and I think more often, I regret the open heath and the untouched pine wood which stretched in my early recollection to within a few hundred yards of the Bath Hotel at Bournemouth, and I hate the gasworks straddling the river and the bungalows shutting in the main roads out of Oxford; then I agree with Mill that it is well that population should become stationary long before necessity compels it.

After all, the increase must stop some time, and watching the effect of the stoppage will be a very interesting experience which I should like to have been born late enough to enjoy.

19

Notes on Some Probable Consequences of the Advent of a Stationary Population in Great Britain[1]

Lionel Robbins

I

The fact which gives occasion to my remarks this evening, the near approach of a stationary condition of population in Great Britain, is one which should be of peculiar interest to the Political Economy Club, since it was the subject of a very remarkable prediction on the part of one of its most distinguished members. It is now more than a quarter of a century since Professor Cannan predicted that by 1941 the increase of population in this country would have become negligible;[2] and what then might have been regarded as a paradoxical and irresponsible piece of prophecy has now become part and parcel of the expectations of all those who are not deliberately blind to the tendencies of our day. The fall in the corrected birth-rate, which he anticipated, has continued; and, as Professor Bowley has recently shown, we have only to apply recent death-rates to the population now in existence, and to make the very reasonable assumption that the number of births will not increase, for the advent of a stationary population round about the 'forties to be a matter of exact demonstration.[3] No doubt it is true that even now these assumptions may be falsified. No one would claim for the predictions to which they lead more than a moderate degree of certainty. You can never be perfectly sure what will happen to the number of births and deaths. But taking a broad view of the probabilities of the situation, I submit it is not unreasonable to hold that a stationary population in the very near future is a possibility which we do well to take serious account of, and I therefore make no further apology for venturing to raise for your consideration certain consequences which may be expected to accompany its advent.

II

Before I do this, however, I wish to remove certain misapprehensions as to the scope of my intentions. It is no part of my business this evening, as I conceive it, to expound once again the familiar analysis of stationary conditions in general—the stationary state of Adam Smith and Marshall, the static conditions of J.B. Clark and his followers. For it should be obvious that the conditions I wish to examine are not likely to exhibit the phenomena of *total* stationariness. Even though the growth of population comes to an end, it is most improbable that other tendencies to change will suffer a similar extinction. Accumulation may proceed, natural resources be discovered or exhausted, the technique of production may change and there may still be fluctuations in consumers' demand, even though the population be stationary. Indeed, it is one of the assumptions of my discussion that such tendencies to change are still present, and that it is desirable to know what differences in their mode of operation are likely to follow from the cessation of the further complication of the growth of numbers.

Nor, secondly, do I wish merely to investigate the formal conditions of the moving equilibria which we may conceive to arise in such circumstances. Such an investigation, indeed, would not be without theoretical interest. For instance, it could be shown that, granted the supposition of a fixed labour supply, much of what is true in the old theories of rent can with equal justification be asserted of wages. But what I want to do here has a less purely formal character. Taking for granted the generalisations of pure theory concerning the state of affairs we are contemplating, I want to ask what differences we should expect to find between conditions as they will be then, and conditions as they have been when population has been increasing. Such a procedure has a double advantage. Not only does it enable us to generalise more firmly about the future: it also compels us to re-examine very thoroughly our beliefs about the present. It is possible, I think, that we have been too apt to assume as permanent facts of the economic system, things which in reality are only the transitory phenomena of a time when population is growing. The mode of inquiry I propose may make us more alive to the true nature of our assumptions.

Finally, it is perhaps necessary for me to say that, in so far as I do not expressly confine myself to mere statements of what seem to me to be probabilities, in everything that follows, I shall be discussing *tendencies*. When, for instance, I argue, as I shall, that there will tend to be less mobility of labour, with a stationary population, I do not mean to commit myself to the prediction that the mobility of labour will be *actually* less. Of course, changes which I do not discuss may counterbalance the tendency in question. All that I mean is that there will be present factors which would produce a diminution of mobility, if other things not obviously consequentially connected with the change I am discussing were to remain unchanged. This, of course, is a qualification which will be taken for granted by all who are familiar with the technique of economic analysis, but the number of intelligent men who are not so familiar is not yet sufficiently small for it to be safe to generalise without stating it explicitly.

III

I come now to the first of the two main divisions of my inquiry. What will be the effect of the cessation of growth of population on production?

A. Look first at the aggregate volume of production. I do not think that we ignore the probabilities of the situation if we predict that the rate of growth of this aggregate will show some diminution. Of course, this is not in any way necessary. But accumulation and improvements in the technique of production will have to proceed at a rate quite unprecedented in history, if, without additions to the population, production is to grow as fast as it has done with them. If this does not take place, then we may expect that the various indices which afford a rough guide to the fluctuations of production, the volume of imports and exports, the physical index of production, and so on, will show a tendency to flag.

Now, of course, so far as the fixed charges on the national revenue are concerned, this does possess some negative significance. If it is true, then there is no prospect of a progressive easing of their burden per head from an increase in the number of producers. What to our fathers was one of the main liberators from the dead hand of the past will not be accessible to our children. But outside this comparatively narrow sphere, a slackening of growth of aggregate production *due to this cause* has no significance whatever. No doubt that section of the public which is apt to be moved by the crude magnitude, rather than by the real significance of official statistics, will be seriously alarmed. But since, public finance apart, it is *average* and not *aggregate* production which matters, this attitude will not be justified. There is no significance in an aggregate of production until it is related to those who have produced it.

B. But what then may we expect to be the effect on average production? This is a matter about which prediction is vastly more difficult.

1. So far as changes resulting from the mere quantitative relation of numbers to material equipment are concerned, the utmost caution is necessary. I have discussed elsewhere my reasons for thinking that our present state of knowledge is inadequate to enable us to make precise statements about this matter, and I will not repeat them here.[4] But I will say that, taking a broad view of our resources and the present technique of production, I do find it very hard to believe that there are many advantages to be gained by further increase, which would not be more than counterbalanced by the obvious disadvantages. If this view be correct, then it would follow that a condition of stationariness in the labour supply, accompanied by continued accumulation and technical progress, would be more favourable to production per head than a condition of further growth. But all this is mere conjecture—there is no agreement among economists on this matter.

2. Thus far analysis is comparatively sterile. We are on firmer ground, I think, when we turn to questions relating to the quality of the population.

(a) Thus, in the first place, if we grant the probability of the cessation of the growth of population at all, it is possible to make certain very definite predictions with regard to the age composition of the population. Indeed, as all those who are acquainted with the work of Professors Bowley and Cannan[5] must realise, it was by way of examination of the future of different age groups that the wider prediction was arrived at. It is quite clear, I think, that we must look forward to a time in which there will be more old people—more absolutely than there are now, more proportionately to the other age groups in the population. Professor Bowley's estimate, for example, for 1971 gives 5.1 millions for the age groups 65 and over, as compared with 2.6 millions for 1921, the age group 15-65 having in the meantime increased only from 14.9 to 16.2 millions. And, of course, these figures underestimate this aspect of the situation, for what increase there is in the group 15-65 occurs almost entirely in the upper reaches. The group 20-45 remains practically almost constant (8.643 millions to 8.679).

Now, of course, productive power is essentially a relative conception depending partly on what is desired to produce. It is possible to conceive, therefore, certain social demands to which a population of the same size with a greater proportion of its members in lower age groups. If poetry be the sphere of the relatively young and prose of the relatively old, then it is clear that in this new period of our development a demand for prose could be more adequately supplied per head than in periods when youth was more dominant. If, at the same time that specific power to produce such things increases, consumers demand changes in a similar manner, then, from the purely economic point of view, the change is a matter of indifference. But, if the demand for products which a more youthful population is better fitted to produce, is not thus superseded, then the power of society to satisfy its own demands will have weakened.

Such fears, I suggest, are not without substance. So far as general undifferentiated power to do tasks calling for vigour and endurance are concerned, there can be little question that productive power will tend to diminish. If we assume that work of this sort ceases at the age of 65, then, since what increase is to be expected will be chiefly in the group 65 and over, the productive groups remaining constant, this becomes obvious. To get the average for the whole population, the aggregate produced by the constant age group must be divided by a larger quantity. Nor does the loss seem likely to be less considerable when we turn to the higher functions of leadership and direction. On the contrary, it is here that the prospect is most depressing. The progress of invention may come to render the brute strength of youth and early middle age less and less essential to production. It will not diminish the need for vision and imagination. Already we begin to hear of too great a preponderance of the old in the higher councils of industry. If the statistics I have quoted be correct, this is a cry which will not diminish.

From this point of view we can perceive a probable complication in the course of national finance which is worth while mentioning at this juncture. The probable increase in the number of old people means a probable increase in the number of old age pensioners, a fact which, of course, is recognized in the latest pension scheme. Since, at the same time, the numbers of the productive classes will have remained roughly constant while their age composition will have changed if anything for the worse, this means that there will be a tendency for the burden of taxation to become heavier. Most discussions of the effects of taxation are absurd because they do not take account of the effects on production of the expenditure of the proceeds of taxation. Taxation expended on education or research, for instance, cannot be said necessarily to diminish the volume of production. But we run no risk in assuming that, whatever its other effects, the money we spend on pensions is a dead weight on production. This is not to say that such expenditure is inadvisable. Nor is it to urge an increase in the birth-rate in order to ease the subjective costs of this form of public expenditure.

(b) I now come to a matter of greater theoretical interest. We have seen that our stationary population will tend to be a less vigorous population. It can also be contended, I think, that it will tend to be a less rapidly adaptable population. Other things being equal, the flexibility of the labour supply is likely to be less, and therefore at any given time the distribution of labour between occupations is likely to be further away from the distribution most appropriate to the demand and conditions of production of that time, than it would be if the labour supply were more flexible.

This is perhaps a hard saying, and to those who conceive of the flexibility of the labour supply as depending wholly on the ability and willingness of adult workers to change from one occupation to another, it is likely to be completely unacceptable. And, of course, if this were the only circumstance determining the ease with which the labour force can be relatively strengthened at one point, relatively diminished at another, this attitude would be entirely justifiable. But in fact it is not so. In fact the flexibility which arises from the presence of a free group of workers not yet committed to any industry is at least as important. The new generation forms, as it were, a mobile body of recruits, which, within the limits indicated by the doctrine of non-competing groups, can be directed to those points on the line where they are most needed, without withdrawing any forces already committed. When the population is stationary, this free force is smaller proportionately to the whole than when population is advancing. Hence the rate at which any disequilibrium can be remedied, without transferring workers already committed to any occupation, is likely to be less in the former conditions than it is in the latter.[6] Of course, technical changes and improvements in the organisation of the labour market may so improve mobility between occupations as to offset this factor. That is a matter about which I have no prediction to make in this paper.[7] All that I contend here is that this tendency will be operative.

Considerations of this sort, I venture to suggest, not only provide an interesting topic of speculation with regard to the future, they also throw a new light on certain opinions of the past. It has been the fashion to denounce the economists of the last century for their too ready assumption of an effective mobility of labour. Writers of the Historical School, for instance, exhibit an almost childish pleasure at the discovery that workers do not necessarily move with great alacrity, and an equally childish indignation with those economists who, according to them, believed that they did. Now I do not wish to say anything that would whitewash the older economists. Perhaps my spiritual parentage in *Dogmengeschichte* may be regarded as rendering me immune from that propensity. No doubt some of these writers[8] did overlook the obstacles to movement both between places and between occupations. No doubt, and this was the more serious omission, they tended to neglect the social barriers and disabilities which make it impossible for us to regard the whole working population as competing in one market. But when we reflect that the period in which they lived was one in which the proportion of the annual recruitment to the total working population was relatively high, the rate of increase being great, the assumption of a very considerable degree of potential mobility over relatively short periods does not seem so glaringly out of harmony with the facts as exclusive concentration on the possibility of mere transfer might lead us to imagine. It was a mistake to speak as if such a degree of mobility was always to be expected. It was an omission not to state explicitly the conditions which make it possible. But it was a mistake which sprang from too ready a disposition to regard the facts of the moment as permanent, rather than from a disposition to generalise without having regard to the facts at all.[9]

3. This, however, is a digression. We may conclude our discussion of the effects on productive power of the cessation of the growth of

population, by turning from the effects on the labour force to the effects on saving. Here, as always with this intractable subject, it is difficult to say anything very helpful. It is fairly clear, I think, that the rate of growth of the aggregate volume of accumulation must diminish. Other things being equal, it is clear that a larger population can save more than a smaller, and it is hard to believe that other things, money income per head, etc., will increase so rapidly after stationariness has set in as to counterbalance this factor. But again the more important matter is the average rate of accumulation, and here I do not think general analysis enables us to see far. It is true that there will be a tendency for the average expectation of life of the community (which is *not* the same thing as the expectation of life of the average individual) to diminish; for the presence of proportionately more old people must tend to depress the total; and if, as Cassel suggests,[10] expectation of life is a factor which influences the conditions of supply of saving, then to that extent the rate will tend to be diminished. But, useful as this theory can be in a broad demonstration of the improbability of a fractional or a zero rate of interest, it is doubtful whether its applicability extends to the comparatively small changes we are here contemplating.

IV

So far in this paper I have been considering the effects of the change we are contemplating on productive power, or the conditions of supply. I now wish to make a few comments on some of its effects on consumption, or the conditions of demand. I do not propose to take distribution directly into consideration.

1. We may notice at the outset certain changes in the direction of demand which seem to follow automatically from the changes in age-composition which we have already noted. The change in the relative size of the age groups will involve a change in the weighting of the social demand schedules which we may perhaps crystallise in the phrase—fewer toys, more foot-warmers. A more important manifestation of the same change will be seen in a tendency to a relative diminution in the demand for educational facilities, and a relative increase in the demand for homes for the old, and so on—a tendency which, of course, is already making itself felt in the national finances.

2. Much more interesting from the theoretical point of view is the change which is likely to come about in the movement of demand for

commodities satisfying rapidly satiable wants. It is here, I think, that the value of the mode of inquiry we have adopted becomes most evident. By definition the demand for rapidly satiable wants does not expand rapidly, other things being equal; and if we were considering only the phenomena of a stationary population, that would be all that there would be to be said about the matter. But when we compare this state of affairs with the phenomena of an increasing population, we see that in fact the movement of demand for such commodities must undergo a change of very considerable significance. For, when population is increasing, although the demands of individual purchasers may not extend at all rapidly, the actual quantity demanded may increase very considerably owing to an increase in the number of purchasers. The *aggregate demand* may increase, though the *demand per person* remains constant. Now, of course, such increases are not necessarily absent when population is stationary. Consumption may have been restricted to certain classes of the community and a change of taste or an increase of incomes may bring in new classes of consumers. This would no doubt happen in the case of an increase of money incomes among the poor as regards certain kinds of luxury (it is, of course, a mistake to regard the individual demand for a given luxury as necessarily very expansible). But in so far as the commodity in question is one whose consumption is already almost coterminous with the extent of the population, for instance bread, this source of expansion, expansion by addition to demanders, is excluded when the population becomes stationary. In a much more ultimate sense we can say that demand is inelastic.

Now all this has a very important bearing upon the probable fortunes of the producers of the commodity in question. If the supply of a commodity, the demand for which is not very expansible, increases, value per unit falls more than proportionately, so that the total proceeds of the sales of the larger amount are less than the total proceeds of the sales of the smaller amount. Hence, if in the industries manufacturing such commodities, productive efficiency improves, there will occur an absolute decline of the incomes of the producers in question, so long as their numbers are not diminished.[11] While population is still increasing, increases in productive efficiency, unaccompanied by a change in the size of the industry, may indeed result in a worsening of the relative position of such producers, but it is not necessary that their incomes should cease to rise. All that may happen is that they do not rise as rapidly as other incomes. When this source of expansion is excluded, however, an absolute decline is more probable, and, if it is to be avoided, a diminution in numbers is all the more imperative.

Such generalisations are, of course, of the widest possible order, and very great care is needed in applying them to the circumstances of our small island in the near future—a bucket of stationariness in an ocean of rapid multiplication. We must not think that so soon as our own rate of increase becomes zero, the absolute position of English wheat producers, for instance, will necessarily be worsened. For, producing as he does for a market which is world-wide, the English farmer will not necessarily be conscious of a tendency to a slight downward fluctuation of demand which is due to the cessation of growth of the community of which he is a member. The elasticity of demand for *his* product is virtually infinite. But in so far as there are products saleable only within the national area, and the object of a demand of the kind we are discussing, the position of the producers will be affected in the way I have mentioned. And when the population of the whole world reaches a point of stationariness, the phenomena in question may become of considerable international importance.

3. Finally, we may notice the effect of the change on that very important category of demand, demand for money.

Here the theoretical developments of the last few years enable us to deal with this matter with great expedition. If, following Marshall and Professor Cannan, we regard demand for money as springing from the willingness of persons and institutions to hold certain quantities of legal tender cash, at any given state of the price level, it is easy to see that one of the main factors affecting the total amount demanded will be variations in the size of the population. A cessation in the growth of population will therefore be a most powerful factor in retarding the rate of increase in demand for money in the area in which it takes place. Other factors, such as increases of real income, changes in the distribution of wealth favourable to classes who do not keep banking accounts, anything which tends to break up the financial solidarity of the family, may still continue to bring about an increase in the demand for money. But that growth in demand which for the last century and more has been due to the increase of population, must no longer be expected.

Now if the currency of this country had continued to be based upon inconvertible paper—if, for instance, Mr. Keynes's proposals for a managed paper currency had been adopted, this prospect would have been of great practical significance. Other things being equal, if the price level was to be kept stable, a falling off in the rate of increase of demand for money would have had to be met by a commensurate diminution in the rate of increase of supply. If this were not done, then an upward tendency in the price level would manifest itself. In fact, however, our currency is no longer national in this sense. Under the gold standard, the demand for money is a world demand, and having regard to the dimensions of the area from which it arises, and the probable extensions of that area, I do not think that any spectacular change in world prices is to be expected as a result of the diminution in the rate of increase of our own "requirements." Gold prices will be slightly higher, our share of the world's gold will be slightly less, than would have been the case if our rate of increase had remained positive.

Nevertheless I do not conceive it to have been otiose to have discussed the matter in this connection. For, if the result of our inquiry in this respect is to some extent negative, it does at least emphasise the essential variability in the modern world of one of the main factors determining the course of general prices; and unless this is recognised, successful prediction is impossible. Professor Cassel[12] has calculated that during the period 1850–1910 an increase of 2.8 per cent. per annum in the world's gold supply would have served to keep prices stable, and he has suggested that a figure of this order may be used side by side with estimates of the probable yield of the mines to serve as a basis for predictions as to the future trend of prices. Now I should be very sorry to be thought to underestimate the value of Professor Cassel's suggestion. I do indeed regard it as one of the most remarkable experiments in applied dynamics that have been made in the history of our science. But at the same time, I do think it important to emphasise that whatever the actual validity of the application of a constant multiplier during the century that has passed, *so long as the rate of increase of population varies, so long must such an application only be valid by accident*. This is not to say that the important prospects of development opened up by Professor Cassel's researches are illusory. On the contrary, the variations of the rate of growth of the money-using population being fairly accurately predictable for short periods, it should not be impossible to introduce corresponding modifications into the calculations. All that I contend is that, if the considerations brought to light by the foregoing argument are correct, such corrections are absolutely necessary.

Notes

1. A paper read before the Oxford Political Economy Club, October 27th, 1928.
2. The Probability of the Cessation of the Growth of Population in England and Wales during the Next Century. *Economic Journal*, 1895, p. 505 *seq.*
3. Bowley, Births and Population in Great Britain, *Economic Journal*, June, 1924, pp. 189–92. Professor Bowley assumes that there is no migration.
4. *London Essays in Economics*, edited Dalton and Gregory. The Optimum Theory of Population, pp. 103–134. See also Cannan, *Wealth*, 3rd edition, pp. 59–62.
5. *Op. cit. passim.*
6. Perhaps the clearest way of presenting this doctrine is by means of a diagram. Let two rectangles, I and II, of equal areas, represent two working populations of equal size, but different tendencies to growth, I being stationary, II still advancing.

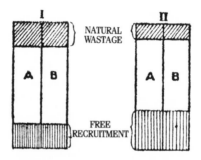

   Let the natural wastage and free recruitment be represented by shaded areas–greatly exaggerated in proportions–at the top and bottom of the respective rectangles, and let an equal division of the populations between two industries, A and B, be represented by the equal division of the intervening areas. If now it is desired to change the *relative proportions* employed in these industries–and of course it is relative proportions rather than absolute numbers which matter in the consideration of equilibrium–it should be obvious that the amount released by shutting down recruitment into A when population is advancing is greater than the amount released by similar measures when population is stationary. Hence it should be clear that a greater relative change per unit of time is possible in the former case than in the latter.
7. It may be contended that modern technique tends to make such movement progressively less difficult (see Cannan, *An Economist's Protest:* War and Commercial Policy, pp. 120-133, especially p. 126). On the other hand, the general Balkanisation of politics since the war and the current tendency to think in terms of the economics of industries rather than the economics of industries, can be said to be less conducive to optimism.
8. Adam Smith was certainly not of their number.
9. If this were a discussion of the cessation of growth of population the world over, we should have to take into account effects on international mobility. Here, I

think, if the stationariness were general and were not the result of a positive rate of multiplication on the part of one race and a negative rate elsewhere, the effect would be favourable. Indeed, it is difficult to conceive anything more favourable to the removal of barriers to migration than the absence of different rates of multiplication on the part of different races.

10. Cassel, *The Nature and Necessity of Interest,* pp. 148–152.
11. On this point see my forthcoming article on "The Economic Effects of Variation of Hours of Labour" in the *Economic Journal.*
12. Cassel, *Theory of Social Economy*, vol. ii, pp. 441–473.

20

Some Economic Consequences of a Declining Population

John Maynard Keynes

I

We know much more securely than we know almost any other social or economic factor relating to the future that, in the place of the steady and indeed steeply rising level of population which we have experienced for a great number of decades, we shall be faced in a very short time with a stationary or a declining level. . . .

II

An increasing population has a very important influence on the demand for capital. Not only does the demand for capital—apart from technical changes and an improved standard of life—increase more or less in proportion to population. But, business expectations being based much more on present than on prospective demand, an era of increasing population tends to promote optimism, since demand will in general tend to exceed, rather than fall short of, what was hoped for. Moreover a mistake, resulting in a particular type of capital being in temporary over-supply, is in such conditions rapidly corrected. But in an era of declining population the opposite is true. Demand tends to be below what was expected, and a state of over-supply is less easily corrected. Thus a pessimistic atmosphere may ensue; and, although at long last pessimism may tend to correct itself through its effect on supply, the first result to prosperity of a change-over from an increasing to a declining population may be very disastrous.

In assessing the causes of the enormous increase in capital during the nineteenth century and since, too little importance, I think, has been given to the influence of an increasing population as distinct from other influences. . . . [T]he demand for capital depends on the number of consumers, the average level of consumption, and the average period of production.

Now it is necessarily the case that an increase in population increases proportionately the demand for capital; and the progress of invention may be relied on to raise the standard of life. But the effect of invention on the period of production depends on the type of invention which is characteristic of the age. . . .

Now, if the number of consumers is falling off and we cannot rely on any significant technical lengthening of the period of production, the demand for a net increase of capital goods is thrown back into being wholly dependent on an improvement in the average level of consumption or on a fall in the rate of interest. I will attempt to give a few very rough figures to illustrate the order of magnitude of the different factors involved.

Let us consider the period of just over fifty years from 1860 to 1913. I find no evidence of any important change in the length of the technical period of production. Statistics of quantity of real capital present special difficulties. But those which we have do not suggest that there have been large changes in the amount of capital employed to produce a unit of output. Two of the most highly capitalized services, those of housing and of agriculture, are old-established. Agriculture has diminished in relative importance. Only if people were to spend a decidedly increased proportion of their incomes on housing, as to which there is indeed a certain amount of evidence for the post-war period, should I expect a significant lengthening of the technical period of production. For the fifty years before the war, during which the long-period average of the rate of interest was fairly constant, I feel some confidence that the period was not lengthened by much more than 10 per cent., if as much.

Now during the same period the British population increased by about 50 per cent., and the population which British industry and investment was serving by a much higher figure. And I suppose that the standard of life must have risen by somewhere about 60 per cent. Thus the increased demand for capital was primarily attributable to the increasing population and to the rising standard of life, and only in a minor degree to technical changes of a kind which called for an increasing capitalization per unit of consumption. To sum up, the population figures, which are reliable, indicate that about half the increase in capital was required to serve the increasing population. Perhaps the figures were about as follows, though I would emphasize that these conclusions are very rough and to be regarded only as broad pointers to what was going on:

	1860	1913
Real capital	100	270
Population	100	150
Standard of life	100	160
Period of Production	100	110

It follows that a stationary population with the same improvement in the standard of life and the same lengthening of the period of production would have required an increase in the stock of capital of only a little more than half of the increase which actually occurred. Moreover, whilst nearly half of the home investment was required by the increase in population, probably a substantially higher proportion of the foreign investment of that period was attributable to this cause.

On the other hand it is possible that the increase in average incomes, the decline in the size of families, and a number of other institutional and social influences may have raised the proportion of the national income which tends to be saved in conditions of full employment. I do not feel confident about this, since there are other factors, notably the taxation of the very rich, which tend in the opposite direction. But I think we can safely say—and this is sufficient for my argument—that the proportion of the national income which would be saved to-day in conditions of full employment lies somewhere between 8 per cent. and 15 per cent. of the income of each year. What annual percentage increase in the stock of capital would this rate of saving involve? To answer this we have to estimate how many years of our national income the existing stock of capital represents. This is not a figure which we know accurately, but it is possible to indicate an order of magnitude. You will probably find when I tell you the answer that it differs a good deal from what you expect. The existing national stock of capital is equal to about four times a year's national income. That is to say, if our annual income is in the neighbourhood of £4,000 millions, our stock of capital is perhaps £15,000 millions. (I am not here including foreign investment, which would raise the figure to, say, four and a half times.) It follows that new investment at a rate of somewhere between 8 per cent. and 15 per cent. of a year's income means a cumulative increment in the stock of capital of somewhere between 2 per cent. and 4 per cent. per annum.

Let me recapitulate the argument. Please take note that I have been making so far two tacit assumptions—namely that there is no drastic change in the distribution of wealth or in any other factor affecting the proportion of income that is saved; and further, that there is no large change in the rate of interest sufficient to modify substantially the length of the average period of production. To the removal of these two assumptions we shall return later. On these assumptions, however, with our existing organization, and in conditions of prosperity and full employment, we shall have to discover a demand for net additions to our stock of capital amounting to somewhere between 2 per cent. and 4 per cent. annually. And this will have to continue year after year indefinitely. Let us in what follows take the lower estimate—namely 2 per cent.—since if this is too low the argument will be *a fortiori*.

Hitherto the demand for new capital has come from two sources, each of about equal strength: a little less than half of it to meet the demands of a growing population; a little more than half of it to meet the demands of inventions and improvements which increase output per head and permit a higher standard of life.

Now past experience shows that a greater cumulative increment than 1 per cent. per annum in the standard of life has seldom proved practicable. Even if the fertility of invention would permit more, we cannot easily adjust ourselves to a greater rate of change than this involves. There may have been one or two decades in this country during the past hundred years when improvement has proceeded at the rate of 1 per cent. per annum. But generally speaking the rate of improvement seems to have been somewhat less than 1 per cent. per annum cumulative.

I am here distinguishing, you will see, between those inventions which enable a unit of capital to yield a unit of product with the aid of less labour than before, and those which lead to a change in the amount of capital employed *more* than in proportion to the resulting output. I am assuming that the former class of improvements will proceed in the future as in the recent past, and am ready to take as my assumption that they will proceed in the near future up to the best standard we have ever experienced in any previous decade; and I calculate that inventions falling under this head are not likely to absorb much more than half of our savings, assuming conditions of full employment and a stationary population. But in the second category some inventions cut some way and some the other, and it is not clear—assuming a constant rate of interest—that the net result of invention changes demand for capital per unit of output one way or the other.

It follows, therefore, that to ensue equilibrium conditions of prosperity over a period of years it will be essential, *either* that we alter our institutions and the distribution of wealth in a way which causes a smaller proportion of income to be saved, *or* that we reduce the rate of interest sufficiently to make profitable very large changes in technique or in the direction of consumption which involve a much larger use of capital in proportion to output. Or, of course, as would be wisest, we could pursue both policies to a certain extent.

III

What relation do these views bear to the older Malthusian theory that more capital resources per head (chiefly envisaged by the older writers in the shape of Land) must be of immense benefit to the standard of life, and that the growth of population was disastrous to human standards by retarding this increase? It may seem at first sight that I am contesting this old theory and am arguing, on the contrary, that a phase of declining population will make it immensely more difficult than before to maintain prosperity.

In a sense this is a true interpretation of what I am saying. But if there are any old Malthusians here present let them not suppose that I am rejecting their essential argument. Unquestionably a stationary population does facilitate a rising standard of life; but on one condition only—namely that the increase in resources or in consumption, as the case may be, which the stationariness of population makes possible, does actually take place. For we have now learned that we have another devil at our elbow at least as fierce as the Malthusian—namely the devil of unemployment escaping through the breakdown of effective demand. Perhaps we could call this devil too a Malthusian devil, since it was Malthus himself who first told us about him. For just as the young Malthus was disturbed by the facts of population as he saw them round him and sought to rationalize that problem, so the older Malthus was no less disturbed by the facts of unemployment as he saw them round him and sought—far less successfully so far as his influence on the rest of the world was concerned—to rationalize that problem too. Now when Malthusian devil P. is chained up, Malthusian devil U. is liable to break loose. When devil P. of Population is chained up, we are free of one menace; but we are more exposed to the other devil U. of Unemployed Resources than we were before.

With a stationary population we shall, I argue, be absolutely dependent for the maintenance of prosperity and civil peace on policies of increasing consumption by a more equal distribution of incomes and of forcing down the rate of interest so as to make profitable a substantial change in the length of the period of production. If we do not, of set and determined purpose, pursue these policies, then without question we shall be cheated of the benefits which we stand to gain by the chaining up of one devil, and shall suffer from the perhaps more intolerable depredations of the other.

Yet there will be many social and political forces to oppose the necessary change. It is probable that we cannot make the changes wisely unless we make them gradually. We must foresee what is before us and move to meet it half-way. If capitalist society rejects a more equal distribution of incomes and the forces of banking and finance succeed in maintaining the rate of interest somewhere near the figure which ruled on the average during the nineteenth century (which was, by the way, a little *lower* than the rate of interest which rules to-day), then a chronic tendency towards the under-employment of resources must in the end sap and destroy that form of society. But if, on the other hand, persuaded and guided by the spirit of the age and such enlightenment as there is, it permits—as I believe it may—a gradual evolution in our attitude towards accumulation, so that it shall be appropriate to the circumstances of a stationary or declining population, we shall be able, perhaps, to get the best of both worlds—to maintain the liberties and independence of our present system, whilst its more signal faults gradually suffer euthanasia as the diminishing importance of capital accumulation and the rewards attaching to it fall into their proper position in the social scheme.

A too rapidly declining population would obviously involve many severe problems, and there are strong reasons lying outside the scope of this evening's discussion why in that event, or in the threat of that event, measures ought to be taken to prevent it. But a stationary or slowly declining population may, if we exercise the necessary strength and wisdom, enable us to raise the standard of life to what it should be, whilst retaining those parts of our traditional scheme of life which we value the more now that we see what happens to those who lose them.

In the final summing up, therefore, I do not depart from the old Malthusian conclusion. I only wish to warn you that the chaining up of the one devil may, if we are careless, only serve to loose another still fiercer and more intractable.

21

Economic Progress and Declining Population Growth

Alvin H. Hansen

One may ask: "Is there any special reason why in the year 1938 we should devote our attention as economists to the general subject "The Changing Character of the American Economy"? Throughout the modern era, ceaseless change has been the law of economic life. Every period is in some sense a period of transition. The swift stream of events in the last quarter century offers, however, overwhelming testimony in support of the thesis that the economic order of the western world is undergoing in this generation a structural change no less basic and profound in character than that transformation of economic life and institutions which we are wont to designate loosely by the phrase "the Industrial Revolution." We are passing, so to speak, over a divide which separates the great era of growth and expansion of the nineteenth century from an era which no man, unwilling to embark on pure conjecture, can as yet characterize with clarity or precision. We are moving swiftly out of the order in which those of our generation were brought up, into no one knows what.

Overwhelmingly significant, but as yet all too little considered by economists, is the profound change which we are currently undergoing in the rate of population growth. In the decade of the nineteen-twenties the population of the United States increased by 16,000,000—

an absolute growth equal to that of the pre-war decade and in excess of any other decade in our history. In the current decade we are adding only half this number to our population, and the best forecasts indicate a decline to a third in the decade which we are about to enter.

Inadequate as the data are, it appears that the prodigious growth of population in the nineteenth century was something unique in history. Gathering momentum with the progress of modern science and transportation, the absolute growth in western Europe mounted decade by decade until the great World War; and in the United States it reached the highest level, as I have just noted, in the post-war decade. The upward surge began with relatively small accretions which rapidly swelled into a flood. But the advancing tide has come to a sudden halt and the accretions are dwindling toward zero.

Thus, with the prospect of actual contraction confronting us, already we are in the midst of a drastic decline in the rate of population growth. Whatever the future decades may bring, this present fact is already upon us; and it behooves us as economists to take cognizance of the significance of this revolutionary change in our economic life.

Schooled in the traditions of the Malthusian theory, economists, thinking in terms of static economics, have typically placed an optimistic interpretation upon the cessation of population growth. This indeed is also the interpretation suggested by the National Resources Committee which recently has issued an exhaustive statistical inquiry into current and prospective changes in population growth. In a fundamental sense this conclusion is, I think, thoroughly sound; for it can scarcely be questioned that a continued growth of population at the rate experienced in the nineteenth century would rapidly present insoluble problems. But it would be an unwarranted optimism to deny that there are implicit in the current drastic shift from rapid expansion to cessation of population growth, serious structural maladjustments which can be avoided or mitigated only if economic policies, appropriate to the changed situation, are applied. Indeed in this shift must be sought a basic cause of not a few of the developments in our changing economy.

Adam Smith regarded growth of population as at once a consequence and a cause of economic progress. Increasing division of labor would, he argued, bring about greater productivity, and this would furnish an enlarged revenue and stock, from which would flow an enlarged wages fund, an increased demand for labor, higher wages, and so economic conditions favorable for population growth. Now a growing population, by widening the market and by fostering inventiveness, in turn facilitated, he thought, division of labor and so the production of wealth. Thus he arrived at an optimistic conclusion. Population growth, he held, stimulated progress and this in turn stimulated further growth and expansion. In contrast, the pessimistic analyses of Malthus and Ricardo stressed the limitation of natural resources and the danger of an increasing population's pressing down the margin of cultivation to a point at which real income would be reduced to a bare subsistence level. In this static analysis the more dynamic approach of Adam Smith was quite forgotten. If we wish to get a clear insight into the economic consequences of the current decline in population growth, it is necessary to return to the suggestion of Adam Smith and to explore more fully the causal interconnection between economic progress, capital formation and population growth.

Economic analysis from the earliest development of our science has been concerned with the rôle played by economic progress. Various writers have included under this caption different things; but for our purpose we may say that the constituent elements of economic progress are (a) inventions, (b) the discovery and development of new territory and new resources, and (c) the growth of population. Each of these in turn, severally and in combination, has opened investment outlets and caused a rapid growth of capital formation.

The earlier economists were concerned chiefly with the effect of economic progress upon the volume of output, or in other words, upon the level of real income. For them economic progress affected the economic life mainly, if not exclusively, in terms of rising productivity and higher real income per capita.

Not until the very end of the nineteenth century did an extensive literature arise which stressed the rôle of economic progress as a leading, if not the main, factor causing fluctuations in employment, output, and income. Ricardo had indeed seen that there was some relation between economic progress and economic instability; but it was left for Wicksell, Spiethoff, Schumpeter, Cassel, and Robertson to elaborate the thesis that economic fluctuations are essentially a function of economic progress.

More recently the rôle of economic progress in the maintenance of full employment of the productive resources has come under consideration. The earlier economists assumed that the economic system tended automatically to produce full employment of resources. Some unemployment there was periodically, owing to the fluctuations incident to the business cycle; but in the upswing phase of the cyclical movement the economy was believed to function in a manner tending to bring about full recovery—maximum output and employment. This view was inspired by a century in which the forces of economic progress were powerful and strong, in which investment outlets were numerous and alluring. Spiethoff saw clearly that technological progress, the development of new industries, the discovery of new resources, the opening of new territory were the basic causes of the boom, which in turn was the progenitor of depression. Indeed he believed that once the main resources of the globe had been discovered and exploited, once the whole world had been brought under the sway of the machine technique, the leading disturbing factors which underlie the fluctuations of the cycle would have spent their force and an era of relative economic stability would ensue. But he did not raise the question whether such stability would be achieved at a full-employment and full-income level.

The business cycle was *par excellence* the problem of the nineteenth century. But the main problem of our times, and particularly in the United States, is the problem of full employment. Yet paradoxical as it may seem, the nineteenth century was little concerned with, and understood but dimly, the character of the business cycle. Indeed, so long as the problem of full employment was not pressing, it was not necessary to worry unduly about the temporary unemployment incident to the swings of the cycle. Not until the problem of full employment of our productive resources from the long-run, secular standpoint was upon us, were we compelled to give serious consideration to those factors and forces in our economy which tend to make business recoveries weak and anaemic and which tend to prolong and deepen the course of depressions. This is the essence of secular stagnation—sick recoveries which die in their infancy and depressions which feed on themselves and leave a hard and seemingly immovable core of unemployment.

In every great crisis the struggle of contending groups maneuvering for an advantageous position amidst rapid change whips up the froth and fury of political and social controversy. Always there is present the temptation to explain the course of events in terms of the more superficial phenomena which are frequently manifestations rather than causes of change. It is the peculiar function of the economist however to look deeper into the underlying economic realities and to discover in these, if possible, the causes of the most obstinate problem of our time—the problem of under-employment. Fundamental to an understanding of this problem are the changes in the "external" forces, if I may so describe them, which underlie economic progress—changes in the character of technological innovations, in the availability of new territory, and in the growth of population.

The expanding economy of the last century called forth a prodigious growth of capital formation. So much was this the case, that this era in history has by common consent been called the capitalistic period. No one disputes the thesis that without this vast accumulation of capital we should never have witnessed the great rise in the standard of living achieved since the beginning of the Industrial Revolution. But it is not the effect of capital formation upon real income to which I wish especially to direct attention. What I wish to stress in this paper is rather the rôle played by the process of capital formation in securing at each point in this ascending income scale fairly full employment of the productive resources and therefore the maximum income possible under the then prevailing level of technological development. For it is an indisputable fact that the prevailing economic system has never been able to reach reasonably full employment or the attainment of its currently realizable real income without making large investment expenditures. The basis for this imperious economic necessity has been thoroughly explored in the last half century in the great literature beginning with Tugan-Baranowsky and Wicksell on saving and investment. I shall not attempt any summary statement of this analysis. Nor is this necessary; for I take it that it is accepted by all schools of current economic thought that full employment and the maximum currently attainable income level cannot be reached in the modern free enterprise economy without a volume of investment expenditures adequate to fill the gap between consumption expenditures and that level of income which could be achieved were all the factors employed. In this somewhat truistic statement I hope I have succeeded in escaping a hornets' nest of economic controversy.

Thus we may postulate a consensus on the thesis that in the absence of a positive program designed to stimulate consumption, full employment of the productive resources is essentially a function of the vigor of investment activity. Less agreement can be claimed for the rôle played by the rate of interest on the volume of investment. Yet few there are who believe that in a period of investment stagnation an abundance of loanable funds at low rates of interest is alone adequate to produce a vigorous flow of real investment. I am increasingly impressed with the analysis made by Wicksell who stressed the prospective rate of profit on new investment as the active, dominant, and controlling factor, and who viewed the rate of interest as a passive factor, lagging behind the profit rate. This view is moreover in accord with competent business judgment.[1] It is true that it is necessary to look beyond the mere *cost* of interest charges to the indirect effect of the interest rate structure upon business expectations. Yet all in all, I venture to assert that the rôle of the rate of interest as a determinant of investment has occupied a place larger than it deserves in our thinking. If this be granted, we are forced to regard the factors which underlie economic progress as the dominant determinants of investment and employment.

A growth in real investment may take the form either of a deepening of capital or of a widening of capital, as Hawtrey has aptly put it. The deepening process means that more capital is used per unit of output, while the widening process means that capital formation grows *pari passu* with the increase in the output of final goods. If the ratio of real capital to real income remains constant, there is no deepening of capital; but if this ratio is constant and real income rises, then there is a widening of capital.

According to Douglas[2] the growth of real capital formation in England from 1875 to 1909 proceeded at an average rate of two per cent per annum; and the rate of growth of capital formation in the United States from 1890 to 1922 was four per cent per annum. The former is less than the probable rate of increase of output in England, while the latter is somewhat in excess of the annual rise of production in the United States. Thus, during the last fifty years or more, capital formation for each economy as a whole has apparently consisted mainly of a widening of capital. Surprising as it may seem, as far as we may judge from such data as are available, there has been little, if any, deepening of capital. The capital stock has increased approximately in proportion to real income. This is also the conclusion of Gustav Cassel;[3] while Keynes[4] thinks that real capital formation in England may have very slightly exceeded the rise in real income in the period from 1860 to the World War. If this be true, it follows that, in terms of the time element in production, which is the very essence of the capital concept, our system of production is little more capitalistic now than fifty or seventy-five years ago. It requires, in other words, a period of employ-ment of our productive resources no longer than formerly to reproduce the total capital stock. The "waiting," so to speak, embodied in our capital accumulations is no greater today than half a century or more ago. Capital has indeed grown relative to labor. Thus the technical coefficient of production, with respect to capital, has increased. While this indicates a more intensive application of capital relative to the other factors, it does not necessarily imply any deepening of capital.

In important areas the capital stock has not increased significantly even in relation to population. This is notably true in the service indus-tries. Moreover, in the field of housing real capital has little more than kept pace with population growth. In manufacturing as a whole it is certainly true that real capital formation has not only far outstripped population but has also risen more rapidly than physical product. The studies of Douglas for the United States and Australia show that real fixed capital invested in manufacturing increased more rapidly than physical output of manufactured goods. On the other hand, Carl Snyder's[5] data, which run in terms of value of invested capital and value of product, indicate that for important separate industries, such as textiles, iron and steel, and petroleum, capital has grown little or no faster than output since about 1890. With respect to the automobile industry, according to his findings, capital investment has risen no more rapidly than value of product, while in the electrical industries, invested capital increased at a slower rate than output after 1907. Considering the economy as a whole, including fields of economic activity other than manufacturing, there is no good evidence that the advance of technique has resulted in recent decades, certainly not in any significant measure, in any deepening of capital. Apparently, once the machine technique has been developed in any field, further mecha-nization is likely to result in an increase in output at least proportional to and often in excess of the net additions to real capital. Though the deepening process is all the while going on in certain areas, elsewhere capital-saving inventions are reducing the ratio of capital to output.

In order to get some insight into the effect of population growth upon capital formation, it is necessary to consider the rôle it plays in conjunction with other factors in the widening and deepening process. The widening of capital is a function of an increase in final output, which in turn is due partly to an increase in population and partly to an increase in per capita productivity, arising from causes other than a larger use of capital per unit of output. On the other hand, the deepening of capital results partly from cost-reducing changes in technique, partly (though this is probably a much less significant factor) from a reduction in the rate of interest, and partly from changes in the character of the output as a whole, with special reference to the amount of capital required to produce it.

Now the rate of population growth must necessarily play an important rôle in determining the character of the output; in other words, the composition of the flow of final goods. Thus a rapidly growing population will demand a much larger per capita volume of new residential building construction than will a stationary population. A stationary population with its larger proportion of old people may perhaps demand more personal services; and the composition of consumer demand will have an important influence on the quantity of capital required. The demand for housing calls for large capital outlays, while the demand for personal services can be met without making large investment expenditures. It is therefore not unlikely that a shift from a rapidly growing population to a stationary or declining one may so alter the composition of the final flow of consumption goods that the ratio of capital to output as a whole will tend to decline.

In the beginning stages of modern capitalism both the deepening and the widening processes of capital formation were developing side by side. But in its later stages the deepening process, taking the economy as a whole, rapidly diminished. And now with the rapid cessation of population growth, even the widening process may slow down. Moreover it is possible that capital-saving inventions may cause capital formation in many industries to lag behind the increase in output.

An interesting problem for statistical research would be to determine the proportion of investment in the nineteenth century which could be attributed (a) to population growth, (b) to the opening up of new territory and the discovery of new resources, and (c) to technical innovations. Such an analysis it has not been possible for me to make, and I shall venture only a few rough estimates together with some qualitative judgments. With respect to population growth some insight into the problem may perhaps be gained by considering first the rôle of population growth in the rise of aggregate real income. The various estimates agree that the annual rate of growth of physical output up to the World War was roughly three per cent in western Europe and nearly four per cent in the United States. Of this average annual increase something less than half of the three per cent increase in western Europe can be attributed to population growth, while something more than half of the annual increase in the United States can be assigned to the increase in the labor supply. Thus it appears that per capita output has increased both in western Europe and in the United States at approximately one and one-half per cent per annum. This increase can be attributed mainly to changes in technique and to the exploitation of new natural resources.

We have already noted that capital formation has progressed at about the same rate as the rise in aggregate output. Thus, as a first approximation, we may say that the growth of population in the last half of the nineteenth century was responsible for about forty per cent of the total volume of capital formation in western Europe and about sixty per cent of the capital formation in the United States. If this is even approximately correct, it will be seen what an important outlet for investment is being closed by reason of the current rapid decline in population growth.

Obviously the growth of population affects capital formation most directly in the field of construction, especially residential building. From decade to decade the increase in the number of dwellings had maintained a close relation to the increase in population. In the decade of the twenties, however, the increase in houses ran about twenty-five per cent in excess of previous decennial increases in relation to population. According to Kuznets, during the seven prosperous years 1923 to 1929, a quarter of the net capital formation was residential building. But the effect of population growth on capital formation is, of course, felt in other spheres as well. This is notably true of all the various municipal and public utilities, and also of the manufacture of essential consumers' goods.

An interesting excursus would lead us into a consideration of the problem how far an increase in population itself contributed to a more efficient technique and so was in part responsible for the rise in per capita real income. According to the older Malthusian view, the growth of population would act counter to the effect of technological progress upon per capita productivity, and would thus slow down the rise in per capita real income. If this were correct, population growth considered by itself alone would tend to check the rise in per capita consumption, and this in turn, *via* the so-called *Relation,* would affect the volume of capital formation. According to the optimum population theory, however, it may not infrequently be the case, and indeed probably was during the greater part of the nineteenth century, that population growth itself facilitated mass production methods and accelerated the progress of technique. If this be correct, population growth was itself responsible for a part of the rise in per capita real income, and this, via the influence of a rising consumption upon investment, stimulated capital formation. Thus it is quite possible that population growth may have acted both directly and indirectly to stimulate the volume of capital formation.

It is not possible, I think, to make even an approximate estimate of the proportion of the new capital created in the nineteenth century which was a direct consequence of the opening up of new territory. The development of new countries was indeed so closely intertwined with the growth of population that it would be difficult to avoid double counting. What proportion of new capital formation in the United States went each year into the western frontier we do not know, but it must have been very considerable. Apparently about one-fourth of the total capital accumulations of England were invested abroad by 1914, and one-seventh of those of France.

These figures, while only suggestive, point unmistakably to the conclusion that the opening of new territory and the growth of population were together responsible for a very large fraction—possibly somewhere near one-half—of the total volume of new capital formation in the nineteenth century. These outlets for new investment are rapidly being closed. The report on *Limits of Land Settlement* by President Isaiah Bowman and others may be regarded as conclusive in its findings that there are no important areas left for exploitation and settlement. So far as population is concerned, that of western Europe has already virtually reached a standstill; but that in eastern Europe, notably in Russia, is still growing, and so also is that in the Orient. And much of this area will probably experience a considerable industrialization. But it is not yet clear how far the mature industrial countries will participate in this development through capital export. Russia still has a long way to go before she becomes completely industrialized; but foreign capital is not likely to play any significant rôle in this process. India will offer some opportunity for British investment, but the total is likely to be small relative to the volume of British foreign investments in the nineteenth century. China and the Orient generally offer, in view of the present and prospective turmoil in that area, relatively meager investment opportunities. At all events, no one is likely to challenge the statement that foreign investment will in the next fifty years play an incomparably smaller role than was the case in the nineteenth century.

Thus the outlets for new investment are rapidly narrowing down to those created by the progress of technology. To be sure, the progress of technology itself played in the nineteenth century a decisive rôle in the opening of new territory and as a stimulus to population growth. But while technology can facilitate the opening of new territory, it cannot create a new world or make the old one bigger than it is. And while the advance of science, by reducing the death rate, was a major cause of the vast nineteenth-century increase in population, no important further gains in this direction can possibly offset the prevailing low birth rate. Thus the further progress of science can operate to open investment outlets only through its direct influence on the technique of production.

We are thus rapidly entering a world in which we must fall back upon a more rapid advance of technology than in the past if we are to find private investment opportunities adequate to maintain full employment. Should we accept the advice of those who would declare a moratorium on invention and technical progress, this one remaining avenue for private investment would also be closed. There can be no greater error in the analysis of the economic trends of our times than that which finds in the advance of technology, broadly conceived, a major cause of unemployment. It is true that we cannot discount the problem of technological unemployment, a problem which may be intensified by the apparently growing importance of capital-saving inventions. But, on the other side, we cannot afford to neglect that type of innovation which creates new industries and which thereby opens new outlets for real investment. The problem of our generation is, above all, the problem of inadequate private investment outlets. What we need is not a slowing down in the progress of science and technology, but rather an acceleration of that rate.

Of first-rate importance is the development of new industries. There is certainly no basis for the assumption that these are a thing of the past. But there is equally no basis for the assumption that we can take for granted the rapid emergence of new industries as rich in investment opportunities as the railroad, or more recently the automobile, together with all the related developments, including the construction of public roads, to which it gave rise. Nor is there any basis, either in history or in theory, for the assumption that the rise of new industries proceeds inevitably at a uniform pace. The growth of modern industry has not come in terms of millions of small increments of change giving rise to a smooth and even development. Characteristically it has come by gigantic leaps and bounds. Very often the change can best be described as discontinuous, lumpy, and jerky, as indeed D. H. Robertson has so vividly done. And when a revolutionary new industry like the railroad or the automobile, after having initiated in its youth a powerful upward surge of investment activity, reaches maturity and ceases to grow, as all industries finally must, the whole economy must experience a profound stagnation, unless indeed new developments take its place. It is not enough that a mature industry continues its activity at a high level on a horizontal plane. The fact that new railroad mileage continued to be built at about the same rate through the seventies, eighties and nineties was not sufficient. It is the *cessation of growth* which is disastrous. It is in connection with the growth, maturity and decline of great industries that the principle of acceleration operates with peculiar force. And when giant new industries have spent their force, it *may* take a long time before something else of equal magnitude emerges. In fact nothing has emerged in the decade in which we are now living. This basic fact, together with the virtual cessation of public investment by state and local government bodies, as indicated by a decline of $2,000,000,000 in their net public debt since 1932, explains in large measure the necessary rise in federal expenditures. [6]

Spiethoff was quite right when he argued that a vigorous recovery is not just spontaneously born from the womb of the preceding depression. Some small recovery must indeed arise sooner or later merely because of the growing need for capital replacement. But a full-fledged recovery calls for something more than the mere expenditure of depreciation allowances. It requires a large outlay on new investment, and this awaits the development of great new industries and new techniques. But such new developments are not currently available in adequate volume. It is my growing conviction that the combined effect of the decline in population growth, together with the failure of any really important innovations of a magnitude sufficient to absorb large capital outlays, weighs very heavily as an explanation for the failure of the recent recovery to reach full employment. Other factors are certainly significant and important, particularly our failure to control the cost structure and to grapple effectively with specific situations, such as those presented by the railroads and by building construction.

We have noted that the approaching cessation of population growth and the disappearance of new territory for settlement and exploitation may cut off a half or more of the investment outlets which we were wont to make in the past. We are thus compelled to fall back upon that measure of capital formation which is associated with the advance of technique and the rise in per capita output. But current institutional developments are restricting even this outlet. The growing power of trade unions and trade associations, the development of monopolistic competition, of rivalry for the market through expensive persuasion and advertising, instead of through price competition, are factors which have rightly of late commanded much attention among economists. There is, moreover, the tendency to block the advance of technical progress by the shelving of patents.

Under vigorous price competition, new cost-reducing techniques were compulsorily introduced even though the scrapping of obsolete but undepreciated machinery entailed a capital loss. But under the monopoly principle of obsolescence new machines will not be introduced until the undepreciated value of the old machine will at least be covered by the economies of the new technique. Thus progress is slowed down, and outlets for new capital formation, available under a more ruthless competitive society, are cut off. Capital losses which could not be avoided under rigorous price competition can be and are avoided under an economic system more closely integrated by inter-corporate association and imperfect competition. If we are to save the one remaining outlet for private capital formation, deliberate action of a far bolder character than hitherto envisaged must be undertaken in order to make the price system and free enterprise sufficiently responsive to permit at least that measure of capital formation to which the rate of technological progress had accustomed us in the past.

Yet even though this much was achieved, it is necessary to recognize that such a rate of progress would not provide sufficient investment outlets to give us full employment of our resources. With a stationary population we could maintain as rapid a rise in per capita real income as that experienced in the past, by making annually only half the volume of new investment to which we have been accustomed. A volume of investment adequate to provide full employment could give us an annual percentage increase in per capita output greatly in excess of any hitherto attained.

Various measures have been offered to maintain full employment in the absence of an adequate rate of technological progress and of the development of new industries. Consumption may be strengthened by the relief from taxes which drain off a stream of income which otherwise would flow into consumption channels. Public investment may usefully be made in human and natural resources and in consumers' capital goods of a collective character designed to serve the physical, recreational and cultural needs of the community as a whole. But we cannot afford to be blind to the unmistakable fact that a solution along these lines raises serious problems of economic workability and political administration.

How far such a program, whether financed by taxation or by borrowing, can be carried out without adversely affecting the system of free enterprise is a problem with which economists, I predict, will have to wrestle in the future far more intensely than in the past. Can a rising public debt owned internally be serviced by a scheme of taxation which will not adversely affect the marginal return on new investment or the marginal cost of borrowing? Can any tax system, designed to increase the propensity to consume by means of a drastic change in income distribution, be devised which will not progressively encroach on private investment?[7]

As so often in economic life, we are confronted by a dilemma. Continued unemployment on a vast scale, resulting from inadequate private investment outlets, could be expected sooner or later to lead straight into an all-round regimented economy. But so also, by an indirect route and a slower process, might a greatly extended program of public expenditures. And from the standpoint of economic workability the question needs to be raised how far such a program can be carried out in a democratic society without raising the cost structure to a level which prevents full employment. Thus a challenge is presented to all those countries which have not as yet submitted to the yoke of political dictatorship. In one of our round tables we are discussing divergencies in the success of governmental spending in democratic countries and in totalitarian states. Totalitarian states have the great advantage that they can rigorously check the advance of costs, including wage rates, while engaging in an expansionist program of public investment. Democratic countries cannot in modern times escape from the influence exerted by organized groups upon the operation of the price system. From the standpoint of the workability of the system of free enterprise, there emerges the problem of sovereignty in democratic countries confronted in their internal economies with powerful groups—entrepreneurial and wage-earning—which have robbed the price system of that impersonal and non-political character idealized in the doctrine of laissez-faire. It remains still to be seen whether political democracy can in the end survive the disappearance of the automatic price system.

Thus we are confronted with various alternatives. On the one side, there is the proposal to risk a negative governmental policy in the expectation that the recuperative forces to which we have long been accustomed will, in the absence of political interference, reassert themselves. On the other side, there is the proposal to go forward under full steam with unrestrained governmental expansion until full employment has been reached. Those who have no doubts whatever about the correctness of their economic analyses will not hesitate to make a bold choice of policy. But others, impressed with the stubborn economic realities of a rapidly changing world, on the one side, and the frailties of human nature in its power to make the appropriate adaptation to change, on the other, will not be so sure, and may prefer to take a course that risks neither a negative policy nor a breakdown of collective management.

With respect to the permissible rôle of public expenditures, I should like to suggest that the problem might usefully be posed in terms of the national income. In 1929 our national income was about $80,000,000,000. Taking account of the prevailing lower level of prices, on the one side, and the additions to the labor force, on the other, we may perhaps set the income which should currently give us approximately full employment at about $80,000,000,000. At the bottom of the Great Depression the national income had fallen from $80,000,000,000 to $40,000,000,000. So drastic a decline in the national income we could not again afford to risk. The consequences for the vitality and workability of the economic system are too serious to contemplate. I suggest—the figures are only a rough approximation—that we cannot afford to let our income fall materially below $65,000,000,000, or say $60,000,000,000 as a minimum. A scale of net income-creating governmental expenditures adequate to prevent a fall in income below this level can, it seems to me, scarcely be questioned, and would currently, I believe, command the support of most economists. As the national income, however, approaches $70,000,000,000,

I suggest that the net income-creating governmental expenditures ought to be tapered off. As we approach this income level, the economic situation becomes increasingly explosive. Bottle-necks begin to appear. Costs rise. Labor aggressively demands wage increases. Rising costs lead to inventory speculation. We encounter the familiar vicious spiral of rising costs and rising prices with growing inefficiency. At this level the spending program becomes relatively ineffective as a means to raise the real income of the community. This danger point is clearly reached sooner in a democratic country than in a totalitarian state. At what precise point it is reached depends upon the degree of discipline and self-restraint which the various economic groups have achieved or can achieve under democratic institutions. What I am suggesting is that in the United States the upper limit of tolerance in terms of social and economic stresses and strains may be set at around $70,000,000,000. At the $60,000,000,000 income level we can afford to spend heavily to forestall any further decline.

The objection will almost certainly be raised that the argument which I have directed against continued governmental spending to the point of full employment, could equally well be directed against private investment, once the upper danger zone has been reached. I should doubt the validity of this criticism. If the government continues to pour out funds at a lavish rate, wage-earners and employers alike are prone to take the easy course which leads to higher costs and higher prices. But if reliance could not be placed upon a stream of purchasing power external to business itself, we could expect, I think, a more vigorous resistance to uneconomic cost-raising demands. Public spending is the easiest of all recovery methods, and therein lies its danger. If it is carried too far, we neglect to attack those specific maladjustments without the removal of which we cannot attain a workable cost-price structure, and therefore we fail to achieve the otherwise available flow of private investment.

There are no easy answers to the problems that confront us. And because this is true, economists will not perform their function if they fail to illuminate the rapidly shifting course of economic development, and through such neglect unwittingly contribute to a dangerous lag in adjustments to change. Equally they will not perform their function if they fail to disclose the possible dangers which lurk in the wake of vastly enlarged governmental activities. Choices indeed must be made, and scientific analysis and painstaking research can aid by exploring the probable consequences of alternative choices. The problems which I have raised offer a challenge to our profession. The great transition, incident to a rapid decline in population growth and its impact upon capital formation and the workability of a system of free enterprise, calls for high scientific adventure along all the fronts represented by the social science disciplines.*

Notes

*   [With the second edition of this volume, Professor Hansen has added the following postscript:

In essence, my stagnation thesis contends that the U.S. propensity to save outruns the inducement to invest. Vast governmental outlays induced partly by three wars, have indeed in large part filled the gap. Still, despite the greatly enlarged role of government, we averaged 4.7 per cent unemployment in 1947-1968 inclusive. No one can claim that the "self-sustaining economy" has proven its capacity to produce full employment.—*Ed.*]

1.   *Cf.* J. E. Meade and P. W. S. Andrews, "Summary of Replies to Questions on Effects of Interest Rates," *Oxford Econ. Papers*, no. 1; also J. Franklin Ebersole, "The Influence of Interest Rates upon Entrepreneurial Decisions in Business—A Case Study," *Harvard Bus. Rev.*, vol. xvii, pp. 35–39. The indirect effect on valuation is perhaps overlooked.

2.   Paul H. Douglas, *The Theory of Wages*, Macmillan, 1934, pp. 464–5.

3.   Gustav Cassel, *On Quantitative Thinking in Economics*, Oxford, 1935, chapter 6.

4.   J. M. Keynes, "Some Economic Consequences of a Declining Population," *Eugenics Review*, April, 1937.

5.   Carl Snyder, "Capital Supply and National Well-Being," *Am. Econ. Rev.*, June, 1936.

6.   *Debts and Recovery* 1929 *to* 1937, The Twentieth Century Fund, 1938, p. 230.

7.   Joseph J. Spengler, "Population Movements, Employment, and Income," *Southern Econ. Jour.*, Oct., 1938.

22

The Number of Members as Determining the Sociological Form of the Group

Georg Simmel

It will be conceded at the first glance, without hesitation, that the sociological structure of a group is essentially modified by the number of the individuals that are united in it. It is an everyday experience—yes, it is almost to be construed from the most general social-psychological presuppositions—that a group of a certain extent and beyond a certain stage in its increase of numbers must develop for its maintenance certain forms and organization which it did not previously need; and that, on the other hand, more restricted groups manifest qualities and reciprocal activities which, in the case of their numerical extension, inevitably disappear. A double significance attaches itself to the quantitative determination: first, the negative significance that certain forms which are necessary or possible from the contents or the conditions of life can come to realization only before or after a certain numerical extension of the elements; the positive significance that other forms are promoted directly through definite and purely quantitative modifications of the group. As a matter of course, these do not emerge in every case, but they depend upon other social circumstances in the group. The decisive matter, however, is that the forms in question never spring from these latter conditions alone, but are produced from them only through the accompanying numerical factor. Thus it may be demonstrated that quite or nearly communistic formations have up to the present day been possible only in relatively small circles, while they have always failed in large groups. The presumption of such socialistic groups—namely, justice in the distribution of effort and of enjoyment—can no doubt be established in a small group, and, what is at least quite as important, it can be observed and controlled by the individuals. What each does for the totality, and wherewith the totality rewards him, is in such cases close at hand, so that comparison and equalization easily occur. In a great group this practice is hindered, particularly by the unavoidable differentiation of persons within it, of their functions and of their claims. A very large number of people can constitute a unity only with decisive division of labor, not merely on the obvious grounds of economic technique, but because this alone produces that interpenetration and interdependence of persons which puts each through innumerable intermediaries in combination with each, and without which a widely extended group would break apart on every occasion. Consequently the more intimate the unity demanded in the same, the more exact must be the specialization of individuals, in order that the individuals may be the more immediately responsible to the whole, and the whole may be dependent upon the individuals. The communism of a great community would thus promote the sharpest differentiation of the personalities which would naturally extend over and beyond their labor, to their feeling and desiring. Hence a comparison of services with each other, of rewards with each other, and equilibration of the two, is infinitely difficult; but upon this the feasibility of approximate communism for small, and therefore undifferentiated, circles rests. What limits such circles, under advanced culture, by a sort of logical necessity, so to speak, to restricted numerical extent, is their dependence upon goods which under their peculiar productive conditions can never be furnished. So far as my knowledge goes, there is in present Europe only a single approximately socialistic organization, namely, the Familistère de Guise, a great iron foundry, founded by a disciple of Fourier in 1888, according to the principle of complete guardianship for every workman and his family, security of a minimum standard of living, of gratuitous care and education of the children, of collective production of the income. This society gave work in the last decade of the nineteenth century to 2,000 people, and has proved that it is capable of life. This is evidently the case, however, only because it is surrounded by a totality existing under entirely different conditions of life. From this environment the organization can cover the necessarily remaining gaps in the means of satisfaction which are left by its own production. For human needs cannot be so rationalized as is the case with production. A previously calculated, mechanically working life-system, in which every detail is regulated according to general principles, can be applied, to be sure, in a small circle which can draw from a greater one whatever it requires for the establishment of its internal equilibrium. But human needs appear to contain an accidental or incalculable element, and this fact permits their satisfaction only at the cost of carrying on parallel activities which produce countless irrational and unavailable by-products. A circle, therefore, which avoids this, and confines itself to complete responsibility and utility in its activities, must always remain minute, because it has need of a greater group in order to be reinforced with the requisite capacity for life.

Moreover, there are group-formations of the ecclesiastical sort which, from the very fact of their sociological structure, permit no application to large numbers; thus the sects of the Waldenses, Mennonites, and Herrnhuter. Where dogma forbids, for example, the oath, military service, occupation of civil offices; where quite personal matters, such as modes of earning a living and the division of the hours of the day, are subject to the regulation of the community; where a special type of dress separates the faithful from all others, and distinguishes them as belonging together; where the subjective experience of an immediate relationship to Jesus constitutes the principal solder of the community—in such cases, evidently, expansion into large circles would snap the bond of union, which consists largely in their exceptional and antithetical attitude toward larger bodies. At least in this sociological respect is the claim of these sects to represent primitive Christianity not unjustified; for precisely this early form of faith, manifesting a yet undifferentiated unity of dogma and form of life, was possible only in those small communities within a greater one which served them at once for supplying their external necessities, and also as an antithesis in contrast with which they were conscious of their peculiar nature. Consequently, the extension of Christianity to the whole state has necessarily changed completely its sociological character not less than its psychical content.

Moreover, that an aristocratic body can have but a relatively narrow compass is given in its very idea. But, besides this trivial consequence of the dominance over masses, there appears to be here also a numerical limitation, which, although in large extent variable, is yet in kind absolute. I mean by this that not only does a definite proportion exist, which would always permit that with increasing number of the ruled the ruling aristocracy would likewise increase *pro rata* and beyond any limit; but that there is an absolute limit beyond which the aristocratic group-form can no longer be maintained intact. This limit will be determined partly by external and partly by psychological conditions. An aristocratic group must be capable of survey by the individual member; each must be able to have a personal acquaintance with each; relationships of blood and marriage must ramify through the whole body, and must be traceable. If, therefore, the historical aristocracies, from Sparta to Venice, have a tendency to the utmost possible numerical limitation, this is not merely the egoistic disinclination to partition of control, but it is the instinct that the conditions of the life of an aristocracy can be fulfilled only with a not merely relative, but also absolute, restriction of the number of its elements. The unlimited right of primogeniture, which is of aristocratic nature, constitutes the means for such prevention of expansion; under its presumption alone was the ancient Theban law possible, that the number of landed estates should not be increased, and also the Corinthian, that the number of families must always remain the same. It is, therefore, entirely characteristic that Plato once, when he spoke of the ruling ojlivgoi, designated the same directly as the mh; pol;loiv.

When an aristocratic body gives place to the democratic centrifugal tendencies, which constitute the unavoidable trend of very large communities, it involves itself in such fatal contradictions of its own life-principle as, for example, the nobility of Poland before the division exemplified. In more fortunate cases such a contradiction resolves itself simply through transformation into the unified democratic social form; for example, the ancient free German community, with its complete personal equality of the members, was aristocratic throughout, and yet became in its continuation in the civic communities the source of democracy. If this is to be avoided, nothing remains except to draw, at a definite point of increase in numbers, a hard and fast line, and to oppose to all elements approaching from beyond this line, even though they were otherwise qualified for admission, the quantitative completeness of the structure. Frequently the aristocratic nature of the same appears only at this point; it becomes conscious for the first time in this closing up of itself against the demand for extension. Accordingly, the old constitution of the "gens" seems to have turned into a real aristocracy for the reason that a new population, alien to the members of the gens, pressed in upon them in too large numbers for gradual absorption into the associations of like strata. In opposition to this increase of the total group, the groups of gentes, which, by their very nature, were limited in numbers, could conduct themselves only as an aristocracy. In quite the same way the *Cölnische Schutzgilde Richerzeche* consisted originally of the totality of the free burghers. In the degree, however, in which the population increased, it became an aristocratic society which closed itself against all intruders. A group which constitutes a totality and, like the gens for instance, is in its whole nature quantitatively limited, will be able to preserve itself within a new and very extended totality only in the form of an aristocracy.

The tendency of political aristocracies leads, to be sure, as a rule, not to the maintenance of the existing status, but to decline in numbers and disappearance. Not merely on account of physiological causes, but small and narrowly exclusive groups are in general distinguished from greater ones in this that the very same destiny which strengthens and renews the latter destroys the former. A disastrous war, which ruins a petty city-state, may regenerate a great state. This occurs not merely from the quite evident external reasons, but because the relation of the reserves of power to the active energies in the two cases is different. Small and centripetally organized groups usually call out and employ to their full extent the energies available within them; in greater groups, on the other hand, much more energy, not merely absolutely but also relatively, remains in a latent condition. The demand of the whole does not seize upon every member constantly and completely, and it permits much power to remain unused which then, in extreme cases, may be mobilized and actualized. The decisive thing in this case is, as indicated, the social centripetalism, that is, the ratio in which the energies present in the society are harnessed for its purposes. When it, therefore, occurs that a lower and smaller group allows its members much autonomy and independence, the latter then often develop energies which are not used socially, and, therefore, in case the appeal to the common interests occurs, they represent a considerable available recourse. This was for a long time the case, for example, with the nobility of the Scotch highlands. Likewise, on the other hand, where dangers, which demand an unused quantity of social energy, are excluded by the circumstances, means of numerical limitation, which extend even beyond endogamy, may be quite appropriate. In the highlands of Thibet polyandry prevails and, as even the missionaries recognize, to the advantage of society; for the soil is there so unfruitful that a rapid increase of the population would produce the greatest misery. To prevent this, polyandry is an efficient means. When we hear that among the Bushmen, on account of the sterility of the soil, very often even families must separate, the rule that the families must limit themselves to numbers corresponding with the possibilities of food production appears to be precisely in the interest of their unity, and highly appropriate when this and its social significance are considered. The dangers of the quantitative limitation are provided against by the external conditions of the life of the group, and their consequences for its inner structure.

Where the small group absorbs the personalities in considerable measure into its unity, especially in political groups, it strives, precisely for the sake of its unity, for definiteness of status toward persons, material tasks, and other societies. The large group, with the number and variety of its elements, demands or tolerates such definiteness much less. The history of the Greek and of the Italian cities, as of the Swiss cantons, shows that small communities, in case they do not proceed to federation, habitually live in open or latent hostility to each other. Moreover, warfare and martial law are between them much more bitter and sharp, and especially more radical, than between great states. It is precisely that absence of organs, of reserves, of undefined and transitional elements, which makes modification and adaptation difficult for them, and, apart from their external conditions, forces them, on account of their fundamental sociological configuration, much oftener to confront the question, "To be or not to be?" . . .

In general we may, in a very essential degree, explain the structures which are peculiar to large communities, as such, from the fact that they produce with these structures a substitute for the personal and immediate cohesion which is peculiar to the smaller circles. In the case of the large group, the question is one of correlating centers which are channels and mediators of the reciprocal action of the elements, and which thus operate as independent bearers of the societary unity, after this is no longer produced by immediate relationship of person to person. For this purpose magistracies and representatives grow up, laws and symbols of the group-life, organizations and social generalizations. At this point I have only to emphasize their connection with the numerical point of view. They all occur purely and maturely, so far as the main point is concerned, only in large circles, *i.e.,* as the abstract form of group-dependence, whose concrete form can no longer exist after a certain extension of the community has been reached. Their utility, ramifying into a thousand social qualities, 2ests in the last analysis upon numerical presuppositions. The character of the superpersonal and objective with which such incorporations of the group-energies face the individual is derived directly from the *multiplicity* of the variously operative individual elements; for only through their multiplicity is the individual element in them paralyzed, and from the same cause the universal mounts to such a distance from the individual that it appears as something existing entirely by itself, not needing the individual, and possibly even antagonistic to the individual—somewhat as the *concept,* which, composed of singular and various phenomena of the common, is the higher above every one of these details, the more it includes; so that precisely the universal ideas which rule the greatest circumference of particulars—the abstractions with which metaphysics reckons—attain a life apart, whose norms and developments are often alien, or hostile, to those of the tangible particulars. The great group thus gains its unity— as it expresses itself in its organs and in its law, in its political ideas and in its ideals—only at the price of a wide distance of all those structures from the individual, his views and needs, which find immediate activity and consideration in the social life of a small circle. From this relation there arises the typical difficulty of organizations in which a series of minor combinations are included within a larger one; viz., the fact is that the situations can be readily seen, and treated with interest and care, only close at hand; while, on the contrary, only from the distance which the central position holds can a just and regular relation of all the details to each other be established. This is a discrepancy which, for example, always emerges in the treatment of poverty, in the organization of labor, and in educational administration. The relationships of person to person, which constitute the life-principle of smaller circles, are not easily compatible with the distance and coolness of the objective-abstract norms without which the great group cannot exist.

Note

1. Translated by A. W. Small.

Part 4

Natural Resources

23

The Coal Question

W. Stanley Jevons

The difficulty and cost of winning and working coal-mines form an aspect of the question that obviously contains the solution of the whole.

In a free industrial system, such as we are developing and assisting to spread, everything is a question of cost. We have heard of moral and physical impossibilities, but we ought to be aware that there are also *commercial impossibilities*. We must ask, in undertaking a work, not only whether it can be done, or is physically possible, but also whether it will pay to do it—whether it is *commercially possible*. The works of the two Brunels were, in a mechanical point of view, at least as successful and wonderful as those of the Stephensons; but, commercially speaking, they were disastrous failures, which no one would have undertaken had the consequences been foreseen. Commerce and industry cannot be carried on but by gain—by a return exceeding the outlay.

Now, in coal-mining, we must discriminate the physical and commercial possibilities. The second presupposes the first, but does not follow from it. The question is a twofold one:—Firstly, is it physically possible to drive our coal-mines to the depth of 4,000, 5,000, or 6,000 feet ? and, secondly, is it commercially possible when in other parts of the world coal is yet being worked in the light of day? The very existence of Britain, as a great nation, is bound up in these questions.

TABLE 1

Depth in feet	Increase of temperature of rock	Actual temperature of rock
50	0°	50°
1,000	14°	64°
2,000	28°	78°
3,000	42°	92°
4,000	56°	106°
5,000	71°	121°

Now I apprehend that there is not the least danger of our reaching any fixed limit of deep mining, where physical impossibility begins. In mines already 2,000 or 2,500 feet deep, there is no special difficulty felt in going deeper. But we must consider the matter a little, because the *Quarterly Review* has confidently asserted that 2,500 feet is the limit,[1] and Mr. Hull, after an express inquiry into the matter, thinks that 4,000 feet may be taken as the limit.[2] It has often been suggested that the increase of temperature of the earth's crust as we descend into it will prove an insuperable obstacle, and Mr. Hull and others have been inclined to hold that beyond a depth of 4,000 or 5,000 feet the temperature will entirely prevent further sinking.

The increase of temperature varies in different mines from one degree in 35 to one degree in 88 feet. The increase in the deep Monkwearmouth Pit was one degree for 60 feet; but the observations of Mr. Astley in the sinking of the Dukinfield Deep Pit showed an average increase of one degree in 83 feet, nearly the lowest rate known.[3] If with Mr. Hull we take one degree in 70 feet as a safe average rate of increase, we easily form the following table, starting from the depth of 50 feet from the surface, at which depth in this country an uniform temperature of about 50° Fahr. is found to exist. (See Tables 1 and 2.)

The air in mines, independently of the rock, is also warmer than at the surface, owing to its greater density; for just as in ascending a mountain the barometer falls and the air grows rare and cold, so in descending a mine the barometer rises and the air grows warmer. The barometer, roughly speaking, varies about an inch for every 1,000 feet of elevation, and the temperature about one degree for every 300 feet. On these data the following table is roughly calculated (as in Table 3).

TABLE 2

Date	Place	Depth in feet from surface	Temperature of rock	Average feet per degree
1880	Dukinfield Colliery	2,700	86.5°	68.4
1881	Ashton Moss Colliery	2,790	85.3°	72.8
1902	Abram Colliery, Wigan	2,700	96°	58.7
"	Agecroft Colliery, Manchester	2,940	95.5°	68.2
"	Rams Mine, Pendelton	3,483	100.5°	67.9
"	Sneyd Collieries, Burslem	2.625	87.5°	68.7
"	Harris Navigation, S. Wales.	2,295	77.5°	76
"	Dowlais Cardiff Colliery	2,590	74°	106
"	" " "	2,600	77°	94.5
"	Niddrie Collieries, Portobello	2,488	73.6°	103.3
"	" " "	2,623	74°	107.2
1904	Mons, Belgium	3,773	116.6°	55.9

If air, then, of the temperature of 50° at the surface descend 5,000 feet, it will acquire the temperature of 67°. The rocks at that depth will have the temperature of 121°, and will therefore warm the air as it circulates through the mine up to their own temperature. [The less active the circulation of air maintained in the mine the more nearly will the temperature of the air approach that of the neighbouring rocks.] The temperature of the air may be reduced by plentiful ventilation,[4] or by letting out in the mine air compressed and cooled at the surface, as is done in the new coal-cutting machines. Now, as men can work at temperatures exceeding 100°, we are not likely to encounter the physical limit of sinking on this account.

But the cost of sinking and working deep pits is quite another matter. The growing temperature will enervate, if it does not stop the labourers. Thus it is stated[5] that in one Cornish mine men work in an atmosphere varying from 110° to 120° Fahr. But then they work only for twenty minutes at a time, with nearly naked bodies, and cold water frequently thrown over them. They sometimes lose eight or ten pounds in weight during a day's work. Much increased ventilation will be a matter of expense and difficulty; the hardening[6] of the coal and rocks will render hewing more costly; creeps and subsidences of the strata will be unavoidable, and will crush a large portion of the coal or

TABLE 3

Depth in feet	Height of Barometer	Increase of temperature of air	Actual temperature of air
0	30°0	0°	50°
1,000	31°0	3°	53°
2,000	32°0	7°	57°
3,000	33°0	10°	60°
4,000	34°0	13°	63°
5,000	35°0	17°	67°

render it inaccessible; while explosions, fires, floods, and the hundred unforeseen accidents and disappointments to which mining is always subject, will lie as a burden on the whole enterprise, a risk which no assurance company will venture upon. In addition to these special difficulties, the whole capital and current expenditure of the mine naturally grows in a higher proportion than the depth. The sinking of the shaft becomes a long and costly matter; both the capital thus sunk has to be redeemed and interest upon it paid. The engine powers for raising water, coals, miners, etc., increase, and, beyond all, the careful ventilation and management of the mine render a large staff of mechanics, viewers, and attendants indispensable.

Much may be done by working larger areas from the same shaft; by forming consolidated companies for economical drainage; by perfecting machinery, and organizing labour to contend with the growing cost. But increased areas and distances of working, though comparatively diminishing the capital expense of the shafts and works above ground, will increase the current expenses of drainage, ventilation, and general maintenance. . . .

An account of the South Hetton Colliery establishment, a well-arranged mine, throws light on this subject. It is published in a little work of the *Traveller's Library*,[7] remarkable for the amount of information it contains on the subject of coal.

Of 529 men employed in or about the colliery, 140 only are hewers of coal, representing the productive power of the establishment. We may divide the staff as follows:—

Hewers of coal	140
Putters, screeners, &c.	227
Employed in administration and maintenance of mine	123
Boys, variously employed	39

The "putters," "screeners," and others, to the number of 227, are occupied in pushing the coal along the tramways from the hewer to the shaft; in raising it to the surface; screening it, and removing the stones; and, finally, loading it into the railway waggon or ship's hold. They represent, as it were, the trading part of the community, while the administration represents the government; consisting of a manager, viewers, engineers, clerks, and a surgeon, with a great number of joiners, sawyers, enginewrights, smiths, masons, carters, waggon-wrights, and common labourers, as well as ventilators, shifters, fore-men, and others of responsible duties underground; all occupied in keeping the mine, the ventilation, machinery, engines, and the works generally in repair.[8]

Now, if coal were quarried at the surface, and wheeled straight away, each hewer would scarcely require more than one subsidiary labourer. In a deep mine we find that nearly three subsidiary labourers are required, so that four only accomplish what two would do at the surface, to say nothing of the timber and other materials consumed, and the great capital sunk in the shafts engines, and works of the deep mine.

As mines become deeper and more extended, the system of management necessary to facilitate the working and diminish the risk of accidents, must become more and more complicated. The work is not of a nature to be made self-acting, and capable of execution by machinery. Even in the West Ardsley Colliery, belonging to the patentees of the coal-cutting machine, who naturally carry out its use to the utmost possible extent, this machine is found[9] to diminish the staff only *ten per cent.* The labour saved is only that of twenty-seven hewers, while other branches of the staff must be rather increased than diminished. So different, too, are the conditions of coal-mining, that in many collieries the use of coal-cutting machines is perhaps impracticable.

The deeper a mine the more fiery it in general becomes. Carburet-ted gas, distilled from the coal in the course of geological ages, lies pent up in the fissures at these profound depths, and is ever liable to blow off and endanger the lives of hundreds of persons. It was supposed that George Stephenson and Sir H. Davy had discovered a true safety lamp. But, in truth, this very ingenious invention is like the compass that Sir Thomas More describes in his *Utopia* as given to a distant people. It gave them such confidence in navigation that they were "farther from care than danger."

No lamp has been made, or, perhaps, can be made, that will prevent accidents when a feeder of gas is tapped, or a careless miner opens his lamp, or a drop of water cracks a heated glass, or a boy stumbles and breaks his lamp. The miner's lamp, in fact, is never a safety lamp, except when carefully used in a perfectly ventilated mine. Long experience shows that perfect ventilation is the only sure safeguard against explosion. But it is no easy matter to ventilate near a hundred miles of levels, inclines, stalls, and goaves in a fiery mine.

The amount of drainage required in deepening our mines is another point of the greatest importance. The coal-measures themselves, containing many beds of clay and shale, are dry enough in general, except where interrupted by faults which allow the water to penetrate. Thus, the lower parts of deep mines will in general be dry enough, but the passage through the overlying Permian and New Red Sandstone beds may often be extremely costly, or almost impossible. . . .

In the continuous working of pits, even where "tubbing" is used to keep the water out of the shaft as much as possible, the quantity of water is not unusually seven or eight times as great as that of the coal raised.[14] At the Friar's Goose Colliery, near Gateshead, 6,000 tons of water are raised from the mine every day, about twenty times as much as the weight of the coal extracted. In some, such as Percy Main and Wylam collieries, it reaches thirty times the weight of the coal.

Now, when it becomes necessary to sink, not only through the Magnesian Limestone, but through the New Red Sandstone, in order to reach new supplies of coal, may not the water be found overpowering? . . .

A question of secondary importance concerns the limit of thinness of workable coal seams. This is, of course, a question of the cost of mining. It is found that, at the present price of coal, it is not profitable to work seams of less than 18 or 24 inches thickness.[16] The reason is obvious. In working a four-foot seam little rock has to be mined, since the spaces from which the coal has been removed furnish the levels and communications of the mine. In working a two-foot seam, however, large quantities of rock have to be removed in addition to the coal, and while the cost is hardly less than in a four-foot seam, the produce of coal is only one half. A one-foot seam, again, would be worked at a very great cost, and would furnish less than one-fourth of the produce of a four-foot seam. Either the larger seam must yield extraordinary profits, or else the thinner seam cannot be worked.

In estimates of existing coal, 24 or 18 inches is taken as the limit of workable seams[17]; how will this limit be affected by probable changes in the conditions of coal-mining? A considerable advance in the price of coal will, of course, enable thinner seams to be worked with profit. Thus, to some extent, the rise of prices will be slackened. The higher the price rises, the more thoroughly will the coal-measures be worked, and the more coal becomes workable. As, however, the high price of coal constitutes the evil of exhaustion, the dreaded results are only somewhat mitigated, not prevented. And it would be wholly erroneous to suppose that when once the thicker seams of a coal district have been worked out, we can readily, at a future time, work out the thinner seams, when the increased price of coal warrants it. For it must be observed, that a very large part of the cost of mining consists in the cost of draining, ventilation, and maintenance of the shaft, and works at the bank, which we may call the general mining expenses. Now, when these expenses are undertaken for the purpose of working a thick and valuable seam, it is often possible to work thin seams of less than 24 inches without any considerable increase in the general expenses. In short, the thick seam pays the general expenses of the mine as well as its own cost of hewing, while it is sufficient if the thin seam leaves a small profit on the expenses of hewing only. But the price of coal must rise in a very extreme degree, that an unworked thin seam should, at a future time, pay the general costs of drainage, ventilation, and maintenance, as well as the cost of hewing.

The same is true of immense masses of coal left underground during the former working of mines, as small or crushed coal, as pillars and barriers, or as outlying portions rendered difficult to mine by faults, or other mining troubles. If such portions of coal could not pay for removal when the mine was in full working efficiency, they cannot pay the whole costs of restoring and maintaining the mine in a workable condition, not at least until the price of coal has risen manifold.

All, then, that we can hope from thin seams, or abandoned coal, *is a retardation of the rise of price after a considerable rise has already taken place. T*his will hardly prevent the evils apprehended from exhaustion.

Nor will the use of the coal-cutting machine much affect this question. By reducing the cost of hewing and the waste of coal in the "kirving," or cut made by the hewer, it will, undoubtedly, to some extent, allow thinner seams to be worked. At the same time, it will not affect the cost of removing large masses of profitless rock, which is essential in working thin seams, nor the general cost of the maintenance of the mine. If seams of 18 inches are now occasionally workable, the coal-cutting machine may reduce the limit a few inches; but it is evident that seams of less than 12 inches could never be worked while the price of coal remained at all tolerable.[18]

Coal-mining is a fair fight with difficulties, and just as the balance inclines between the difficulties and the powers we possess to overcome them, will the cost of coal and the prospects of this country oscillate. What we can do to cheapen extraction, indeed, is chiefly effected by turning the powers of coal against itself, by multiplying steam power to pump and wind, and cut and draw the coal. But then the greater part of the work within the colliery is of a kind that cannot be executed by machinery, just as the building of houses, or the digging of holes, never has been, and scarcely can be, done wholly by machinery.

But be the difficulties what they may, we would have ingenuity and energy enough to overcome them, were the question one of a simple absolute amount of difficulty. But in reality we must consider our mines not by themselves, but in comparison with those of other countries. Our main branches of iron industry grew up at places like Wednesbury, in South Staffordshire, "where there being but little earth lying over the measure of coal, the workmen rid off the earth and dig the coal under their feet, and carry it out in wheelbarrows, there being no need for windlass, rope, or corf."[19]

Our industry will certainly last and grow until our mines are commonly sunk 2,000 or 3,000, or even 4,000 feet deep. But when this time comes, the States of North America will still be working coal in the light of day, quarrying it in the banks of the Ohio, and running it down into boats alongside. The question is, *how soon will our mines approach the limit of commercial possibility, and fail to secure us any longer that manufacturing supremacy on which we are learning to be wholly dependent?*

Notes

1. Vol. cx., p. 329.
2. *Coal-fields,* etc., 2nd ed., p. 219. About 1845 the greatest depth reached was 1,794 feet at Monkwearmouth (R. C. Taylor, *Statistics of Coal*). In 1859 a depth of 2,151 feet was reached at Dukinfield. The 1871 Commission had evidence as to three pits of over 2,000 feet in depth, the deepest at that time being the Rose

Bridge Colliery, Wigan, 2,376 feet. The recent Commission received evidence as to several pits of about 2,500 feet in depth, and a few about 3,000 feet. The deepest reported was that at Pendleton, 3,483 feet deep. All the coal won from this pit in 1902 was from depths exceeding 3,000 feet (cf. *First Report,* vol. ii, p. 16). Evidence relating to a pit near Mons, Belgium, 3,773 feet deep, was received (cf. *Final Report, p*art x, p. 354).

3. The following summary of more recent observations shows the temperatures observed in some of the deeper coal pits (cf. *First Report of Commission on Coal Supplies, especially Professor Dixon's evidence, pp. 114–6).*

   In a deep boring at Schladebach, temperatures were observed to a depth of 5,630 feet in 1889. The average rate of increase was one degree in 67•1 feet. Temperatures for 4,000 feet and 5,000 feet were 108•8° and 124 2°.

   The average temperature gradient accepted by the Argyll Commission was one degree in 60 feet, which has been adopted by Mr. Hull since the date of that Commission's report. The Allerton Commission states that one degree in rather less than 64 feet is indicated. The local geological conditions cause considerable variations from the average, and the rate at which the temperature increases is not uniform at all depths. The temperature in the Rams mine increased, at the greater depths, at about one degree in 661/2 feet, which would give 108•3° at 4,000 feet. The figures of the table in the text may therefore be retained as the general basis of the argument.

4. The temperature of the air in the working places in the Rams mine was but 93•5° where the rock had a temperature of 100•5°. In the deep Belgian colliery, the air temperature was 103°, or 13•6° less than that of the rock. The air current had a velocity of 6 to 9 feet per second in this case. The maintenance of an air temperature 6° or 7° below that of the strata is recognized as quite feasible.

5. *Report of Royal Commission on Mines,* 1864.

   The effect of high temperatures on the efficiency of workmen depends largely on the amount of moisture present in the air. Deep pits are generally dry as compared with pits of moderate depth. The enervating effect of the heat is thus less than might otherwise be expected, since dry heat is less destructive of working energy than moist heat. It is stated that the miners work a full nine-hour shift in the deep Belgian pit.

   An inquiry into the case referred to in the text was made for the Argyll Commission by Dr. J. Burdon Sanderson. He reported that "no man remained for more than fifteen minutes in the heat at one time, and not always so long. . . . Each miner, after taking his turn in the heat, retreated into the comparatively cold air behind, where the temperature was about 81°."

6. On this point the evidence before the recent Coal Commission points to a conclusion differing somewhat from that expressed in the text. The Report thus summarizes the information received:—

   "The increase of pressure with depth has some advantages as well as disadvantages; it may increase the percentage of small coal, and the cost of maintaining the roadways and of timbering, but it assists the working of the coal" (*Final Report,* § 19). Thus, though the particular point of the hardening of the coal with depth is not supported, the general argument as to increase of cost is fully confirmed.

7. *Our Coal and Our Coal-pits.* The Traveller's Library, vol. 23. London: 1856.

8. Similar facts for a recent date are represented in the following return of mine workers in all the anthracite collieries in the State of Pennsylvania during 1901.

Inside foremen, or mine bosses	539
Fire bosses	830
Miners	37,804
Miners' labourers	26,268
Drivers and runners	10,894
Door boys and helpers	3,148
All other employees	18,951
Total inside	98,434
Superintendents, book-keepers, and clerks	804
Outside foremen	379
Blacksmiths and carpenters	2,331
Engineers and firemen	4,615
Slate pickers	19,564
All other employees	21,524
Total outside	49,217
Total inside and outside	147,651

As many as 108 different classes of labour are mentioned as employed by one mining company (cf. *Bulletin of The U.S. Department of Labour,* May, 1903, pp. 455 and 478).

9. Prof. H. D. Rogers, in *Good Words,* April, 1864, p. 338.

The improvement of coal-cutting machines has greatly increased the saving of labour which they effect over that attained when Jevons wrote. Mr. W. E. Garforth, of Normanton, stated in evidence before the Allerton Commission that the use of machines enabled 280 men to get as much coal as would need 384 miners by hand-work in the Silkstone seam (4 feet thick, depth 960 feet); and that 233 men got 900 tons daily in the Diamond seam ($3^{1}/_{4}$ feet thick, depth 1,500 feet), an amount which would need 400 men at handwork. Of the numbers mentioned, 60 per cent. were colliers and fillers, the remainder being engaged in other work directly in connection with the winning of the coal. Haulage and road repairs are not covered by any of the numbers (*First Report,* vol. ii. p. 110).

The advantage of coal-cutting machines has been found in Great Britain to be greatest in working thin seams. In adding to the safety of the miners, and to the proportion of large coal secured, further advantage from their use is found.

10. *Trans. of the North of England Institute of Mining Engineers, vol. v.*

11. *Brit. Assoc. Report,* 1863, pp. 726, 727.

12. *Our Coal and our Coal Pits, p.* 113.

13. *Our Coal and our Coal Pits, p.* 115.

14. Sir James Joicey stated in evidence before the recent Commission that, in the pits with which he was connected, the coal raised was about 5,000,000 tons yearly, and 15,000,000 tons of water were pumped (*Final Report,* part x, p. 146). Mr. H. Mungall, speaking of some Lothian collieries, stated that as much as 40 per cent. of the total output of coal was consumed in pumping. The percentage was reduced to 12 by increasing the output. In the Fifeshire Coal Company's colliery, 2,250,000 tons of coal per annum was raised, and ten tons of water pumped for each ton of coal raised (*loc. cit.,* pp. 212, 213, 216). Mr. J. Gemmell stated that in Scotland "occasionally you will find that the quantity of water pumped is 20 to 30 times as much as the coal drawn" (*First Report,* vol, ii. p. 150). In South Staffordshire, it was stated that, under the general drainage scheme, 26 or 27 tons of water have

been pumped for every ton of coal won for the last twenty years (*Final Report,* part x, p. 219).

15. *Manchester Memoirs,* 3rd series, 1861-2. Vol. ii, pp. 256, 257.

16. Cf. *ante,* p. 42, footnote.

17. The estimate of resources prepared for the Coal Commission of 1871 included all seams of not less than one foot in thickness. Some of the Committees charged with preparing district reports distinguished between the contents of seams of different thicknesses, while others omitted to separate the totals into such classes. The estimates of the later Commission generally distinguish between the resources of seams 12 to 15 inches, 15 to 18 inches, 18 to 24 inches, and over 24 inches in thickness. They note that 79•3 per cent. of the available coal estimated to exist at depths less than 4,000 feet in proved coal-fields is contained in seams of 2 feet thick and upwards, and 91•6 per cent. in seams of 18 inches and upwards, so far as the distinction can be made. Only a little over 4 per cent. of the total reported was not separated according to thickness of seams. As to actual current practice, it was given in evidence that about 17•7 per cent. of the output of 1900 in Great Britain came from seams 3 feet and under in thickness. In East Lancashire, of a total of about 10,000,000 tons, about 3,000,000 tons were from seams not exceeding 3 feet in thickness, about 860,000 tons being from seams of 2 feet and less, and 290,000 tons from seams not over 18 inches thick. Seams less than a foot thick contributed only 1 5,000 tons (*First Report,* vol. ii, pp. 25-6).

18. It is for the purpose of supplying special local markets that most thin seams which are not worked in conjunction with other seams are exploited: they are workable "where there is little or no competition with thicker seams" (cf. *Final Report of Commission on Coal Supplies,* § 28). See also footnote p. 67, *ante.*

19. Dr. Plot's *Natural History of Staffordshire,* quoted in the *History of Wednesbury,* p. 101.

24

The Economic Consequences
of the Peace

John Maynard Keynes

Europe before the War

Before 1870 different parts of the small continent of Europe had specialized in their own products; but, taken as a whole, it was substantially self-subsistent. And its population was adjusted to this state of affairs.

After 1870 there was developed on a large scale an unprecedented situation, and the economic condition of Europe became during the next fifty years unstable and peculiar. The pressure of population on food, which had already been balanced by the accessibility of supplies from America, became for the first time in recorded history definitely reversed. As numbers increased, food was actually easier to secure. Larger proportional returns from an increasing scale of production became true of agriculture as well as industry. With the growth of the European population there were more emigrants on the one hand to till the soil of the new countries, and, on the other, more workmen were available in Europe to prepare the industrial products and capital goods which were to maintain the emigrant populations in their new homes, and to build the railways and ships which were to make accessible to Europe food and raw products from distant sources. Up to about 1900 a unit of labor applied to industry yielded year by year a purchasing power over an increasing quantity of food. It is possible that about the year 1900 this process began to be reversed, and a diminishing yield of Nature to man's effort was beginning to reassert itself. But the tendency of cereals to rise in real cost was balanced by other improvements; and—one of many novelties—the resources of tropical Africa then for the first time came into large employ, and a great traffic in oil-seeds began to bring to the table of Europe in a new and cheaper form one of the essential foodstuffs of mankind. In this economic Eldorado, in this economic Utopia, as the earlier economists would have deemed it, most of us were brought up.

That happy age lost sight of a view of the world which filled with deep-seated melancholy the founders of our Political Economy. Before the eighteenth century mankind entertained no false hopes. To lay the illusions which grew popular at that age's latter end, Malthus disclosed a Devil. For half a century all serious economical writings held that Devil in clear prospect. For the next half century he was chained up and out of sight. Now perhaps we have loosed him again.

What an extraordinary episode in the economic progress of man that age was which came to an end in August, 1914! The greater part of the population, it is true, worked hard and lived at a low standard of comfort, yet were, to all appearances, reasonably contented with this lot. But escape was possible, for any man of capacity or character at all exceeding the average, into the middle and upper classes, for whom life offered, at a low cost and with the least trouble, conveniences, comforts, and amenities beyond the compass of the richest and most powerful monarchs of other ages. The inhabitant of London could order by telephone, sipping his morning tea in bed, the various products of the whole earth, in such quantity as he might see fit, and reasonably expect their early delivery upon his doorstep; he could at the same moment and by the same means adventure his wealth in the natural resources and new enterprises of any quarter of the world, and share, without exertion or even trouble, in their prospective fruits and advantages; or he could decide to couple the security of his fortunes with the good faith of the townspeople of any substantial municipality in any continent that fancy or information might recommend. He could secure forthwith, if he wished it, cheap and comfortable means of transit to any country or climate without passport or other formality, could despatch his servant to the neighboring office of a bank for such supply of the precious metals as might seem convenient, and could then proceed abroad to foreign quarters, without knowledge of their religion, language, or customs, bearing coined wealth upon his person, and would consider himself greatly aggrieved and much surprised at the least interference. But, most important of all, he regarded this state of affairs as normal, certain, and permanent, except in the direction of further improvement, and any deviation from it as aberrant, scandalous, and avoidable. The projects and politics of militarism and imperialism, of racial and cultural rivalries, of monopolies, restrictions, and exclusion, which were to play the serpent to this paradise, were little more than the amusements of his daily newspaper, and appeared to exercise almost no influence at all on the ordinary course of social and economic life, the internationalization of which was nearly complete in practice.

It will assist us to appreciate the character and consequences of the Peace which we have imposed on our enemies, if I elucidate a little further some of the chief unstable elements, already present when war broke out, in the economic life of Europe.

* * *

European Russia increased her population in a degree even greater than Germany—from less than 100,000,000 in 1890 to about 150,000,000 at the outbreak of war;[1] and in the year immediately preceding 1914 the excess of births over deaths in Russia as a whole was at the prodigious rate of two millions per annum. This inordinate growth in the population of Russia, which has not been widely noticed in England, has been nevertheless one of the most significant facts of recent years.

The great events of history are often due to secular changes in the growth of population and other fundamental economic causes, which, escaping by their gradual character the notice of contemporary observers, are attributed to the follies of statesmen or the fanaticism of atheists. Thus the extraordinary occurrences of the past two years in Russia, that vast upheaval of Society, which has overturned what seemed most stable—religion, the basis of property, the ownership of land, as well as forms of government and the hierarchy of classes—may owe more to the deep influences of expanding numbers than to Lenin or to Nicholas; and the disruptive powers of excessive national fecundity may have played a greater part in bursting the bonds of convention than either the power of ideas or the errors of autocracy.

* * *

The Relation of the Old World to the New

The accumulative habits of Europe before the war were the necessary condition of the greatest of the external factors which maintained
the European equipoise.

Of the surplus capital goods accumulated by Europe a substantial
part was exported abroad, where its investment made possible the
development of the new resources of food, materials, and transport,
and at the same time enabled the Old World to stake out a claim in the
natural wealth and virgin potentialities of the New. This last factor
came to be of the vastest importance. The Old World employed with
an immense prudence the annual tribute it was thus entitled to draw.
The benefit of cheap and abundant supplies, resulting from the new
developments which its surplus capital had made possible, was, it is
true, enjoyed and not postponed. But the greater part of the money
interest accruing on these foreign investments was reinvested and allowed to accumulate, as a reserve (it was then hoped) against the less
happy day when the industrial labor of Europe could no longer purchase on such easy terms the produce of other continents, and when
the due balance would be threatened between its historical civilizations and the multiplying races of other climates and environments.
Thus the whole of the European races tended to benefit alike from the
development of new resources whether they pursued their culture at
home or adventured it abroad.

Even before the war, however, the equilibrium thus established between old civilizations and new resources was being threatened. The
prosperity of Europe was based on the facts that, owing to the large
exportable surplus of foodstuffs in America, she was able to purchase
food at a cheap rate measured in terms of the labor required to produce
her own exports, and that, as a result of her previous investments of
capital, she was entitled to a substantial amount annually without any
payment in return at all. The second of these factors then seemed out
of danger, but, as a result of the growth of population overseas, chiefly
in the United States, the first was not so secure.

When first the virgin soils of America came into bearing, the proportions of the population of those continents themselves, and consequently of their own local requirements, to those of Europe were very
small. As lately as 1890 Europe had a population three times that of
North and South America added together. But by 1914 the domestic

requirements of the United States for wheat were approaching their production, and the date was evidently near when there would be an exportable surplus only in years of exceptionally favorable harvest. Indeed, the present domestic requirements of the United States are estimated at more than ninety per cent of the average yield of the five years 1909–1913.[2] At that time, however, the tendency towards stringency was showing itself, not so much in a lack of abundance as in a steady increase of real cost. That is to say, taking the world as a whole, there was no deficiency of wheat, but in order to call forth an adequate supply it was necessary to offer a higher real price. The most favorable factor in the situation was to be found in the extent to which Central and Western Europe was being fed from the exportable surplus of Russia and Roumania.

In short, Europe's claim on the resources of the New World was becoming precarious; the law of diminishing returns was at last reasserting itself, and was making it necessary year by year for Europe to offer a greater quantity of other commodities to obtain the same amount of bread; and Europe, therefore, could by no means afford the disorganization of any of her principal sources of supply.

Much else might be said in an attempt to portray the economic peculiarities of the Europe of 1914. I have selected for emphasis the three or four greatest factors of instability,—the instability of an excessive population dependent for its livelihood on a complicated and artificial organization, the psychological instability of the laboring and capitalist classes, and the instability of Europe's claim, coupled with the completeness of her dependence, on the food supplies of the New World.

The war had so shaken this system as to endanger the life of Europe altogether. A great part of the Continent was sick and dying; its population was greatly in excess of the numbers for which a livelihood was available; its organization was destroyed, its transport system ruptured, and its food supplies terribly impaired.

It was the task of the Peace Conference to honor engagements and to satisfy justice; but not less to re-establish life and to heal wounds. These tasks were dictated as much by prudence as by the magnanimity which the wisdom of antiquity approved in victors. We will examine in the following chapters the actual character of the Peace.

Notes

1. Including Poland and Finland, but excluding Siberia, Central Asia, and the Caucasus.
2. Even since 1914 the population of the United States has increased by seven or eight millions. As their annual consumption of wheat per head is not less than 6 bushels, the pre-war scale of production in the United States would only show a substantial surplus over present domestic requirements in about one year out of five. We have been saved for the moment by the great harvests of 1918 and 1919, which have been called forth by Mr. Hoover's guaranteed price. But the United States can hardly be expected to continue indefinitely to raise by a substantial figure the cost of living in its own country, in order to provide wheat for a Europe which cannot pay for it.

25

The Isolated State

Johann Heinrich von Thünen

The Role of Population Density

The question: How . . . does the denser or sparser population of the various districts affect the distribution of the country towns as regards their size and distance from each other?, brings me to the following problems, which have not yet been discussed.

1. What is the effect on land rent of the distance of a farm from the small country town whence it buys its recurrent needs?
2. What is the effect of population density on farming costs?

Suppose now:

1. that the advantages of association in trades and industries allow of no town with a population of less than 2000 souls;
2. that 1500 people per square mile are employed in agriculture in the section of the ring of the improved system nearest to the Town, but only 500 per square mile at the edge of the cultivated plain;
3. that a town of 2000 people is required for every 10,000 employed on the land;
4. that the supply region of each town, that is, the district buying its necessities from the town, forms a square. Hence the region of a town in district A is equal to 10,000/1800, or 5·55 square miles, and in B, the remoter district, it is 10,000/600, or 16·66 square miles.[1] In district A,

211

the distance between the towns comes to $\sqrt{(5·55)}$, or 2·36 miles; in district B to $\sqrt{(16·66)}$, or 4·08 miles.

A farm lying halfway between two towns is distant from either town,

in district A 2·36/2 = 1·18 miles
in district B 4·08/2 = 2·04 miles

Difference   0·86 miles

There are two possibilities in this situation.

1. All agricultural work is performed with the same thoroughness in both regions, and in both the people employed in farming enjoy the same comforts and conveniences.
2. In both regions the same amount of money is spent on the maintenance of the buildings and equipment, the labourers' keep, the children's education, and medical care.

In B, the following, amongst other services, will be more expensive than in A.

1. If the farm has to send a messenger to the town twice a week to fetch the recurrent requirements, the farm lying centrally between two towns in district B will have to pay its messenger a wage which is higher by the extra distance of 1·72 miles (2 x 0·86) than the wage the farm in district A need pay its messenger.
2. The craftsmen from the towns who work on the farms have to make a longer journey, for which they must be remunerated.
3. Higher fees have to remunerate the doctor who is called out to attend the sick for the greater expense of his journey and the additional time loss.

In B, the buildings and equipment will be in a worse state of repair, the workers will live less comfortably, and in particular the doctor will be summoned to attend only the more serious cases.

The effect of sparse population on the rural areas in region B as compared with region A

This is particularly well illustrated in religious instruction and in the schooling of the children. If 150 people live on a farm one-tenth of a square mile in district A, but only 50 on one of equivalent size in district B, and in both the schooling is equally good, then education on the farm in B will be three times as expensive per head as in A. The same applies to the preacher's salary, and so on.

If the costs per head of religious and school instruction are to be the same in both regions, three farms must in B combine to maintain one school; in the bad road and weather conditions of winter the children will have to walk across the fields to go to school, which is liable to affect their health, and certain to reduce attendance.

If the densely populated district has one church and one preacher to the square mile, and the costs per head are to be the same in the densely and the sparsely populated district, the latter will be able to afford only one church and preacher to every three square miles. This makes it much more inconvenient to go to church and reduces attendance; it means, moreover, that the minister has a far more difficult task and will not be able to perform his duties, particularly the supervision of the schools, as efficiently as a minister in district A.

What happens in practice?

Neither tendency will probably be fully realised, and their conflict will give rise to a compromise situation.

It would be interesting to discover what principles—if rational choices may be assumed—decide this process in reality; though the matter contains far too many difficulties for me to undertake the task.

I can state, though, that here too, immediate material interest is likely to be the guiding principle. People will put up with a broken window pane if the repair seems comparatively too expensive; and in a situation resembling that of region B they will probably accept a less comfortable mode of life, inferior dress and education than are enjoyed by people in a situation akin to that of A; but if the day labourer's wage expressed in rye is everywhere the same, they will probably eat rather better food, in particular a greater quantity of meat.[2]

Human nature will be torn between different appetites, and people will weigh up and compare the various pleasures they may purchase.

If one particular non-essential article becomes too costly, we make do with less of it and spend the money saved on something that seems to bring us relatively greater satisfaction. But the pleasure and enjoyment of life as a whole is the object and control of human action. Different peoples, at different stages of prosperity and development, will necessarily have differing valuations for the goods of life: for in this already every individual human being acts according to the wildest whim.

But it is impossible to deny that education and learning belong to a class of goods or pleasures the consumption of which is restricted or ceases when they become too costly and conflict with other pleasures, such as for instance the possession of decent clothes. And since we have seen that the education of the common man becomes progressively more difficult and costly the sparser is the population, we arrive at the painful conclusion that even within the restricted confines of the Isolated State, the level of education and intelligence will differ in the different districts. How much more so must this be true then of the vast spaces of our globe!

This explains why the natives of thinly peopled regions so often are primitive and savage.

North America is here an honourable exception. But it is a country inhabited by immigrants, who bring with them a respect for knowledge and education impossible for a people that is working itself out of a state of barbarism. Besides, the ease with which the settler may make a living in America does much to preserve and spread this attitude to learning.

*　*　*

Let us see now whether the provincial towns will all be of the same size in the Isolated State. It seems likely that in this matter also, diverging tendencies will yield a compromise; for the advantages of association grow with the increasing size of towns, whereas the increasing distance between the towns, a corollary of their growth in size, is a drawback for the country. In all probability the provincial towns near the capital will not be at a regular distance of 4·08 miles from each other, and their population will not be limited to 2000; they will be closer to each other, and also larger.

Nearer the capital, their larger size, together with the increasingly busy traffic along the roads, will make the provincial towns progressively more suitable as industrial centres; and the industries will in turn contribute to the growth of these towns.

It is worth noting that railway construction will rob of all their force the arguments against the development of the capital, and will strengthen those in favour of such growth.

Thus we may say with certainty that railways will make an important contribution to the development of the large towns, and that, *but for the fact that railways will promote also the prosperity of the rural districts surrounding the provincial towns*, the latter would decay in consequence.

Notes

1. This is evidently a slip. Thünen must have thought that he had written 1800 and 600 two paragraphs above, instead of 1500 and 500.
2. Because they will be able to buy meat at net farm price, without added transport costs. They are worse off in relation to town-produced products but better off in relation to other farm products.

Part 5

The Determinants
of Population Growth
and Density

26

An Essay on the Principle of Population as it Affects the Future Improvement of Society (First Edition)

Thomas R. Malthus

It is said that early marriages very generally prevail through all the ranks of the Chinese. Yet Dr. Adam Smith supposes that population in China is stationary. These two circumstances appear to be irreconcilable. It certainly seems very little probable that the population of China is fast increasing. Every acre of land has been so long in cultivation that we can hardly conceive there is any great yearly addition to the average produce. The fact, perhaps, of the universality of early marriages may not be sufficiently ascertained. If it be supposed true, the only way of accounting for the difficulty, with our present knowledge of the subject, appears to be that the redundant population, necessarily occasioned by the prevalence of early marriages, must be repressed by occasional famines, and by the custom of exposing children, which, in times of distress, is probably more frequent than is ever acknowledged to Europeans. Relative to this barbarous practice, it is difficult to avoid remarking, that there cannot be a stronger proof of the distresses that have been felt by mankind for want of food, than the existence of a custom that thus violates the most natural principle of the human heart. It appears to have been very general among ancient nations, and certainly tended rather to increase population.

In examining the principal states of modern Europe, we shall find that though they have increased very considerably in population since they were nations of shepherds, yet that at present, their progress is but slow, and instead of doubling their numbers every twenty-five years they require three or four hundred years, or more for that purpose. Some, indeed, may be absolutely stationary, and others even retrograde. The cause of this slow progress in population cannot be traced to a decay of the passion between the sexes. We have sufficient reason to think that this natural propensity exists still in undiminished vigour. Why then do not its effects appear in a rapid increase of the human species? An intimate view of the state of society in any one country in Europe, which may serve equally for all, will enable us to answer this question, and to say that a foresight of the difficulties attending the rearing of a family acts as a preventative check, and the actual distresses of some of the lower classes, by which they are disabled from giving the proper food and attention to their children, acts as a positive check to the natural increase of population.

England, as one of the most flourishing states of Europe, may be fairly taken for an example, and the observations made will apply with but little variation to any other country where the population increases slowly.

The preventive check appears to operate in some degree through all the ranks of society in England. . . . [T]he preventive check to population in this country operates, though with varied force, through all the classes of the community. The same observation will hold true with regard to all old states. The effects, indeed, of these restraints upon marriage are but too conspicuous in the consequent vices that are produced in almost every part of the world, vices, that are continually involving both sexes in inextricable unhappiness.

*   *   *

The positive check to population by which I mean the check that represses an increase which is already begun, is confined chiefly, though not perhaps solely, to the lowest orders of society. This check is not so obvious to common view as the other I have mentioned, and, to prove distinctly the force and extent of its operation would require, perhaps, more data than we are in possession of. But I believe it has been very generally remarked by those who have attended to bills of mortality that of the number of children who die annually, much too great a proportion belongs to those who may be supposed unable to give their offspring proper food and attention, exposed as they are occasionally to severe distress and confined, perhaps, to unwholesome habitations and hard labour.

27

An Essay on the Principle of Population, or A View of Its Past and Present Effects on Human Happiness (Second Edition)

Thomas R. Malthus

The fundamental cause of the low state of population in Turkey, compared with its extent of territory, is undoubtedly the nature of the government. Its tyranny, its feebleness, its bad laws and worse administration of them, together with the consequent insecurity of property, throw such obstacles in the way of agriculture that the means of subsistence are necessarily decreasing yearly, and with them, of course, the number of people. . . .

To complete the ruin of agriculture, a maximum is in many cases established, and the peasants are obliged to furnish the towns with corn at a fixed price. It is a maxim of Turkish policy, originating in the feebleness of the government and the fear of popular tumults, to keep the price of corn low in all the considerable towns. In the case of failure in the harvest, every person who possesses any corn is obliged to sell it at the price fixed, under pain of death; and if there be none in the neighbourhood, other districts are ransacked for it. When Constantinople is in want of provisions, ten provinces are perhaps famished for a supply. At Damascus, during the scarcity in 1784, the people paid only one penny farthing a pound for their bread, while the peasants in the villages were absolutely dying with hunger.

The effect of such a system of government on agriculture need not be insisted upon. The causes of the decreasing means of subsistence are but too obvious; and the checks, which keep the population down to the level of these decreasing resources, may be traced with nearly equal certainty, and will appear to include almost every species of vice and misery that is known. . . .

There is certainly a considerable difference in the healthiness of different countries, arising partly from the soil and situation, and partly from the habits and employment of the people. When, from these or any other causes whatever, a great mortality takes place, a proportional number of births immediately ensues, owing both to the greater number of yearly marriages from the increased demand for labour, and the greater fecundity of each marriage from being contracted at an earlier, and naturally a more prolific age.

On the contrary, when from opposite causes the healthiness of any country or parish is extraordinarily great; if, from the habits of the people, no vent for an overflowing population be found in emigration, the absolute necessity of the preventive check will be forced so strongly on their attention, that they must adopt it or starve; and consequently the marriages being very late, the number annually contracted will not only be small in proportion to the population, but each individual marriage will naturally be less prolific. . . .

But the English North-American colonies, now the powerful people of the United States of America, far outstripped all the others in the progress of their population. To the quantity of rich land which they possessed in common with the Spanish and Portuguese colonies, they added a greater degree of liberty and equality. Though not without some restrictions on their foreign commerce, they were allowed the liberty of managing their own internal affairs. The political institutions which prevailed were favourable to the alienation and division of property. Lands which were not cultivated by the proprietor within a limited time, were declared grantable to any other person. In Pennsylvania there was no right of primogenture; and in the provinces of New England, the eldest son had only a double share. There were no tithes in any of the States, and scarcely any taxes. And on account of the extreme cheapness of good land, and a situation favourable to the exportation of grain, a capital could not be more advantageously employed than in agriculture; which, at the same time that it affords the greatest quantity of healthy work, supplies the most valuable produce to the society.

The consequence of these favourable circumstances united, was a rapidity of increase almost without parallel in history.